UNIVERSITY CASEBOOK SERIES®

2020 SUPPLEMENT TO

HART AND WECHSLER'S

THE FEDERAL COURTS AND THE FEDERAL SYSTEM

SEVENTH EDITION

RICHARD H. FALLON, JR.
Story Professor of Law
Harvard Law School

JACK L. GOLDSMITH
Learned Hand Professor of Law
Harvard Law School

JOHN F. MANNING
Morgan and Helen Chu Dean and Professor of Law
Harvard Law School

DAVID L. SHAPIRO
Late William Nelson Cromwell Professor of Law, Emeritus
Harvard Law School

AMANDA L. TYLER
Shannon Cecil Turner Professor of Law
University of California, Berkeley School of Law

FOUNDATION
PRESS

The publisher is not engaged in rendering legal or other professional advice, and this publication is not a substitute for the advice of an attorney. If you require legal or other expert advice, you should seek the services of a competent attorney or other professional.

University Casebook Series is a trademark registered in the U.S. Patent and Trademark Office.

© 2016–2019 LEG, Inc. d/b/a West Academic
© 2020 LEG, Inc. d/b/a West Academic
    444 Cedar Street, Suite 700
    St. Paul, MN 55101
    1-877-888-1330

Printed in the United States of America

ISBN: 978-1-68467-978-2

PREFACE

This supplement brings the Seventh Edition up to date by discussing judicial decisions that have come down, statutes that have been enacted, and secondary literature that has been published since the Seventh Edition went to the publisher in January 2015. The most important changes from the 2019 Supplement involve decisions from the Supreme Court's 2019 Term. This supplement also furnishes summaries of, and in some cases responsive commentary on, some of the past year's most notable contributions to the Federal Courts literature.

As in the past, material in footnotes is intended primarily for scholars and researchers. We announce to our own classes that they need not read the footnotes in the editorial Notes unless we specifically assign them. (Students should of course read footnotes that we have included in principal cases.)

We are grateful to a large number of outstanding research assistants running back to 2015. Special thanks for help during this past year go to Alexander Cave, Lana El-Farra, Emily Massey, and Seanhenry VanDyke.

In looking backward to record debts, we mourn the death of our beloved senior colleague David L. Shapiro. This is the first Hart & Wechsler Supplement in which David has not participated since he became an editor of the casebook's Second Edition in 1973. David was a giant in the field and a friend and mentor to all of us personally. Despite David's absence, his influence pervades this cumulative supplement, as it will continue to pervade future editions of the casebook.

RHF
JLG
JFM
ALT

July 2020

SUMMARY OF CONTENTS

TABLE OF CONTENTS

TABLE OF CASES

The principal cases are in bold type.

TABLE OF AUTHORITIES

UNIVERSITY CASEBOOK SERIES®

2020 SUPPLEMENT TO

HART AND WECHSLER'S

THE FEDERAL COURTS AND THE FEDERAL SYSTEM

SEVENTH EDITION

CHAPTER I

THE DEVELOPMENT AND STRUCTURE OF THE FEDERAL JUDICIAL SYSTEM

———

INTRODUCTORY NOTE: THE JUDICIARY ARTICLE IN THE CONSTITUTIONAL CONVENTION AND THE RATIFICATION DEBATES

Page 1. Add at the end of footnote 1:

One of the most important sources for the Convention debates is James Madison's Notes on the 1787 Constitutional Convention. Bilder, Madison's Hand: Revising the Constitutional Convention (2015), reveals that Madison's revisions to his notes over the course of the decades that followed the Convention were far more extensive than scholars have previously recognized. By comparing the version of Madison's notes first published in 1840 to earlier sources, including a copy made of Madison's then-existing notes in 1790 for Thomas Jefferson, and using technology to date Madison's many revisions, Bilder shows the evolution of Madison's thinking on many important issues debated at the Convention while calling into question the reliability of his description of the debates regarding certain topics. For discussion emphasizing the significance of Bilder's findings and probing the conclusions she draws, consult Rakove, *A Biography of Madison's Notes of Debates*, 30 Const.Comment. 317 (2016).

Page 3. Add at the end of footnote 14:

A recent addition to the literature on the Convention, and on the decision to move beyond amending the Articles, Klarman, The Framers' Coup: The Making of the United States Constitution (2017), describes the relevant events as effectively an undemocratic coup. For probing analysis, consult Fried, *The Cunning of Reason: Michael Klarman's* The Framers' Coup, 116 Mich.L.Rev. 981 (2018); Finkelman, *The Nefarious Intentions of the Framers?*, 84 U.Chi.L.Rev. 2139 (2017). Ellis, The Quartet: Orchestrating the Second American Revolution, 1783–1789 (2015), details the roles that Washington, Hamilton, Madison, and Jay played in the transition from the Articles of Confederation to the Constitution, giving special attention to Washington's influence as chair of the Constitutional Convention.

Page 4. Add a new footnote 18a at the end of the carryover paragraph:

[18a] For an overview of the various schools of thought with respect to the continuing influence of the Articles on constitutional meaning and a detailed comparison of the provisions of the Articles and the Constitution, consult Maggs, *A Concise Guide to the Articles of Confederation as a Source for Determining the Original Meaning of the Constitution*, 85 Geo.Wash.L.Rev. 397 (2017).

Page 17. Add at the end of footnote 105:

Mask & MacMahon, *The Revolutionary War Prize Cases and the Origins of Diversity Jurisdiction*, 63 Buff.L.Rev. 477 (2015), argues that the experience of the Continental Congress in entertaining appeals from state tribunals in prize cases, as discussed on p. 6, footnote 36 of the Seventh Edition, persuaded influential Framers of the importance of national courts free of geographic bias. According to the authors, their findings "rehabilitate[] the view that geographic bias was a driving force behind the grant of diversity jurisdiction."

———

NOTE ON THE ORGANIZATION AND DEVELOPMENT OF THE FEDERAL JUDICIAL SYSTEM

Page 24. Add a new footnote 27a at the end of the third sentence of Section A, Paragraph (3)(b):

[27a] Once the potential existed for ties on the circuit courts, see Seventh Edition p. 27 & note 38, the Supreme Court reviewed a number of federal criminal cases over which it would not otherwise have enjoyed appellate jurisdiction. See Nash & Collins, *The Certificate of Division and the Early Supreme Court*, 94 S.Cal.L.Rev. ___ (forthcoming 2021) (documenting that the Court reviewed 44 such cases during the Chief Justiceships of Marshall and Taney).

Page 35. Insert the following in place of the final sentence of the second paragraph of Section G, Paragraph (3):

Appeals of such applications are reviewable by the Foreign Intelligence Surveillance Court of Review, made up of three Article III judges also selected by the Chief Justice.

Page 36. Add at the end of the carryover paragraph at the top of the page:

Congress adopted some of these proposals in the USA FREEDOM Act of 2015, which established procedures for the appointment of amici to appear before the FISC in cases involving "a novel or significant interpretation of the law" or where otherwise appropriate. The Act also provides for the certification of questions of law to higher courts and calls for the declassification of significant FISC decisions, orders, and opinions.[110a]

[110a] See Uniting and Strengthening America by Fulfilling Rights and Ensuring Effective Discipline over Monitoring (USA FREEDOM) Act of 2015, Pub.L.No. 114–23, 129 Stat. 268 (2015), codified at 50 U.S.C. § 1861.

Page 38. Add at the end of footnote 126:

In response to the decision in Kuretski v. Commissioner, 755 F.3d 929, 932 (D.C.Cir.2014), declaring that "[t]he Tax Court exercises Executive authority as part of the Executive Branch," Congress amended various provisions governing the Tax Court and added the following language to the court's chartering provision: "The Tax Court is not an agency of, and shall be independent of, the executive branch of the government." See Protecting Americans from Tax Hikes Act of 2015, Pub.L.No. 114–113, 129 Stat. 2242, codified at 26 U.S.C. § 7441.

Page 39. Add a new footnote 137a at the end of the first paragraph of Section H, Paragraph (2):

[137a] For a discussion of important differences between administrative law judges ("ALJs") and administrative judges ("AJs"), including the procedures by which they are appointed, the protections that they enjoy from removal, and their roles within agencies, along with the view that ALJs are superior to AJs because of their higher likelihood of impartiality and greater insulation from agency pressures, see Barnett, *Against Administrative Judges*, 49 U.C. Davis L.Rev. 1643 (2016) (arguing that AJs are "the real hidden judiciary"). In Lucia v. SEC, 138 S.Ct. 2044 (2018), the Supreme Court held that ALJs presiding over enforcement actions in the Securities and Exchange Commission (SEC) are not merely employees, but "Officers of the United States", a class of government officials subject to the Appointments Clause. See Art. II, § 2, cl. 2. Accordingly, the Court held the appointment of SEC ALJs by SEC staff, rather than the by the Commissioners themselves, ran afoul of that Clause. Relying on Freytag v. Commissioner, 501 U.S. 868 (1991), which reached the same conclusion with respect to special trial judges of the United States Tax Court, the Court emphasized the extensive powers that the SEC ALJs exercise and the potential for their decisions to become final where the Commission declines to review them. See also Buckley v. Valeo, 424 U.S. 1 (1976) (per curiam) (defining officers for Appointments Clause purposes as exercising "significant authority"). The holding in Lucia raises important questions, including how many other ALJs and possibly AJs may fall under its purview depending on how they are appointed. It may also have ramifications

with respect to how ALJs and AJs may be removed by agency heads where the Appointments Clause applies, a matter that the Court declined to take up in Lucia despite the government's invitation to do so. In Lucia's wake, the President issued an executive order declaring that under the decision, "at least some—and perhaps all—ALJs are 'Officers of the United States' and thus subject to the Constitution's Appointments Clause." Accordingly, the order directs that going forward, ALJs shall be exempt from "competitive examination and competitive service selection procedures" through which they had previously been appointed, and be appointed at the discretion of agency heads. Exec. Order No. 13,843, § 1, 83 Fed. Reg. 32,755 (July 13, 2018). The Solicitor General followed the order with separate guidance expanding the order's application to non-ALJs who act as adjudicators and explaining that the Department of Justice will defend existing statutory limitations on the removal of ALJs only insofar as those limitations are construed to be "suitably deferential" to the Department head at issue. Memorandum from the Solicitor General, U.S. Dep't of Justice, to Agency Gen. Counsels, Guidance on Administrative Law Judges After Lucia v. SEC (S. Ct.) (July 2018). Combined, the order and guidance have the potential to introduce extensive changes to the appointment and removal processes governing both ALJs and AJs.

Page 40. Add a new footnote 146a at the end of the last paragraph of Section H, Paragraph (3)(a):

[146a] For broad discussion of the role of magistrates in the Article III framework, consult *Symposium: Magistrate Judges and the Transformation of the Federal Judiciary*, 16 Nev.L.J. 775 (2016).

Page 41. Add a new paragraph at the beginning of Section I and before Paragraph (I)(1):

The Federal Judicial Branch today, "while tiny in comparison to the Executive Branch, is nevertheless a large and complex institution, with an annual budget exceeding $7 billion and more than 32,000 employees." Ayestas v. Davis, 138 S.Ct. 1080 (2018) (citing Administrative Office of the U.S. Courts, The Judiciary FY 2018 Congressional Budget Office Summary Revised 9–10 (June 2017)).

Page 42. Add at the end of footnote 159:

Updated 2018 figures from the Administrative Office of the U.S. Courts reveal that after a decline in 2017, civil filings in the district courts have returned to a level similar to that reported in 2013. (Specifically, the 2018 figure is 282,936.) 2019 figures report a slight increase to 297,877. Meanwhile, after also falling in recent years, criminal filings rose in 2018 to 87,149 and in 2019 to 92,678. (Part of the explanation for this trend is a substantial rise in prosecutions for immigration violations during 2017–2019.) Correlating with these trends, after a substantial decline since 2015, diversity filings in the district courts rose 17% in 2017–2018, to 88,547, and rose further in 2018–2019 to 104,803. Bankruptcy petitions, however, continued to decline during the same period, numbering 773,375 in 2017–2018, and growing less than 1% during 2018–2019. See Administrative Office of the U.S. Courts, 2017 Judicial Business, Analysis & Tables C, C-2, D, D-2, F; Administrative Office of the U.S. Courts, 2018 Judicial Business, Analysis & Tables C, C-2, D, D-2, F; Administrative Office of the U.S. Courts, 2019 Judicial Business, Analysis & Tables C, C-2, D, D-2, F.

Page 43. Add at the end of footnote 163:

For an elaboration of these points and a broader discussion of how the federal courts constitute American lawyers' " 'common intellectual heritage,' " consult Resnik, *Revising Our "Common Intellectual Heritage": Federal and State Courts in Our Federal System*, 91 Notre Dame L.Rev. 1831 (2016) (from a Symposium honoring Daniel Meltzer) (quoting Meltzer, *The Judiciary's Bicentennial*, 56 U.Chi.L.Rev. 423, 427 (1989)).

Page 45. Add at the end of footnote 172:

Updated 2016 figures from the Administrative Office of the U.S. Courts revealed a 14.5% increase from the prior year in filed appeals, although the total number, 60,357, remained below the high of 2006. Figures in 2017, 2018, and 2019 reversed this trend, revealing a decline in filings in 2017 of 16%, followed by a decline of 2% in 2018, and a further decline in 2019 of 2%, bringing the figure to 48,486. In the year spanning 2015–2016, *pro se* appeals increased by 18%, with the result that they accounted for 52% of court of appeals filings. Between 2016 and 2018, *pro se* appeals dropped over 20%, yet they still accounted for half of all court of appeals filings. Almost half of *pro se* filings in 2018–2019 were by prisoners. See Administrative Office of the U.S. Courts, 2016 Judicial Business, Analysis & Tables B, B-9; Administrative Office of the U.S. Courts, 2017 Judicial Business, Analysis & Tables B, B-9; Administrative Office of the U.S. Courts, 2018 Judicial Business, Analysis & Tables B, B-9; Administrative Office of the U.S. Courts, 2019 Judicial Business, Analysis & Tables B, B-9.

Page 47. Insert the following in place of the second paragraph of Section I, Paragraph (3):

The number of cases filed annually in the Court has risen over time, though it has fallen in recent years. During the 2018 Term, which ended in June 2019, the Court docketed 7,623 cases[185] (in comparison with 1,957 in the 1960, 3,419 in the 1970, 4,174 in the 1980, 5,502 in the 1990, 7,924 in the 2001, and 8,580 in the 2013 Terms). Of the total in the 2018 Term, 11 came within the Court's original jurisdiction.[186]

[185] *The Supreme Court, 2018 Term—The Statistics*, 133 Harv.L.Rev. 412, 420 (2019).

[186] See *id.*

Page 47. Insert the following in place of the second sentence of the third paragraph of Section I, Paragraph (3):

The Court rendered opinions in 72 cases in the 2018 Term,[187] in comparison with 132 in the 1960, 141 in the 1970, 159 in the 1980, 129 in the 1990, 95 in the 1994, and 88 in the 2001 Terms.

[187] This figure includes 66 signed opinions and six per curiam decisions (p. 412).

Page 47. Add at the end of footnote 187:

An empirical study of 93,000 certiorari petitions filed between the 2001 Supreme Court Term and the start of the 2015 Term found that factors influencing the probability of a petition being granted include whether the federal government supports a grant, the attorneys involved, and the lower court that rendered the decision. See Feldman & Kappner, *Finding Certainty in Cert: An Empirical Analysis of the Factors Involved in Supreme Court Certiorari Decisions from 2001–2015*, 61 Vill.L.Rev. 795 (2017).

CHAPTER II

THE NATURE OF THE FEDERAL JUDICIAL FUNCTION: CASES AND CONTROVERSIES

---

1. INTRODUCTION AND HISTORICAL CONTEXT

NOTE ON MARBURY V. MADISON

Page 69. Add to footnote 4:

For a defense of Marbury on nearly every point, including a rejection of the claim that the opinion was "disingenuously manipulative * * * in order to create an occasion for the exercise of judicial review," see Treanor, *The Story of Marbury v. Madison: Judicial Authority and Political Struggle*, in Federal Courts Stories (Jackson & Resnik eds. 2010), at 29.

NOTE ON MARBURY V. MADISON AND THE FUNCTION OF ADJUDICATION

Page 79. Add at the end of Paragraph (7)(b):

See also Sessions v. Morales-Santana, 137 S.Ct. 1678 (2017), also discussed pp. 18, 20, *infra*, in which the Court ruled a provision of the immigration laws invalid on equal protection grounds even though applicable remedial law precluded an award of citizenship to the complaining party, who therefore remained subject to removal from the United States. To remedy the equal protection violation, the Court concluded that the Government, in the absence of other corrective action by Congress, should eliminate the disparity of which the respondent complained by ceasing to confer citizenship on others on a gender-discriminatory basis. To a protest from Justice Thomas, joined by Justice Alito, that the equal protection ruling was "unnecessary" in light of the Court's remedial determination, Justice Ginsburg's majority opinion rejoined: "[D]iscrimination itself . . . perpetuat[es] 'archaic and stereotypic notions' incompatible with the equal treatment guaranteed by the Constitution." Does the Justices' disagreement turn on what it means for constitutional rulings to be unnecessary? If so, in what way?

Page 81. Add at the end of Paragraph (7)(c):

Divisions among the Justices about whether a construction is sufficiently plausible to trigger the avoidance canon are not infrequent. See, *e.g.*, Jennings v. Rodriguez, 138 S.Ct. 830 (2018) (involving a division, by 5–3, about whether three immigration provisions could plausibly be read to require periodic bond hearings for long-term detainees). See also Katyal & Schmidt, *Active Avoidance: The Modern Supreme Court and Legal Change*, 128 Harv.L.Rev. 2109 (2015) (arguing that recent decisions invoking the avoidance doctrine have engaged in "constitutional adventurism of a uniquely pernicious sort" by announcing new rules of constitutional law and relying on them as a predicate for substantially rewriting statutes).[13]

[13] Fish, *Constitutional Avoidance as Interpretation and as Remedy*, 114 Mich.L.Rev. 1275 (2016), argues for re-conceptualizing avoidance doctrine as including not only an interpretive component, but also a remedial one, through which courts seek to save statutes from facial invalidity. Courts have traditionally dealt with judicial responses to identified statutory overbreadth or vagueness via separability doctrine. For discussion, see Seventh Edition pp. 170–74.

----

2. ISSUES OF PARTIES, THE REQUIREMENT OF FINALITY, AND THE PROHIBITION AGAINST FEIGNED AND COLLUSIVE SUITS

NOTE ON HAYBURN'S CASE

Page 86. Add at the end of Paragraph (4):

Pfander & Birk, *Article III Judicial Power, the Adverse-Party Requirement, and Non-Contentious Jurisdiction*, 124 Yale L.J. 1346 (2015), seek comprehensively to revise long-settled assumptions that Article III jurisdiction requires adverse parties in all cases. The authors trace a history of "non-contentious" jurisdiction from Roman times through the English Court of Chancery sitting in Westminster to colonial and early American courts that had sundry powers to rule on ex parte or otherwise uncontested petitions to establish or register legal rights or interests. According to the authors, historical or modern residues of that tradition can be seen not only in naturalization proceedings (as in Tutun), but also, inter alia, in uncontested prize and salvage cases in admiralty, appointments of bankruptcy trustees, issuances of warrants, entries of default judgments, class action settlements, and consent decrees. In the authors' view, Article III requires adverse parties in "controversies", but not necessarily in all "cases", some of which can be non-contentious. "The lesson of Hayburn's Case", they write, "is not that the federal courts lack power to hear ex parte proceedings, but that they can act only where their decision will have a binding, legally determinative effect." Seeking to distill normative lessons from historical practice, Pfander & Birk conclude: "[W]hile no adverse party need appear in non-contentious proceedings, federal courts should exercise jurisdiction only if the party invoking federal power has a concrete interest in the recognition of a legal claim. * * * The courts also should exercise non-contentious jurisdiction only where they have been called upon to employ judicial judgment in the application of law to the facts and only where their decisions will enjoy the finality long viewed as essential to the federal judicial role. The courts must be especially mindful of the potential for cases heard on the non-contentious side of their dockets to affect the rights of absent parties, and due process will continue to require that third parties receive notice of, and an opportunity to participate in, matters that concern them."

Pfander & Birk are unquestionably correct that federal courts routinely act on ex parte motions and render uncontested rulings in a number of contexts. As the authors acknowledge, many of these rulings come in proceedings that are potentially contested (as in Tutun) or are ancillary to the resolution of live disputes (as, for example, in the appointment of bankruptcy trustees). That said, their study generates an important question: Is there a large enough residual category to warrant the development of forward-looking principles—such as those that they propose—to identify, limit, and structure exercises of "non-contentious jurisdiction" under Article III.

Woolhandler, *Adverse Interests and Article III*, 111 Nw.U.L.Rev. 1025 (2017), answers in the negative. According to Professor Woolhandler, the examples adduced by Pfander and Birks show at most that Article III does not require adverse arguments in every case; the authors fail to refute the more fundamental proposition that Article III jurisdiction always requires parties with adverse interests. Pfander & Birk, *Adverse Interests and Article III: A Reply*, 111 Nw.U.L.Rev. 1067 (2017), retort that Woolhandler adopts a conceptualization of Article III's requirements that emerged only in the late nineteenth century and that she offers no theory adequate to explain earlier discussion of and practice involving non-contentious jurisdiction.

---

3. SOME PROBLEMS OF STANDING TO SUE

A. PLAINTIFFS' STANDING

NOTE ON STANDING TO SUE

Page 119. Add at the end of Paragraph (3)(c):

(d) Trump v. Hawaii, 138 S.Ct. 2392 (2018), upheld the standing of three U.S. citizens or permanent residents to challenge a presidential proclamation that restricted entry into the United States by nationals of six predominantly Muslim countries. In doing so, the Court declined to decide whether injury to a "claimed dignitary interest" in being free from religious establishments and the designation of a "disfavored faith" sufficed for standing. The individual plaintiffs had alleged adequate injury in the "real-world effect that the Proclamation has had in keeping them separated from certain relatives who seek to enter the country."

Page 119. Add to footnote 15:

In cases under the Establishment Clause challenging governmental displays of crèches, crosses, and the Ten Commandments, the Supreme Court has often ruled on the merits, typically without discussion of standing. In American Legion v. American Humanist Ass'n, 139 S.Ct. 2067 (2019), which rejected a challenge to the display of a cross as a war memorial, the majority took no notice of any standing issue. But Justice Gorsuch, in an opinion concurring in the judgment that Justice Thomas joined, would have dismissed on standing grounds. More broadly, he would have rejected "the plaintiffs' 'offended observer' theory of standing" and, further, would have held the implied recognition of standing in a number of prior religious display cases to be error. According to Justice Gorsuch, the plausibility of the "offended observer" theory depends on a mistaken test of substantive constitutional validity, under which displays of religious symbols are unconstitutional if a "reasonable observer" would perceive them as "endorsing" religion. See, *e.g.*, County of Allegheny v. American Civil Liberties Union, Greater Pittsburgh Chapter, 492 U.S. 573, 620–21 (1989) (opinion of Blackmun, J.); *id.* 631 (O'Connor, J., concurring in part and concurring in the judgment). In Justice Gorsuch's view, the Article III standing requirement of injury-in-fact renders the "offended observer" theory untenable, and he would have rejected that theory along with the "endorsement" test (and the test of Lemon v. Kurtzman, 403 U.S. 602 (1971), on which it sometimes functioned as a gloss). Justice Ginsburg's dissenting opinion, which Justice Sotomayor joined, described "Justice Gorsuch's 'no standing' opinion [as] startling in view of the many religious-display cases this Court has resolved on the merits." She also suggested that it would have intolerable consequences. Without further elaboration, Justice Ginsburg approvingly cited an amicus brief that she described in a parenthetical as "explaining why offended observer standing is necessary and proper."

In demanding that the Court reject "offended observer" standing, Justice Gorsuch traced the mismatch between the Court's Establishment Clause jurisprudence and the Article III demand for injury-in-fact to the Court's "misadventure" in seeking "a 'grand unified theory' of the Establishment Clause [that] left us only a mess." Would it be just as fair to direct the same criticism at the Court's effort to develop a "grand unified theory" of Article III standing built on a demand for injury-in-fact? Cf. Fallon, *The Fragmentation of Standing*, 93 Tex.L.Rev. 1061, 1062 (2015) ("Since the Court began in the 1970s to characterize standing as turning almost entirely on a single, transubstantive, tripartite test * * * commentators have complained about inconsistencies and anomalies in application.").

Page 124. Add to footnote 19:

See also Boddie, *The Sins of Innocence,* 68 Vand.L.Rev. 297 (2015) (arguing that presumed injuries to white plaintiffs seeking to enjoin affirmative action programs rely on racialized conceptions of innocence and make standing both a product and an instrument of racial inequality).

Page 125. Add to footnote 20:

Town of Chester v. Laroe Estates, Inc., 137 S.Ct. 1645 (2017), applied the principle that plaintiffs must separately demonstrate standing for all forms of relief that they seek to intervenors as of right under Fed.R.Civ.P. 24(a)(2) who seek relief not requested by the plaintiffs.

Hessick, *The Separation-of-Powers Theory of Standing*, 95 N.C.L.Rev. 673 (2017), argues from the premise that standing doctrine exists solely to protect the separation of powers to the conclusion that there should be no Article III standing barrier to suits that do not present separation-of-powers concerns, including actions to enforce either "private" or "public" rights against state officials. Notwithstanding supporting dicta in a few Supreme Court decisions, is the premise of Professor Hessick's argument sounder than a number of the decisions with which his conclusion would conflict?

Page 125. Add at the end of Paragraph (5)(c):

In Department of Commerce v. New York, 139 S.Ct. 2551 (2019), the Court ruled that some plaintiff states and possibly other parties had standing to challenge the citizenship question in the 2020 census questionnaire. In an opinion by Chief Justice Roberts, the Court upheld standing based on the prediction that the "citizenship question would result in noncitizen households responding to the census at lower rates than other groups, which in turn would cause them to be undercounted and lead to" such harms to the states as "los[ing] out on federal funds that are distributed on the basis of state population." For a Court that was unanimous on this point, the Chief Justice reasoned: "The Government invokes our steady refusal to 'endorse standing theories that rest on speculation about the decisions of independent actors,' Clapper v. Amnesty Int'l USA, 568 U.S. 398, 414 (2013), particularly speculation about future unlawful conduct, Los Angeles v. Lyons, 461 U.S. 95, 105 (1983). But * * * evidence at trial established that noncitizen households have historically responded to the census at lower rates than other groups, and the District Court did not clearly err in crediting the Census Bureau's theory that the discrepancy is likely attributable at least in part to noncitizens' reluctance to answer a citizenship question. Respondents' theory of standing thus does not rest on mere speculation about the decisions of third parties; it relies instead on the predictable effect of Government action on the decisions of third parties." Compare Allen v. Wright, Seventh Edition p. 103, and Simon v. Eastern Ky. Welfare Rights Org., Seventh Edition p. 124, both denying standing on the ground that anticipated harm resulting from actions by third parties was too speculative to support standing.

Page 127. Add at the end of Paragraph (6):

In a survey of standing doctrine under the Roberts Court, Fallon, *The Fragmentation of Standing,* 93 Tex.L.Rev. 1061 (2015), traces standing's "fragmentation", which the author defines as "the division of standing law into multiple compartments", since the articulation of the modern, three-part (injury, causation, and redressability) test in the 1970s. In the author's view, "large generalizations" about standing, including those offered in Supreme Court opinions, are characteristically either empty or misleading. Nevertheless, he writes, the Court's decisions tend to form patterns defined by interconnections among such features as: (a) the provision under which a plaintiff brings suit, (b) the nature and sensitivity of the remedy that a plaintiff seeks, (c) whether the plaintiff sues to enforce a substantive or a procedural right, (d) whether the plaintiff is a private citizen or a governmental body or official, and (e) the presence or absence of congressional authorization. These patterns, Professor Fallon claims, "frequently exhibit an implicit normative logic" and enable predictions of future outcomes, but require scholars and judges to look behind the Court's words to "the kinds of facts that actually drive decisions in practice". Professor Fallon suggests that his "doctrinal Realist credo affords a note of hope, not despair" for those seeking ordered consistency among leading decisions. Is there any reason why the verbal formulae in which the Supreme Court couches standing doctrine should be less reliable than judicial articulations of other legal doctrines?

―――――

NOTE ON SPECIALIZED STANDING DOCTRINES: TAXPAYER AND LEGISLATOR STANDING

Page 132. Add to footnote 4:

Compare Nash, *A Functional Theory of Congressional Standing,* 114 Mich.L.Rev. 339 (2015) (arguing that congressional standing should be based on a broader view of injury than mere vote nullification and should extend to injuries involving Congress's "constitutional functions" such as impediments to information gathering and certain diminishments of bargaining power). For further discussions of congressional standing, see Campbell, *Executive Action and Nonaction,* 95 N.C.L.Rev. 553 (2017) (arguing that Congress should have standing to challenge presidential failures to enforce the law when "congressional votes resulting in the passage of a law have been completely nullified"); Sant'Ambrogio, *Legislative Exhaustion,* 58 Wm. & Mary L.Rev. 1253 (2017) (coining the term "Legislative Exhaustion" to describe the argument that Congress ought to have standing only when it lacks nonjudicial methods of resolving a dispute with the executive branch, as when the President declines to enforce federal law based on constitutional objections); Grove, *Standing Outside of Article III*, 162 U.Pa.L.Rev. 1311 (2014) (identifying Article I and Article II as well as Article III limits on the standing of Congress and the executive branch); Jackson, *Congressional Standing to Sue: The Role of Courts and Congress in U.S. Constitutional Democracy*, 93 Ind.L.J. 845 (2018) (canvasing competing considerations and concluding that, although there should be no categorical preclusion of congressional standing, "most controversies between the branches are best addressed through political mechanisms").

Page 132. Add a new Paragraph (3)(d):

(d) In an opinion by Justice Ginsburg (joined by Justices Kennedy, Breyer, Sotomayor, and Kagan), the Court in Arizona State Legislature v. Arizona Independent Redistricting Comm'n, 135 S.Ct. 2652 (2015) ("AIRC"), held that the Arizona State Legislature had standing to challenge a state ballot initiative that transferred to an independent commission the legislature's previous authority to redistrict Arizona's seats in the U.S. House of Representatives. The state legislature argued, *inter alia*, that this shift violated the Elections Clause, U.S. Const. art. I, § 4, cl. 1, which gives "the Legislature" of each state the power to prescribe the "Time, Places and Manner" of federal legislative elections. Although ultimately rejecting that claim on the merits, the Court found that the suit asserted a concrete and legally cognizable injury caused by the initiative's alleged infringement of the legislature's constitutionally assigned role.

The Court distinguished Raines v. Byrd, Seventh Edition, p. 131, on the ground that, in that case, "six *individual Members* of Congress" challenged the Line Item Veto Act and that neither the House nor the Senate had authorized suit by those Members. In contrast, the Arizona Legislature in AIRC sued as "an institutional plaintiff asserting an institutional injury, and * * * commenced this action after authorizing votes in both of its chambers." Quoting Coleman v. Miller, Seventh Edition, pp. 130–31, the Court in AIRC further noted that the challenged Arizona initiative would " 'completely nullif[y]' " the legislature's votes on federal redistricting. This consideration, said the Court, made the injury analogous to that of the twenty state senators who had been granted standing in Coleman to argue that their votes against ratifying a constitutional amendment were nullified, in violation of Article V, by the lieutenant governor's tie-breaking vote in favor.

In a dissenting opinion in AIRC, Justice Scalia (joined by Justice Thomas) contended that the traditional Anglo-American conception of "cases" or "controversies" does not "include suits between units of government regarding their legitimate powers." Even if such a suit was sufficiently "concrete" to permit effective adjudication, Justice Scalia concluded that the "separation of powers" precludes federal adjudication of interbranch disputes unless necessary to redress some resultant "concrete harm" to "a private party". Limiting the judicial power in this way, he added, "keeps us minding our own business." While acknowledging that Coleman seemed at odds with his position, Justice Scalia viewed that decision as an outlier whose true holding was far from clear.[5]

Would the Court's approach in AIRC justify congressional standing if Congress itself (or even a particular House) authorized Members to sue to vindicate an alleged "institutional injury" to Congress? Justice Ginsburg's opinion reserved that question, noting that "a suit between Congress and the President would raise separation-of-powers concerns absent here." Justice Scalia replied that if the Framers would have disfavored congressional standing, they presumably would have been *"all the more averse* to unprecedented judicial meddling by federal courts with the branches of their state governments." How should the Court sort out such competing contentions about implied limits on federal judicial power?

[5] Grove, *Government Standing and the Fallacy of Institutional Injury*, 167 U.Pa.L.Rev. 611 (2019), also maintains that Coleman should not be followed. According to her, Coleman relied on "a now outdated rule of appellate standing" that permitted Supreme Court review of state court decisions of federal claims that a federal district court could not have entertained. Professor Grove argues more broadly that claims of standing predicated on "institutional injuries" are incompatible with a constitutional design that allocates rights to individuals, not institutions, and relies on individuals to assert their own rights. She would allow only narrow exceptions to permit government bodies to perform functions that they could not perform without resort to a court, such as imposing sanctions (including for contempt of legislative bodies).

Page 132. Add a new Paragraph (3)(e):

(e)   In Virginia House of Delegates v. Bethune-Hill, 139 S.Ct. 1945 (2019), the Court held, by 5–4, that the Virginia House of Delegates lacked standing to appeal from a lower court ruling that a state redistricting plan (adopted by the state House and Senate) constituted a forbidden racial gerrymander. The issue arose when the State Attorney General, after defending the plan in the lower court, decided not to pursue an appeal, and the state House, which had previously participated as an intervenor, sought Supreme Court review. Justice Ginsburg's opinion, in which Justices Thomas, Sotomayor, Kagan, and Gorsuch joined, first ruled that the House lacked authority under Virginia law to represent the state's interests. Though Virginia could have "designated the House to represent its interests," it had not done so. Justice Ginsburg's opinion then held that a single house of a bicameral legislature suffered no sufficiently distinctive injury from the invalidation of a state law, including a districting statute, to support standing. In so ruling, the Court distinguished Sixty-seventh Minnesota State Senate v. Beens, 406 U.S. 187 (1972) (per curiam), which allowed the Minnesota Senate to challenge a lower court ruling in a malapportionment case that reduced the Senate's size from 67 to 35. "Cutting the size of the legislative chamber in half would necessarily alter its day-to-day operations" in a way that a mere change in district lines and membership would not, she reasoned: "[T]he House as an institution has no cognizable interest in the identity of its members." Justice Alito's dissenting opinion deemed it unnecessary to "address the [majority's] first" holding that "Virginia law does not authorize the House to defend the invalidated redistricting plan on behalf of the Commonwealth". In his view, it was "obvious" that the Virginia House, like "any group consisting of members who must work together to achieve the group's aims has a keen[, constitutionally cognizable] interest in the identity of its members [and] in how its members are selected." Accordingly, he thought it decisive that "neither the Court nor the Virginia Solicitor General has provided any support for the proposition that Virginia law bars the House from defending, in its own right, the constitutionality of a districting plan."

The majority and dissenting opinions appear ultimately to agree that state law is capable of controlling whether one branch of a bicameral legislature has standing to defend a state districting plan—either as a representative of the state or, according to the dissent, in its own right. To the extent that state law is controlling, which side should bear the burden of establishing a state-law authorization or prohibition?

Page 132. Add a Paragraph (5):

(5) Actions by Voters. In Gill v. Whitford, 138 S.Ct. 1916 (2018), the Supreme Court held unanimously that challengers to an alleged partisan gerrymander of the Wisconsin Legislature had failed to establish the "concrete and particularized" injury needed for standing: "We have long recognized that a person's right to vote is 'individual and personal in nature.' Reynolds v. Sims, 377 U.S. 533, 561 (1964). Thus, 'voters who allege facts showing disadvantage to themselves as individuals have standing to sue' to remedy that disadvantage. Baker v. Carr, 369 U.S. [186, 206 (1962)]. The plaintiffs in this case alleged that they suffered such injury from partisan gerrymandering, which works through 'packing' and 'cracking' voters of one party to disadvantage those voters. That is, the plaintiffs claim a constitutional right not to be placed in legislative districts deliberately designed to 'waste' their votes in elections where their chosen candidates will win in landslides (packing) or are destined to lose by closer margins (cracking). To the extent the plaintiffs' alleged harm is the dilution of their votes, that injury is district specific", and "results from the boundaries of the particular district[s] in which [they] reside[ ]. And a plaintiff's remedy must be 'limited to the inadequacy that produced [his] injury in fact.' Lewis v. Casey, 518 U.S. 343, 357 (1996). * * * For similar reasons, we have held that a plaintiff who alleges that he is the object of a racial gerrymander * * * has standing to assert only that his own district has been so gerrymandered. See United States v. Hays, 515 U.S. 737, 744–45 (1995)."[6]

Although "[f]our of the plaintiffs * * * pleaded a particularized [injury]" of having been deliberately placed in districts where their votes would be wasted, they "failed to meaningfully pursue their allegations of individual harm" and "instead rested their case at trial—and their arguments before this Court—on [a] theory of statewide injury to Wisconsin Democrats" through the wasting of Democratic votes on a statewide basis. As thus framed, the case was "about group political interests, not individual legal rights", and the plaintiffs' proposed measure of impermissible gerrymandering—an "efficiency gap" theory that compares each party's "wasted" votes on a statewide basis—gauged harms "to the fortunes of political parties", not the kinds of concrete injuries to individuals that are necessary for standing.

---

[6] For criticism of the standing analyses in the Court's racial gerrymandering cases involving deliberate attempts to create majority-minority districts, see Issacharoff & Karlan, *Standing and Misunderstanding in Voting Rights Law*, 111 Harv.L.Rev. 2276 (1998) (arguing that the Court has failed to develop a coherent theory of what injury, if any, such districting inflicts). *Cf.* Ely, *Standing to Challenge Pro-Minority Gerrymanders*, 111 Harv.L.Rev. 576, 587 (1997) (maintaining that whites included in a majority-minority district "are being denied the opportunity to elect one of 'their own' ").

Having identified these defects in the plaintiffs' claims to standing, the Court remanded to the district court to give some of them the opportunity to adduce evidence "that would tend to demonstrate a burden on their individual votes." Justices Thomas and Gorsuch, concurring and part and concurring in the judgment, would have remanded with instructions to dismiss on the ground that the plaintiffs had already had "a more-than-ample opportunity to prove their standing under [established] principles."

Justice Kagan, joined by Justices Ginsburg, Breyer, and Sotomayor, concurred. She noted first that if the plaintiffs could establish personal injury arising from a constitutionally forbidden partisan gerrymander of their own districts, the violations "might warrant a statewide remedy": "with enough plaintiffs joined together—attacking all the packed and cracked districts in a statewide gerrymander—th[e] obligatory revisions could amount to a wholesale restructuring of the State's districting plan."

Justice Kagan also maintained that although the case had mostly been litigated on a vote-dilution theory, partisan gerrymanders may "inflict other kinds of constitutional harm" that would be cognizable under a theory alleging infringement of First Amendment rights of political association: "Justice Kennedy explained the First Amendment associational injury deriving from a partisan gerrymander in his concurring opinion in Vieth [v. Jubelirer, 541 U.S. 267 (2004)]", in which he explained that " '[r]epresentative democracy' is today 'unimaginable without the ability of citizens to band together' to advance their political beliefs. That means significant 'First Amendment concerns arise' when a State purposely 'subject[s] a group of voters or their party to disfavored treatment.' "

Justice Kagan continued: "As so formulated, the associational harm of a partisan gerrymander is distinct from vote dilution. * * * [Even if their own districts were 'left untouched' by a gerrymander, members] of the 'disfavored party' in the State, deprived of their natural political strength by a partisan gerrymander, may face difficulties fundraising, registering voters, attracting volunteers, generating support from independents, and recruiting candidates to run for office (not to mention eventually accomplishing their policy objectives)." Chief Justice Roberts' opinion for the Court responded: "We leave for another day consideration of other possible theories of harm not presented here and whether those theories might present justiciable claims giving rise to statewide remedies."

Justice Kagan's articulation of a theory of standing based on injury to associational rights, which she developed almost entirely from suggestive remarks in Justice Kennedy's opinion concurring in the judgment in Vieth, seemed clearly framed for the purpose of winning Justice Kennedy's vote, either in a future case or upon further review of the Gill case. And the standing question in partisan gerrymandering cases seems closely connected to the political question issue that the Court, in Gill, found it unnecessary to confront after holding that the plaintiffs had failed to establish standing. In Vieth, Seventh Edition p. 253, four Justices had ruled that challenges to partisan gerrymanders presented nonjusticiable political questions due to the absence of judicially manageable standards for determining when a gerrymander went "too far." Justice Kennedy, concurring, concluded only that no judicially manageable standards had yet "emerged". In Gill, the plaintiffs sought to advance a judicially manageable standard by relying on a state-wide "efficiency gap." Would it be anomalous for a voting scheme that creates a statewide efficiency gap to give rise to "concrete and particularized" injuries under the First Amendment but not the Equal Protection Clause? Justice Kagan maintained that it would not: "Standing, we have long held, 'turns on the nature and source of the claim asserted.' Warth v. Seldin, 422 U.S. 490, 500 (1975)."

———————

NOTE ON CONGRESSIONAL POWER TO CONFER STANDING TO SUE

Page 151. Add a new Paragraph (2)(c):

(c) In Spokeo, Inc. v. Robins, 136 S.Ct. 1540 (2016), the Court reaffirmed the framework that it had developed in Lujan v. Defenders of Wildlife, Seventh Edition p. 133, to define congressional authority to confer standing, but divided 6–2 over how to apply that framework. The Fair Credit Reporting Act requires consumer reporting agencies to "follow reasonable procedures to assure maximum possible accuracy of" consumer reports and provides that " '[a]ny person who willfully fails to comply with any requirement [of the Act] with respect to any [individual] is liable to that [individual]' ". Robins brought suit under the Act against Spokeo, a "people search engine" that maintained an inaccurate report about him on its website. In evaluating Robins' standing, the Court, in an opinion by Justice Alito, reaffirmed that "a bare procedural violation, divorced from any concrete harm", would not satisfy the Article III injury requirement "without [harm to] some concrete interest that is affected by the deprivation". The question thus became "whether the particular procedural violations alleged in this case entail a degree of risk sufficient to meet" the requirements of Article III. According to Robins, Spokeo falsely reported, inter alia, that he was in his fifties, had a graduate degree, and was economically well off, when in fact he was out of work and seeking employment. Robins maintained that Spokeo's report damaged his employment prospects by making him appear overqualified for jobs that he might have obtained otherwise.

In appraising that claim Justice Alito emphasized that Article III requires plaintiffs to allege injuries that are both "particularized" and "concrete", which he defined as meaning " 'real, and not 'abstract.' " He then quoted Lujan's recognition that "Congress may 'elevat[e] to the status of legally cognizable injuries concrete, de facto injuries that were previously inadequate in law.' " Against this background, Justice Alito concluded that Robins had alleged an injury particularized to him, but noted that "not all inaccuracies cause harm or present any material risk of harm." As an example, the majority offered the dissemination of an incorrect zip code, which it thought unlikely to "work any concrete harm." The lower court, the majority found, had focused its standing analysis exclusively on the requirement of particularized injury and thus failed to analyze "whether the particular procedural violations alleged in this case"—which the plaintiff said resulted in the publication of misinformation about him—"entail a degree of risk sufficient to meet the concreteness requirement." Accordingly, the Court vacated and remanded for further proceedings without deciding whether Robins "adequately alleged an injury in fact". Justice Thomas, who joined the Court's opinion, also concurred separately.

Justice Ginsburg, joined by Justice Sotomayor, dissented. Although Justice Ginsburg "agree[d] with much of the Court's opinion", she would have affirmed the lower court's decision to uphold standing without a remand, based on the allegation in Robins' complaint that "Spokeo's misinformation 'cause[s] actual harm to [his] employment prospects.' "

The principal significance of Spokeo appears to lie in the affirmation in the majority opinion—which six Justices joined and with which the dissenting Justices registered no express disagreement—that "Congress' role in identifying and elevating intangible harms does not mean that a plaintiff automatically satisfies the injury-in-fact requirement whenever a statute grants a person a statutory right and purports to authorize that person to sue to vindicate that right." It may also be significant that a majority of the Justices thought that application of the correct legal standard required a remand despite the district court's already having developed a factual record.

Page 151. Add a new Paragraph (2)(d):

(d)   In Thole v. U.S. Bank N.A., 140 S.Ct. 1615 (2020), the Court held (by 5–4) that retired participants in the Bank's defined-benefit retirement plan lacked standing to challenge alleged mismanagement of the plan, despite a provision of the Employee Retirement Income Security Act (ERISA) authorizing suits by plan beneficiaries. Because the plaintiffs had been paid all benefits due in the past, and were "legally and contractually entitled to receive * * * [fixed] monthly payments for the rest of their lives", they had suffered no cognizable injury, the Court reasoned. Absent a concrete injury, the statute's attempted conferral of a right to sue failed to satisfy Article III.

Justice Sotomayor, joined by Justices Ginsburg, Breyer, and Kagan, dissented. She argued that "[b]ecause ERISA requires that retirement-plan assets be held in trust," beneficiaries had "equitable interests" in the plan's assets—analogous to those recognized by the traditional law of trusts—the alleged harms to which constituted actionable injuries.[5a] The dissent also argued, inter alia, that the statutory authorization to sue effectively assigned the plan's claims to the petitioners. By contrast, the Court emphasized that no formal assignment had occurred.

The majority did not appear to dispute that if Congress had formally assigned the claims of the retirement plan to the plan's beneficiaries or had otherwise authorized plan beneficiaries to sue as the plan's representatives, its doing so would have conferred Article III standing. Was it appropriate to require such a formal assignment when Congress had explicitly sought to endow plan beneficiaries with rights to sue?

[5a]   Justice Thomas, joined by Justice Alito, concurring, criticized prior decisions' use of "the common law of trusts as 'the starting point' for interpreting ERISA."

Page 151. Add to footnote 6:

But see Pfander, *Standing, Litigable Interests, and Article III's Case-or-Controversy Requirement*, 65 UCLA L.Rev. 170 (2018) (questioning the Westminster paradigm in light of early assignment to Article III courts of "noncontentious" cases arising under federal law, including naturalization petitions, and arguing that eighteenth-century Scottish practice provides a better model for understanding early American analogues to modern standing doctrine).

Page 152. Add at the beginning of footnote 9:

Pfander, *Standing, Litigable Interests, and Article III's Case-or-Controversy Requirement*, 65 UCLA L.Rev. 170 (2018), argues that Congresses and courts of the early republic distinguished between "controversies," which required parties with concretely adverse interests, and "cases," which could encompass noncontentious federal business that involved no injury, such as petitions for naturalization. According to Pfander, that practice mirrored features of Scots law, in which distinctive limitations—not unlike the statutory qualifications sometimes attached to modern citizen-suit provisions—applied to public actions involving broadly shared injuries. He argues, however, that a more historically accurate account of standing would accord Congress broader powers to confer jurisdiction in the absence of modern notions of injury in fact, "especially where Congress has taken [alternative] steps to protect the government's enforcement primacy and the defendant's interest in the avoidance of duplicative litigation."

Page 156. Add a new footnote 17a at the end of Paragraph (5):

[17a] See also Gilles & Friedman, *The New Qui Tam: A Model for the Enforcement of Group Rights in a Hostile Era*, 98 Tex.L.Rev. 489 (2020) (assessing state utilization of qui tam statutes to enforce state protections for vulnerable groups and noting different federal challenges that differently drafted statutes would encounter).

Page 156. Add to footnote 15:

Beck, *Qui Tam Litigation Against Government Officials: Constitutional Implications of a Neglected History*, 93 Notre Dame L.Rev. 1235 (2018), argues that from the fourteenth through the late eighteenth centuries, the British Parliament, colonial and then state legislatures, and the U.S. Congress all enacted qui tam legislation authorizing "informers" to sue public officials—such as tax collectors—for monetary penalties for failing to perform their duties. Drawing parallels between his findings and those of Professor Louis Jaffe and Raoul Berger, Seventh Edition p. 151–52, Professor Beck asserts that the Supreme Court has predicated standing doctrine, and particularly its demand for personalized injury, on a misapprehension of historical practices relevant to interpretation of Article III. At the same time, Beck notes important distinctions between historical qui tam actions and modern citizen suit provisions. Among them, qui tam plaintiffs had a pecuniary stake in the outcome of their legal actions, which were predicated in specific allegations of past wrongdoing. Professor Beck's article makes no claims about which historical facts should count for how much in determining whether modern standing doctrine should be overhauled. (For general discussion of the relevance of history to constitutional decisionmaking, see Fallon, *The Many and Varied Roles of History in Constitutional Adjudication*, 90 Notre Dame L.Rev. 1753 (2015).)

Page 160. Add at the end of Paragraph (7):

The disputes in ASARCO and Hollingsworth occur against the background of the long-settled rule that a plaintiff suing in federal court, even on a state law claim, must satisfy federal standing rules. For a challenge to that assumption as applied to diversity cases not raising federal questions, see Hessick, *Cases, Controversies, and Diversity,* 109 Nw.L.Rev. 57 (2015), arguing that application of state justiciability rules in diversity actions "would better achieve diversity jurisdiction's goals of providing an alternative forum for resolving state claims involving out-of-state litigants." According to Professor Hessick, "the reasons underlying federal justiciability doctrines" largely involve avoidance of judicial interference with other branches under the federal separation of powers and have no application to diversity cases. Do you agree?

———

B. STANDING TO ASSERT THE RIGHTS OF OTHERS AND RELATED ISSUES INVOLVING "FACIAL CHALLENGES" TO STATUTES

NOTE ON ASSERTING THE RIGHTS OF OTHERS

Page 165. Add to footnote 2:

For a suggestion that the Court should return to the traditional approach of sharply limiting third-party standing, coupled with a specific protest that the Court has gone astray in allowing doctors and abortion clinics to invoke women's abortion rights, see Whole Woman's Health v. Hellerstedt, 136 S.Ct. 2292, 2321 (2016) (Thomas, J., dissenting).

Page 166. Add at the end of Paragraph (3):

The Court divided sharply about third-party standing in June Medical Services LLC. v. Russo, 140 S.Ct. 2103 (2020), which invalidated a Louisiana statute that required any doctor who performs abortions to have admitting privileges at a nearby hospital. In allowing abortion doctors to assert the rights of their patients, Justice Breyer's plurality opinion for four Justices— with which the Chief Justice agreed with regard to standing—interwove several strands of argument: (1) the rule against third-party standing is prudential and therefore waivable; (2) the state had waived its objection in the lower courts; and (3) in any event, the Court "generally permitted plaintiffs to assert third-party rights where the 'enforcement of the challenged restriction against the litigant would result directly in the violation of third parties' rights'", as reflected in prior cases that had "permitted abortion providers to invoke the rights of their actual or potential patients".

Justice Alito, joined in relevant part by Justices Thomas and Gorsuch, disagreed about waiver on factual grounds. Further, he did not think that the plaintiffs qualified for third-party standing under traditional principles, due to the absence of a close relationship between the parties and the ability of women seeking abortion to assert their own rights. Additionally, Justice Alito insisted that conflict-of-interest principles, as recognized in cases including Elk Grove Unified School Dist. v. Newdow, Seventh Edition p. 158, precluded doctors from claiming third-party standing to challenge a law that the state defended as designed to protect the health of women whose rights the doctors sought to assert.

In response to the conflict-of-interest argument, Justice Breyer maintained that plaintiffs commonly are allowed to challenge statutes that were ostensibly enacted for the benefit of the parties whose rights they invoke. As examples, he cited Craig v. Boren, Seventh Edition p. 161, in which the state statute sought to protect young men from the perils of driving while intoxicated, and several prior abortion cases.

In a case of actual conflict of interest, should a challenger to a statute be able to invoke a third-party's rights? In a case in which the challenger seeks to assert the rights of a large number of absent parties, how should a court ascertain whether an actual conflict of interest exists?

Besides joining much of Justice Alito's opinion, Justice Thomas dissented separately to argue that the Court lacked subject matter jurisdiction because third-party standing was incompatible with historical understandings of Article III. With regard to third-party standing, Justice Kavanaugh, dissenting, said only that the district court should address the state's "new argument (raised for the first time in this Court)" on remand.

Page 168. Add at the end of footnote 7:

For the argument that private parties lack rights under most structural constitutional provisions and therefore should ordinarily have no standing to complain of violations, see Huq, *Standing for the Structural Constitution*, 99 Va.L.Rev. 1435 (2013). But see Barnett, *Standing for (and up to) Separation of Powers*, 91 Ind.L.J. 665 (2016) (arguing that structural challenges are analogous to "procedural" challenges for which causation and redressability requirements are relaxed and that injured parties may come within the zone of interests that structural provisions protect).

Page 168. Add a new footnote 7a at the end of Paragraph (4)(c):

[7a] Without reference to the Lexmark case, the Court applied traditional third-party standing analysis in Sessions v. Morales-Santana, 137 S.Ct. 1678 (2017). Justice Ginsburg's majority opinion held that a party seeking to establish U.S. citizenship could assert his father's equal protection rights in challenging a statute that preferred unwed citizen mothers over unwed citizen fathers in passing on their citizenship to children born abroad.

PRELIMINARY NOTE ON AS-APPLIED AND FACIAL CHALLENGES AND THE PROBLEM OF SEPARABILITY

Page 172. Add a new Paragraph (4)(c):

(c) Whole Woman's Health v. Hellerstedt, 136 S.Ct. 2293 (2016), held, by 5–3, that the district court had correctly upheld a facial challenge (which the Fifth Circuit subsequently rejected) to two provisions of Texas law that the Court found to constitute undue burdens on abortion rights: (1) a requirement that doctors performing abortions have admitting privileges at a hospital within 30 miles of the abortion facility, and (2) a mandate that all abortion facilities must meet "the minimum" statutory standards applicable to "ambulatory surgical centers" under state law. The Court ruled the provisions facially invalid despite a severability clause providing that "every provision, section, subsection, sentence, clause, phrase, or word in this Act, and every application of the provision [sic] in this Act, are severable from each other." The clause further directed that if "any application of any provision * * * is found by a court to be invalid, the remaining applications of that provision to all other persons and circumstances shall be severed and may not be affected." Writing for the Court, Justice Breyer reasoned that the challenged provisions "vastly increase the obstacles confronting women seeking abortions in Texas without providing any benefit to women's health capable of withstanding any meaningful scrutiny" and are therefore "unconstitutional on their face". He continued: "Including a severability provision in the law does not change that conclusion. Severability clauses, it is true, do express the enacting legislature's preference for a narrow judicial remedy. As a general matter, we attempt to honor that preference. But our cases have never required us to proceed application by conceivable application when confronted with a facially unconstitutional statutory provision. * * * Indeed, if a severability clause could impose such a requirement on courts, legislatures would easily be able to insulate unconstitutional statutes from most facial review. * * * A severability clause is not grounds for a court to 'devise a judicial remedy that * * * entail[s] quintessentially legislative work.' Ayotte v. Planned Parenthood of Northern New Eng., 546 U.S. 320, 329 (2006). * * * We reject Texas' invitation to pave the way for legislatures to immunize their statutes from facial review. * * * Texas' attempt to broadly draft a requirement to sever 'applications' does not require us to proceed in piecemeal fashion when we have found the statutory provisions at issue facially unconstitutional."

Justice Alito, joined by Chief Justice Roberts and Justice Thomas, dissented: "Federal courts have no authority to carpet-bomb state laws, knocking out provisions that are perfectly consistent with federal law, just because it would be too much bother to separate them from unconstitutional provisions. * * * By forgoing severability, the Court strikes down numerous provisions that could not plausibly impose an undue burden. For example, [under the provisions of Texas law that apply to ambulatory surgery centers,] [c]enters must maintain fire alarm and emergency communications systems, and eliminate '[h]azards that might lead to slipping, falling, electrical shock, burns, poisoning, or other trauma'. [The enforcement of these and other unexceptionable provisions is now] * * * enjoined. * * * If the Court is unwilling to undertake the careful severability analysis required, * * * [t]he proper course would be to remand to the lower courts."

Does the Court opinion effectively reject the assumption that state law determines the separability of state statutes, possibly on the ground that federal law determines facial invalidity and that total invalidation (rather than separation) is sometimes a necessary remedy, also as a matter of federal law? If so, how could the majority square that conclusion with cases such as Yazoo & Mississippi Valley R.R. v. Jackson Vinegar Co., Seventh Edition p. 168, which seem to presuppose that whether a state statute is subject to a facial challenge depends on state separability law? Does the Court impliedly hold that the particular severability clause at issue is unconstitutional in light of the challenged provisions' substantive content and effects, possibly on the ground that requiring piecemeal analysis would constitute an "undue burden" on abortion rights? If so, in what sense?

Most of the Court's substantive analysis in Whole Woman's Health rests on the ground that the challenged provisions are invalid based on their effects, but the opinion also quoted language affirming that statutes can be invalid if they have "the purpose of presenting a substantial obstacle to a woman seeking an abortion". The decision regarding facial challenges and non-severability might have fit better with seemingly settled doctrine if the Court had concluded that the challenged provisions had the forbidden purpose of unduly burdening abortion rights and that that forbidden purpose rendered them invalid in all possible applications. Would it be tenable to interpret the decision as resting on that basis despite the absence of textual evidence that the Court intended it so to be read?

Page 173. For the third sentence of Paragraph (5)(b), substitute the following:

(In Heckler, the Court found no constitutional violation and thus no need to provide a remedy of any kind.)

Page 173. Add to Paragraph (5)(b):

Sessions v. Morales-Santana, 137 S.Ct. 1678 (2017), also discussed pp. 5, 18, *supra*, echoed Califano v. Westcott that when a federal statute unconstitutionally benefits one class in preference to another, "the preferred rule in the typical case is to extend favorable treatment". But the Court, in an opinion by Justice Ginsburg, also recognized that withdrawal of benefits from the favored class is a constitutionally permissible remedy for equal protection violations, and it affirmed that "[t]he choice between these outcomes is governed by the legislature's intent, as revealed by the statute at hand." Turning to the statutory scheme at issue, the Court concluded that Congress would not have wanted to extend a provision of the immigration laws that made it easier for unwed citizen mothers than for either unwed citizen fathers or for married couples to pass on their citizenship to children born abroad: "Put to the choice, Congress, we believe, would have abrogated [the] exception [that favors unmarried citizen mothers who have resided in the U.S. only for short periods over otherwise similarly situated unwed fathers and married couples], preferring preservation of the general rule." Until and unless Congress enacted "a uniform prescription that neither favors nor disadvantages any person on the basis of gender", the Court determined, the otherwise generally applicable rule "should apply, prospectively, to children born to unwed U.S.-citizen mothers."

Why is extension of benefits "the preferred rule" if the choice of remedies "is governed by the legislature's intent"? Is there any basis on which a presumption for extension could be supported? Are there judicially manageable standards for determining what Congress would have done in the absence of a presumption?

The Court again applied severability doctrine to redress what Justice Kavanaugh's plurality opinion termed an "equal-treatment constitutional violation" of the First Amendment's Free Speech Clause in Barr v. American Ass'n of Political Consultants, Inc., 140 S.Ct. 2335 (2020). The Telephone Consumer Protection Act of 1991 generally prohibits robocalls to cell phones but, following a 2015 amendment, excepted robocalls made to collect debts owed to or guaranteed by the United States. In a challenge brought by plaintiffs who wished to make political robocalls, six Justices—though without a majority opinion—concluded that the statute discriminated impermissibly on the basis of content. Again without a majority opinion, seven Justices agreed that the appropriate judicial response was to sever the provision that exempted robocalls involving debts owed to or guaranteed by the government.

Justice Gorsuch, joined by Justice Thomas, dissented from the severability holding. Although he agreed that the statute was invalid as applied to the challengers, he thought that they lacked standing to challenge its application to debt collectors. Believing it problematic under the separation of powers for the Court, by severing a statutory exemption, "to render unlawful conduct that Congress has explicitly made lawful", Justice Gorsuch instead would have enjoined the application of the statute to the challengers. He concluded: "[I]f this is what modern 'severability doctrine' has become, it seems to me all the more reason to reconsider our course."

As Justice Kavanaugh noted in response, Justice Gorsuch's "proposed remedy", when conjoined with stare decisis, "would in effect allow all robocalls to cell phones—notwithstanding Congress's decisive choice to prohibit most robocalls to cell phones." Justice Kavanaugh added: "[T]here is no magic solution to severability that solves every conundrum, especially in equal-treatment cases, but the Court's current approach * * * is constitutional, stable, predictable, and commonsensical."

The severability "conundrum" arose in Barr partly as a result modern First Amendment doctrine that treats all forms of content discrimination as presumptively invalid and thereby gives rise to "equal-treatment constitutional violation[s]". Dissenting on the merits, Justice Breyer proposed reconsidering past decisions that subject all forms of content discrimination to strict judicial scrutiny. Had Justice Breyer prevailed, no severability conundrum would have arisen. Do the difficulties that arise in connection with "equal-treatment constitutional violation[s]" demonstrate a general infirmity in separability doctrine, or are they distinctive? May some of those difficulties result from judicial choices in crafting substantive constitutional tests?

Page 173. Add at the end of Paragraph (5)(c):

In Murphy v. NCAA, 138 S.Ct. 1461 (2018), a majority of the Justices followed the approach of the NFIB v. Sebelius dissent by refusing to sever and uphold what they regarded as secondary statutory provisions after invalidating a central one. In an opinion by Justice Alito, the Court ruled that the Professional and Amateur Sports Protection Act (PASPA) unconstitutionally commandeered state legislatures by forbidding them to authorize gambling on sporting events. Having done so, the majority declined to sever provisions that would have (a) prohibited the States from themselves sponsoring or advertising sports gambling schemes and (b) barred private actors from operating gambling schemes pursuant to state law. Writing for a 6–3 majority, Justice Alito reasoned that if Congress had known that states could authorize gambling by private entities, it would not have "wanted" to bar state lotteries, which "were thought more benign" than private gambling, nor to prohibit only those private gambling operations that the states had authorized. Justice Ginsburg's dissenting opinion, which Justice Sotomayor joined in whole and Justice Breyer in part, complained that "[t]he Court wields an axe to cut down [the challenged statute] instead of using a scalpel to trim [it]": "Deleting the alleged 'commandeering' directions would free the statute to accomplish just what Congress legitimately sought to achieve: stopping sports-gambling regimes while making it clear that the stoppage is attributable to federal, not state, action." Is hypothesizing counterfactual intent (involving what Congress would have wanted, if an unforeseen partial invalidation were to occur) as a basis for declining to sever statutes more or less defensible than appealing to legislative intent as a basis for interpreting statutes? Concurring in Murphy, Justice Thomas raised related questions, and suggested that they had no good answers, but joined the majority in full because "no party in this case has asked us to reconsider [modern severability] precedents". Did the Court's precedents dictate Murphy's approach to severability?

Page 174. Add at the end of Paragraph (5)(d):

Fish, *Severability as Conditionality,* 64 Emory L.J. 1293 (2015), argues that courts lack the authority to hold statutes non-severable except insofar as the legislature, as a matter of statutory interpretation, has explicitly or implicitly made the continuing validity of one part of a statute—defined as one or more words—conditional on another part. According to the author, this approach would recognize that courts lack constitutional competence to make policy-based judgments concerning how statutes ought to operate following the invalidation of an isolable part. Note that issues of statutes' separability arise not only with respect to words that have no valid applications, but also with respect to words or strings of words that may be unconstitutional in some applications but constitutional in others (if invalid applications are deemed severable). For example, a statute that forbids "speaking to a woman within 50 feet of an abortion facility without her consent" would have many invalid applications, but severability doctrine determines whether it could be enforced against an abortion protestor who utters constitutionally prohibitable threats against a woman within 50 feet of an abortion facility.

See also Manheim, *Beyond Severability*, 101 Iowa L.Rev. 1833 (2016) (incisively critiquing a broad menu of approaches to severability, and advocating an approach to "flawed statutes" that would identify and implement whatever "option[ ] the legislature would prefer", but offering no specific guidance on how to discern legislative intent).

Page 175. Add to footnote 4:

For a conceptual survey of judicial approaches to separability and defense of a methodology aimed at preserving statutory purposes, see Fish, *Choosing Constitutional Remedies*, 63 UCLA L.Rev. 322 (2016).

Fish, *Judicial Amendment of Statutes*, 84 Geo.Wash.L.Rev. 563 (2016), argues that when courts find statutes unconstitutional, they often remedy the identified defects through judicial amendment, rather than mere severance of invalid language. As examples, the author cites United States v. Booker, Seventh Edition p. 174, and Heckler v. Mathews, Seventh Edition p. 173. Even if Fish were correct in his analysis of the Supreme Court's rulings in cases such as Booker and Heckler, would it follow, as Fish suggests, that courts have a general power to amend otherwise invalid statutes, rather than that the Court has overstepped its constitutional role in some past cases?

NOTE ON THE SCOPE OF THE ISSUE IN FIRST AMENDMENT CASES AND RELATED PROBLEMS INVOLVING "FACIAL CHALLENGES"

Page 184. Add at the end of the carryover paragraph:

Expressions Hair Design v. Schneiderman, 137 S.Ct. 1144 (2017), reiterated that "a plaintiff whose speech is clearly proscribed cannot raise a successful vagueness claim" even in a First Amendment case.

NOTE ON FACIAL CHALLENGES AND OVERBREADTH BEYOND THE FIRST AMENDMENT

Page 185. Add a new footnote * at the end of the first full paragraph:

* Distinct from whether a court can adjudicate a facial challenge is whether a lower federal court, in upholding one, can issue a universal injunction barring a statute's enforcement against other parties in other districts and other circuits. In a concurring opinion in Trump v. Hawaii, 138 S.Ct. 2392 (2018), Justice Thomas characterized universal injunctions as "a recent development, emerging for the first time in the 1960s and dramatically increasing in popularity only very recently." He questioned whether federal courts have either statutory or constitutional jurisdiction to issue universal injunctions. Justice Gorsuch, joined by Justice Thomas, took up similar themes in an opinion concurring in the Supreme Court's grant of a stay of a universal injunction in Dep't of Homeland Security v. New York, 140 S.Ct. 599 (2020). (The injunction barred the enforcement of a Department of Homeland Security rule defining "public charge" under a federal statute that denied noncitizens admission into the United States if, "in the opinion of" the Attorney General, the noncitizen is "likely at any time to become a public charge." 8 U.S.C. § 1182(a)(4)(A); see 84 Fed.Reg. 41,292 (Aug. 14, 2019) (Rule).) In calling for the Court to "take up some of the underlying equitable and constitutional questions raised by the rise of nationwide injunctions," Justice Gorsuch noted that such remedies can preclude the percolation of issues through multiple circuits. But he also stressed that the stakes for the parties to a suit seeking nationwide relief are asymmetric: "Because plaintiffs generally are not bound by adverse decisions in cases to which they were not a party, there is a nearly boundless opportunity to shop for a friendly forum to secure a win nationwide." (By contrast, if a lower court upheld a constitutional challenge to a rule or statute but did not issue a nationwide injunction, nonmutual offensive issue preclusion would not normally apply against the government. See United States v. Mendoza, 464 U.S. 154 (1984), Seventh Edition p. 1370.)

The opinions by Justices Thomas and Gorsuch both relied in part on two recent articles: Bray, *Multiple Chancellors: Reforming the National Injunction*, 131 Harv.L.Rev. 417 (2017) (arguing that universal injunctions were rare if not nonexistent until recent times and concluding that the Article III "judicial Power" is solely "a power to decide a case for a particular claimant"); and Morley, *De Facto Class Actions? Plaintiff- and Defendant-Oriented Injunctions in Voting Rights, Election Law, and Other Constitutional Cases*, 39 Harv.J.L. & Pub.Pol'y 487 (2016) (mounting a multifaceted attack on the casual issuance of nationwide injunctions against the enforcement of federal statutes, orders, and regulations); see also Siddique, *Nationwide Injunctions*, 117 Colum.L.Rev. 2095 (2017) (arguing that federal courts should, and normally do, adhere to the principle that an injunction should extend no further than necessary to provide "complete relief to the plaintiffs" and proposing an amendment to Rule 65 of the FRCP to codify this requirement).

Responding to the argument that universal injunctions are a recent innovation, Sohoni, *The Lost History of the "Universal" Injunction*, 133 Harv.L.Rev. 920 (2020), offers historical evidence that "Article III courts have issued injunctions that extend beyond just the plaintiff for well over a century." Sohoni's article complements an earlier argument by Frost, *In Defense of Nationwide Injunctions*, 93 N.Y.U.L.Rev. 1065 (2018), that nationwide injunctions lie within the Article III judicial power and that district courts should be able to issue them "in three categories of cases: when they are the only method of providing the plaintiff with complete relief; when they are the only means of preventing irreparable injury to individuals similarly situated to plaintiffs; and when they are the only practical remedy because a more limited injunction would be chaotic to administer and would impose significant costs on the courts or others." Although highly critical of proposals "to outright strip the federal courts of the substantive power to grant" universal injunctions, Professor Sohoni acknowledges that universal injunctions often pose distinctive problems and should rarely issue. She also points out that the Congress of an earlier era responded to perceived abuses of federal equitable powers by channeling suits seeking federal injunctions against state statutes to three-judge district courts. For discussion of a variety of limitations on the award of federal equitable relief—including some imposed by Congress and others crafted by the Supreme Court—see the Seventh Edition, Chapter X.

Page 185. Add at the end of Paragraph (2):

City of Los Angeles v. Patel, 576 U.S. 409 (2015), upheld a facial challenge under the Fourth Amendment to a provision compelling hotel operators to keep records containing specified information about their guests and to make those records available to police on demand. In doing so, Justice Sotomayor's majority opinion noted that the Court had allowed facial challenges "under a diverse array of constitutional provisions" including the Second Amendment, the Due Process Clause, and the Foreign Commerce Clause, as well as the First Amendment. Justice Sotomayor described the formula of United States v. Salerno, Seventh Edition p. 184, under which a statute will be invalidated facially only if it is unconstitutional in all of its applications, as "the most exacting standard that the Court has prescribed for facial challenges". But she found even that standard to be satisfied by reasoning that the challenged provision was "irrelevant" to any case in which the Fourth Amendment itself permitted warrantless searches. Given the provision's irrelevancy in most cases, its only practical effect came when it purported to permit searches that the Fourth Amendment forbade, and it was therefore unconstitutional as applied to all cases in which it mattered.

Writing in dissent, Justice Scalia, joined by Chief Justice Roberts and Justice Thomas, argued that the challenged ordinance constituted a legislative authorization of warrantless searches of historically closely regulated businesses and that it had many valid applications. Justice Alito's separate dissenting opinion, in which Justice Thomas joined, offered a series of hypothetical cases in which the penalty provisions of the challenged ordinance might coerce hotel owners and personnel to cooperate with otherwise valid searches. These cases, he argued, demonstrated that the challenged ordinance was not invalid in all applications in which it had practical effect. For the majority, Justice Sotomayor parried that "[a]n otherwise facially unconstitutional statute cannot be saved from invalidation based solely on the existence of a penalty provision that applies when searches are not actually authorized by the statute." Why not?

Page 192. Add at the end of Paragraph (7):

Johnson v. United States, 135 S.Ct. 2551 (2015), held a penalty-enhancing provision of the Armed Career Criminal Act (ACCA) to be constitutionally invalid on its face due to vagueness. The challenged provision provided enhanced punishment for defendants convicted of being felons in possession of a firearm if they had three or more previous convictions for a "violent felony". The ACCA defines "violent felony" to include certain enumerated crimes such as burglary and arson and any other felony that "involves conduct that presents a serious potential risk of physical injury to another." To apply the ACCA's penalty-enhancement provisions, a prior Court decision had prescribed a "categorical" approach, which "requires a court to picture the kind of conduct that [a prior] crime involves in 'the ordinary case,' and to judge whether that abstraction presents a serious potential risk of physical injury." Against the background of that holding, "[t]wo features of the [challenged] clause conspire[d] to make it unconstitutionally vague." It left "grave uncertainty about how to estimate the risk posed by a [type of] crime." And it created a comparable "uncertainty about how much risk it takes for a crime to qualify as a violent felony." Justice Scalia, speaking for the Court, concluded that because the resulting indeterminacy "both denies fair notice to defendants and invites arbitrary enforcement by judges", the statute violated the demand for clarity that due process imposes in criminal cases. In reaching that conclusion, Justice Scalia rejected an argument, pressed by Justice Alito in dissent, that a facial challenge must fail "because some crimes clearly pose a serious risk of physical injury to another" and the statute therefore must have some valid applications. "[A]lthough statements in some of our opinions could be read to suggest otherwise, our *holdings* squarely contradict the theory that a vague provision is constitutional merely because there is some conduct that clearly falls within the provision's grasp", Justice Scalia wrote. The Court's holding, he insisted, did not threaten the validity of criminal statutes that "use terms like 'substantial risk'" but do not "require[ ] application of the 'serious potential risk' standard to an idealized ordinary case of the crime."

Justices Kennedy and Thomas, in separate opinions concurring only in the judgment, both concluded that the petitioner's conviction for possession of a short-barreled shotgun did not qualify as a violent felony. Justice Alito dissented. He would have interpreted the ACCA to avoid vagueness problems by holding that it requires conduct-specific determinations of whether a defendant's own prior felonies posed a serious risk of physical injury to another. But he contended that even if a categorical approach were used, vagueness challenges not involving the First Amendment had to be addressed "on an as-applied basis" and that some felonies (such as attempted rape) certainly would pose a serious potential risk of physical injury in the ordinary case.

The most obvious significance of Johnson lies in its rejection of the premise that a facial challenge based on vagueness grounds must fail if a statute has any valid applications—a premise that Justice Alito described as "an application of the broader rule", asserted in United States v. Salerno, Seventh Edition p. 184, "that, except in First Amendment cases, we will hold that a statute is facially unconstitutional only if 'no set of circumstances exists under which the Act would be valid.'" Sessions v. Dimaya, 138 S.Ct. 1204 (2018), extended the Johnson rationale from a criminal to a civil case, though Justice Kagan's plurality opinion spoke narrowly on this point by emphasizing the severity of the penalty—the removal from the United States of a lawfully present non-citizen—that was at stake.[6a]

[6a] Sessions v. Dimaya turned on a provision of the Immigration and Naturalization Act that virtually mandated removal of any non-citizen convicted of a "crime of violence" while in the U.S. Finding close similarities to the statute in Johnson, which also required courts to determine whether a crime was likely to be violent in most cases, the plurality rejected suggestions that a more permissive void-for-vagueness standard should apply in civil removal actions than in criminal cases. Concurring in part and in the judgment, Justice Gorsuch agreed that robust void-for-vagueness analysis applied, but he saw no good reason why Congress should need to "speak more clearly when it seeks to deport a lawfully resident alien than when it wishes to subject a citizen to indefinite civil commitment, strip him of a business license essential to his family's living, or confiscate his home." Chief Justice Roberts, joined by Justices Kennedy, Thomas, and Alito, dissented, finding the statute materially less vague than that in Johnson. Justice Thomas filed a separate dissent in which he questioned whether modern vagueness doctrine could be justified as consistent with the original meaning of the Due Process Clause. (Justice Gorsuch's concurring opinion agreed with Justice Thomas about the importance of that question. He concluded, however, that "the vagueness doctrine enjoys a secure footing in the original understanding".)

In United States v. Davis, 139 S.Ct. 2329 (2019), the Court, in an opinion by Justice Gorsuch, found that a statute imposing heightened penalties for felonies "that by [their] nature, involv[e] a substantial risk that physical force * * * may be used" referred to an imagined ordinary instance of the crime and was therefore unconstitutionally vague under *Johnson.* Justice Kavanaugh, in an opinion that three other Justices joined, dissented on statutory interpretation grounds, insisting that the challenged statute called for a permissible, case-specific calculation of the risk posed by a particular defendant's unlawful conduct.

_____

4. MOOTNESS

NOTE ON MOOTNESS: ITS RATIONALE AND APPLICATIONS

Page 201. Add to footnote 3:

In *Fisher v. University of Texas,* 136 S.Ct. 2198 (2016), the Court, without noticing any mootness issue, ruled on an equal protection challenge to affirmative action policies in place in 2008, even though "[p]etitioner long since has graduated from another college, and the University's policy—and the data on which it first was based—may have evolved or changed in material ways."

Page 203. Add a Subparagraph (3)(d):

(d)   *New York State Rifle & Pistol Ass'n, Inc. v. City of New York,* 140 S.Ct. 1525 (2020), arose when the petitioners sought declaratory and injunctive relief from a New York City ordinance that barred possessors of licenses to keep handguns in their homes from transporting their weapons anywhere besides seven firing ranges within the City. The challengers' complaint maintained that the Second Amendment requires "unrestricted access to gun ranges and shooting events." After two lower courts upheld the ordinance and the Supreme Court granted certiorari, the New York Legislature enacted legislation abrogating any local regulation that prevented the holders of "premises licenses" from transporting their guns "directly to or from" an authorized range, competition, or second home. Nearly contemporaneously, the City amended its regulation to conform to the new state law.

The Supreme Court vacated the lower court's decision invalidating the original New York ordinance in a brief *per curiam* opinion that held the petitioners' claim to declaratory and injunctive relief to be moot. Following the changes in New York State and City law, the Court reasoned, "petitioners may now transport firearms to a second home or shooting range outside the city, which is the precise relief that [they] requested." The Court then declined to consider whether mootness might be averted based on a request for damages that the petitioners raised for the first time in the Supreme Court. Instead, it remanded the case for the lower courts to consider whether the petitioners "may still add a claim for damages in this lawsuit."

Justice Alito dissented, joined by Justice Gorsuch in full and Justice Thomas in part. He maintained that New York's newly enacted rule continued to burden the petitioners' asserted right of "unrestricted access" to gun ranges by limiting them to traveling "directly" to and from their homes. Accordingly, he reasoned, they had not received the complete relief that they sought, and their claim to injunctive relief therefore was not moot. Justice Alito concluded that the petitioners' claim to damages relief also sufficed to save the case from mootness. Reaching the merits, he found that the amended New York ordinance violated the Second Amendment.

With regard to mootness, the core disagreement between the *per curiam* opinion and Justice Alito's dissent appeared to lie in divergent understandings of what would constitute a continuing, live claim to judicial "relief" in the absence of damages. The Court's cryptic observation that New York's change of law gave the petitioners "the precise relief that [they] requested" seems not strictly correct. The petitioners sought an injunction against the enforcement of what they maintained was an invalid statute, not a voluntarily enacted change of law that fell short of granting "unrestricted" rights to transport licensed weapons to shooting ranges and gun shows. By contrast, the dissent's conception of the "relief" sought by the petitioners— the absence of which kept the dispute alive—encompassed protection against any regulation, whenever enacted, that denied the broad rights to transport licensed weapons that they claimed under the Second Amendment.

The Justices' divergent understandings of what constitutes a live, continuing claim to injunctive and declaratory "relief" seem likely to matter only in cases on appeal. In the district court, the plaintiffs would undoubtedly have standing to challenge the newly enacted New York City ordinance, in a new action if not through an amendment of their complaint. But if the arguments bearing on the validity of the amended ordinance might differ in material respects from those concerning the original ordinance—for example, if it is arguable that the new ordinance is valid under the Second Amendment even if the old one was not—it is a different question whether the Supreme Court should be the first court to address those arguments. Does mootness doctrine furnish an apt analytical framework for resolving that question? Note, too, that if the Court had deemed the dispute between the parties justiciable based on a damages claim, it presumably would have had to determine the constitutionality of the original New York ordinance, whereas a determination that the plaintiffs suffered a continuing injury would have had to focus on the revised New York ordinance. Under these circumstances, how should the Court have responded to New York's deliberate efforts to render the case moot? Given the complexity of the entwined issues of justiciability and orderly appellate procedure, is the Court fairly subject to criticism for disposing of the case in a terse and sometimes opaque *per curiam* opinion?

Page 203. Add to footnote 6:

A unanimous Court applied the mootness exception for cases capable of repetition, yet evading review in Kingdomware Technologies, Inc. v. United States, 136 S.Ct. 1969 (2016), in which a business owned by a service-disabled veteran challenged the Government's failure to award it short-term contracts pursuant to a narrow interpretation of a statute mandating preferences for service-disabled or other veteran-owned businesses. The contracts whose award Kingdomware Technologies sought to challenge were performed in less than two years, a period "too short to complete judicial review of the lawfulness of the procurement," and Kingdomware had "shown a reasonable likelihood that it would be awarded a future contract if its interpretation" prevailed.

———

NOTE ON MOOTNESS IN CLASS ACTIONS

Page 211. Add at the end of footnote 2:

The Court adopted the theory of Justice Kagan's dissent in Genesis Healthcare Corp. v. Symczyk, Seventh Edition p. 210, in Campbell-Ewald Co. v. Gomez, 136 S.Ct. 663 (2016). Gomez filed a class action complaint in which he alleged that the defendant violated his rights under the Telephone Consumer Protection Act by sending him unauthorized text messages and sought $1,500 in damages, the maximum that he could recover under the Act. Campbell-Ewald made a settlement offer of the full amount, which Gomez refused. Campbell-Ewald then argued that its offer had mooted the case. Writing for five Justices, Justice Ginsburg held that "under basic principles of contract law" the "unaccepted offer" was "a legal nullity, with no operative effect" and that both parties thus "retained the same stake in the litigation they had at the outset." In a potentially important passage at the end of her opinion, however, Justice Ginsburg reserved the question "whether the result would be different if a defendant deposits the full amount of the plaintiff's individual claim in an account payable to the plaintiff, and the court then enters judgment for the plaintiff in that amount." Is there any reason why a defendant who wished to forestall a class action by offering to pay the named plaintiff's claim prior to class certification would not make such a deposit? (If not, has Justice Ginsburg suggested that the defendant may moot any such class action simply by taking one additional step with respect to the named plaintiff?) Justice Thomas concurred on the ground that the defendant had not satisfied the common law standard for a "tender" of complete relief, which required an admission of liability. Chief Justice Roberts, joined by Justices Scalia and Alito, dissented.

Again emphasizing the significance of Rule 23, United States v. Sanchez-Gomez, 138 S.Ct. 1532 (2018), unanimously held that the rationale of Gerstein and Geraghty did not extend to challenges, raised on motions in criminal actions, to a U.S. Marshall Service policy of shackling in-custody defendants for some court appearances. Although the court of appeals had viewed the challenges by four defendants as a "functional class action", the Court found all of the individual cases to be moot on appeal in the absence of any formal mechanism for class certification.

---

5. RIPENESS

NOTE ON "RIPENESS" IN PUBLIC LITIGATION CHALLENGING THE VALIDITY OR APPLICATION OF STATUTES AND REGULATIONS

Page 225. Add at the end of Paragraph (3)(b):

In Knick v. Township of Scott, 139 S.Ct. 2162 (2019), also discussed p. 104, *infra*, the Court, by 5 to 4, partially overruled Williamson County, Seventh Edition p. 224, as based on a substantive misinterpretation of the Takings Clause. Under a proper interpretation, the Court ruled in an opinion by Chief Justice Roberts, a property owner suffers a constitutional violation as soon as "the government takes his property without just compensation, and therefore may bring his claim in federal court under § 1983 at that time." The requirement that the plaintiff pursue compensation in state court first constituted an impermissible requirement to exhaust state remedies that is incompatible with § 1983, the Chief Justice reasoned. The Court did not question Williamson County's alternative holding that a takings claim does not become ripe until a property owner has pursued opportunities for administrative relief from regulatory burdens (such as seeking a variance from a zoning ordinance).

Dissenting, Justice Kagan defended the aspect of Williamson County that the Court overruled as "rooted in" a correct "understanding of the Fifth Amendment's Takings Clause stretching back to the late 1800s." Like the

Chief Justice, Justice Kagan appeared to view Williamson County's reference to ripeness as inseparable from its conclusions about the scope of the Taking Clause's substantive guarantee.

———

6. POLITICAL QUESTIONS

NOTE ON POLITICAL QUESTIONS

Page 249. Add at the end of footnote 3:

Grove, *The Lost History of the Political Question Doctrine*, 90 N.Y.U.L.Rev. 1908 (2015), argues that the modern political question doctrine is a twentieth-century invention. Under the "traditional" doctrine that applied throughout the nineteenth century, Professor Grove writes, "political questions were *factual* determinations made by the political branches that courts treated as conclusive in the course of resolving cases." Based on Professor Grove's evidence, the line between law and fact does not appear sharp, and she acknowledges that the Court breached it, at least in dictum, in Luther v. Borden, Seventh Edition p. 258. Nevertheless, she maintains, the traditional doctrine was not jurisdictional: the Court exercised its jurisdiction to apply the determination of another branch. According to Professor Grove, the modern, jurisdictional doctrine had its first flowering in 1912, in Pacific States Tel. & Tel. Co. v. Oregon, Seventh Edition p. 259, but even the reasoning of that decision was arguably limited to the Guarantee Clause. After gaining traction in some plurality opinions, the modern, general, jurisdictional doctrine emerged only in 1962 in Baker v. Carr, Seventh Edition p. 250. Professor Grove attributes the rise of the modern doctrine largely to casebook authors in the "legal process" school, beginning with then-Professor Felix Frankfurter and later including Henry Hart and Herbert Wechsler, who, she writes, sought more generally to limit the range of properly judicial authority with jurisdictional doctrines that they ascribed to Article III. In Professor Grove's view, the modern political question doctrine is vulnerable to criticism both because it lacks historical foundations and because it gives the Supreme Court too much power, not too little: by reserving "for itself the power to decide which institution decides any constitutional question * * * the Court has most often used its modern political question cases * * * as a vehicle to assert its supremacy over various areas of constitutional law." However one judges a number of Professor Grove's specific claims, the article offers a fascinating study in the possibility of historically evolving understandings of a concept and of the use of that concept to serve shifting agendas.

Page 253. Substitute the following for the second paragraph of Paragraph (4) and the remainder of the Paragraph:

In Rucho v. Common Cause, 139 S.Ct. 2484 (2019), which follows immediately in this Supplement, a majority of the Justices found that challenges to partisan gerrymanders present nonjusticiable political questions due to an absence of judicially manageable standards.

Page 257. After Paragraph (7), add the following principal case and accompanying Notes:

Rucho v. Common Cause

___ U.S. ___, 139 S.Ct. 2484, 204 L.Ed.2d 931 (2019).
Appeal from the United States District Court
for the Middle District of North Carolina.

■ CHIEF JUSTICE ROBERTS delivered the opinion of the Court.

Voters and other plaintiffs in North Carolina and Maryland challenged their States' congressional districting maps as unconstitutional partisan gerrymanders. The North Carolina plaintiffs complained that the State's districting plan discriminated against Democrats; the Maryland plaintiffs complained that their State's plan discriminated against Republicans. The plaintiffs alleged that the gerrymandering violated the First Amendment, the Equal Protection Clause of the Fourteenth Amendment, the Elections Clause, and Article I, § 2, of the Constitution. * * *

I

[All agree that the partisan gerrymanders at issue in the two cases were deliberate and at least initially highly effective. In Rucho, the case from North Carolina,] one of the two Republicans chairing the redistricting committee * * * explained that the map was drawn with the aim of electing ten Republicans and three Democrats because he did "not believe it [would be] possible to draw a map with 11 Republicans and 2 Democrats." One Democratic state senator objected that entrenching the 10–3 advantage for Republicans was not "fair, reasonable, [or] balanced" because, as recently as 2012, "Democratic congressional candidates had received more votes on a statewide basis than Republican candidates." * * * In November 2016, North Carolina conducted congressional elections using the 2016 Plan [at issue in the litigation], and Republican candidates won 10 of the 13 congressional districts. * * *

The second case before us is Lamone v. Benisek. In 2011, the Maryland Legislature—dominated by Democrats—undertook to redraw the lines of that State's eight congressional districts. The Governor at the time, Democrat Martin O'Malley, * * * appointed a redistricting committee to help redraw the map * * *. The Governor later testified that his aim was to "use the redistricting process to change the overall composition of Maryland's congressional delegation to 7 Democrats and 1 Republican by flipping" one district. * * * The 2011 Plan accomplished that by moving roughly 360,000 voters out of the Sixth District and moving 350,000 new voters in. Overall, the Plan reduced the number of registered Republicans in the Sixth District by about 66,000 and increased the number of registered Democrats by about 24,000. The map was adopted by a party-line vote. It was used in the 2012 election and succeeded in flipping the Sixth District. A Democrat has held the seat ever since.

II

A

* * * In these cases we are asked to decide an important question of constitutional law. "But before we do so, we must find that the question is presented in a 'case' or 'controversy' that is, in James Madison's words, 'of a Judiciary Nature.'" DaimlerChrysler Corp. v. Cuno, 547 U.S. 332, 342 (2006) (quoting 2 Records of the Federal Convention of 1787, p. 430 (M. Farrand ed. 1966)). * * * The question here is whether there is an "appropriate role for the Federal Judiciary" in remedying the problem of partisan gerrymandering—whether such claims are claims of *legal* right,

resolvable according to *legal* principles, or political questions that must find their resolution elsewhere.

B

Partisan gerrymandering is nothing new. Nor is frustration with it. * * * The Framers addressed the election of Representatives to Congress in the Elections Clause. Art. I, § 4, cl. 1. That provision assigns to state legislatures the power to prescribe the "Times, Places and Manner of holding Elections" for Members of Congress, while giving Congress the power to "make or alter" any such regulations. * * * [The Court here cited historical examples of congressional regulation before recognizing that only a requirement that states use single-member districts remains in place today.] * * *

Appellants suggest that, through the Elections Clause, the Framers set aside electoral issues such as the one before us as questions that only Congress can resolve. We do not agree. In two areas—one-person, one-vote and racial gerrymandering—our cases have held that there is a role for the courts with respect to at least some issues that could arise from a State's drawing of congressional districts. See Wesberry v. Sanders, 376 U.S. 1 (1964); Shaw v. Reno, 509 U.S. 630 (1993).

But the history is not irrelevant. The Framers were aware of electoral districting problems and considered what to do about them. * * * At no point was there a suggestion that the federal courts had a role to play. Nor was there any indication that the Framers had ever heard of courts doing such a thing.

C

* * * Partisan gerrymandering claims have proved far more difficult to adjudicate [than one-person, one-vote cases and cases involving racial discrimination]. The basic reason is that, while it is illegal for a jurisdiction to depart from the one-person, one-vote rule, or to engage in racial discrimination in districting, "a jurisdiction may engage in constitutional political gerrymandering." Hunt v. Cromartie, 526 U.S. 541, 551 (1999) (citing Bush v. Vera, 517 U.S. 952, 968 (1996); [further citations omitted].

To hold that legislators cannot take partisan interests into account when drawing district lines would essentially countermand the Framers' decision to entrust districting to political entities. The "central problem" is not determining whether a jurisdiction has engaged in partisan gerrymandering. It is "determining when political gerrymandering has gone too far." Vieth [v. Jubelirer, 541 U.S. 267, 296 (2004) (plurality opinion)]. [The Court here recounted its prior confrontations will challenges to political gerrymandering. In Davis v. Bandemer, 478 U.S. 109 (1986)), a majority thought the case was justiciable but splintered over the proper standard to apply. Four Justices (White, Brennan, Marshall, and Blackmun) would have required proof of "intentional discrimination against an identifiable political group and an actual discriminatory effect on that group." Two Justices (Powell and Stevens) would have focused on "whether the boundaries of the voting districts have been distorted deliberately and arbitrarily to achieve illegitimate ends." But Justice O'Connor, joined by Chief Justice Burger and Justice Rehnquist, would have held that partisan gerrymandering claims pose political questions because the Equal Protection Clause simply "does not supply judicially manageable standards for resolving" them.

[Eighteen years later, in Vieth, Justice Scalia's plurality opinion also would have held challenges to gerrymanders nonjusticiable due to an absence of judicially manageable standards.] Justice Kennedy, concurring in the judgment, noted "the lack of comprehensive and neutral principles for drawing electoral boundaries [and] the absence of rules to limit and confine judicial intervention." He nonetheless left open the possibility that "in another case a standard might emerge." Four Justices dissented. * * *

III

[The] question [in appraising political gerrymandering claims] is one of degree: How to "provid[e] a standard for deciding how much partisan dominance is too much." League of United Latin American Citizens v. Perry, 548 U.S. 399, 420 (2006) (opinion of Kennedy, J.). And it is vital in such circumstances that the Court act only in accord with especially clear standards: "With uncertain limits, intervening courts—even when proceeding with best intentions—would risk assuming political, not legal, responsibility for a process that often produces ill will and distrust." Vieth, 541 U.S., at 307 (opinion of Kennedy, J.). * * *

* * * Partisan gerrymandering claims invariably sound in a desire for proportional representation. * * * "Our cases, however, clearly foreclose any claim that the Constitution requires proportional representation * * *." * * * Unable to claim that the Constitution requires proportional representation outright, plaintiffs inevitably ask the courts to make their own political judgment about how much representation particular political parties *deserve*—based on the votes of their supporters—and to rearrange the challenged districts to achieve that end. But federal courts are not equipped to apportion political power as a matter of fairness, nor is there any basis for concluding that they were authorized to do so. * * *

The initial difficulty in settling on a "clear, manageable and politically neutral" test for fairness is that it is not even clear what fairness looks like in this context. * * * Fairness may mean a greater number of competitive districts. * * * On the other hand, perhaps the ultimate objective of a "fairer" share of seats in the congressional delegation is most readily achieved by yielding to the gravitational pull of proportionality and engaging in cracking and packing, to ensure each party its "appropriate" share of "safe" seats. * * * Or perhaps fairness should be measured by adherence to "traditional" districting criteria, such as maintaining political subdivisions, keeping communities of interest together, and protecting incumbents. * * *

Deciding among just these different visions of fairness (you can imagine many others) poses basic questions that are political, not legal. There are no legal standards discernible in the Constitution for making such judgments, let alone limited and precise standards that are clear, manageable, and politically neutral. * * *

Even assuming the court knew which version of fairness to be looking for, there are no discernible and manageable standards for deciding whether there has been a violation. * * * Appellees contend that if we can adjudicate one-person, one-vote claims, we can also assess partisan gerrymandering claims. * * * [But] "vote dilution" in the one-person, one-vote cases refers to the idea that each vote must carry equal weight. * * * That requirement does not extend to political parties. It does not mean that each party must be influential in proportion to its number of supporters.

IV

Appellees and the dissent propose a number of "tests" for evaluating partisan gerrymandering claims, but none meets the need for a limited and precise standard that is judicially discernible and manageable. And none provides a solid grounding for judges to take the extraordinary step of reallocating power and influence between political parties. * * *

A

[The District Court in the North Carolina case used a test that involved a "predominant" legislative purpose coupled with a demand for] a showing "that the dilution of the votes of supporters of a disfavored party in a particular district * * * is likely to persist in subsequent elections such that an elected representative from the favored party in the district will not feel a need to be responsive to constituents who support the disfavored party." * * *

The District Court's "predominant intent" prong is borrowed from the racial gerrymandering context. * * * If district lines were drawn for the purpose of separating racial groups, then they are subject to strict scrutiny because "race-based decisionmaking is inherently suspect." But determining that lines were drawn on the basis of partisanship does not indicate that the districting was improper. A permissible intent—securing partisan advantage—does not become constitutionally impermissible, like racial discrimination, when that permissible intent "predominates."

The District Court tried to limit the reach of its test by requiring plaintiffs to show, in addition to predominant partisan intent, that vote dilution "is likely to persist" to such a degree that the elected representative will feel free to ignore the concerns of the supporters of the minority party. But "[t]o allow district courts to strike down apportionment plans on the basis of their prognostications as to the outcome of future elections . . . invites 'findings' on matters as to which neither judges nor anyone else can have any confidence." Bandemer, 478 U.S., at 160 (opinion of O'Connor, J.). * * *

B

The District Courts also found partisan gerrymandering claims justiciable under the First Amendment, coalescing around a basic three-part test: proof of intent to burden individuals based on their voting history or party affiliation; an actual burden on political speech or associational rights; and a causal link between the invidious intent and actual burden. * * * To begin, there are no restrictions on speech, association, or any other First Amendment activities in the districting plans at issue. * * * The plaintiffs' argument is that partisanship in districting should be regarded as simple discrimination against supporters of the opposing party on the basis of political viewpoint. * * * [But that test] simply describes the act of districting for partisan advantage. It provides no standard for determining when partisan activity goes too far.

As for actual burden, the slight anecdotal evidence found sufficient by the District Courts in these cases shows that this too is not a serious standard for separating constitutional from unconstitutional partisan gerrymandering. * * * How much of a decline in voter engagement is enough to constitute a First Amendment burden? How many door knocks must go unanswered? How many petitions unsigned? How many calls for volunteers unheeded? * * *

C

The dissent proposes using a State's own districting criteria as a neutral baseline from which to measure how extreme a partisan gerrymander is. The dissent would have us line up all the possible maps drawn using those criteria according to the partisan distribution they would produce. Distance from the "median" map would indicate whether a particular districting plan harms supporters of one party to an unconstitutional extent.

As an initial matter, it does not make sense to use criteria that will vary from State to State and year to year as the baseline for determining whether a gerrymander violates the Federal Constitution. The degree of partisan advantage that the Constitution tolerates should not turn on criteria offered by the gerrymanderers themselves. * * *

Even if we were to accept the dissent's proposed baseline, it would return us to "the original unanswerable question (How much political motivation and effect is too much?)." Vieth, 541 U.S., at 296–297 (plurality opinion). Would twenty percent away from the median map be okay? Forty percent? Sixty percent? Why or why not? * * *

The dissent argues that there are other instances in law where matters of degree are left to the courts. True enough. But those instances typically involve constitutional or statutory provisions or common law confining and guiding the exercise of judicial discretion. * * * Here, on the other hand, the Constitution provides no basis whatever to guide the exercise of judicial discretion. * * * The only provision in the Constitution that specifically addresses the matter assigns it to the political branches. See Art. I, § 4, cl. 1. [The Court next dismissed arguments based on the Elections Clause and Article I, § 2.]

V

Excessive partisanship in districting leads to results that reasonably seem unjust. But the fact that such gerrymandering is "incompatible with democratic principles," Arizona State Legislature [v. Arizona Independent Redistricting Comm'n, 135 S.Ct. 2652 (2015)], does not mean that the solution lies with the federal judiciary. * * * Federal judges have no license to reallocate political power between the two major political parties, with no plausible grant of authority in the Constitution, and no legal standards to limit and direct their decisions. * * *

Our conclusion does not condone excessive partisan gerrymandering. Nor does our conclusion condemn complaints about districting to echo into a void. The States, for example, are actively addressing the issue on a number of fronts. * * * [The Court here described state legislation, state ballot initiatives, and state constitutional amendments to limit partisan gerrymandering.] * * *

As noted, the Framers gave Congress the power to do something about partisan gerrymandering in the Elections Clause. * * * [The Court here described several bills introduced in Congress.] * * * We express no view on any of these pending proposals. We simply note that the avenue for reform established by the Framers, and used by Congress in the past, remains open. * * *

■ JUSTICE KAGAN, with whom JUSTICES GINSBURG, BREYER, and SOTOMAYOR join, dissenting.

For the first time ever, this Court refuses to remedy a constitutional violation because it thinks the task beyond judicial capabilities. * * * The partisan gerrymanders in these cases deprived citizens of the most fundamental of their constitutional rights: the rights to participate equally in the political process, to join with others to advance political beliefs, and to choose their political representatives. * * * If left unchecked, gerrymanders like the ones here may irreparably damage our system of government.

And checking them is *not* beyond the courts. The majority's abdication comes just when courts across the country, including those below, have coalesced around manageable judicial standards to resolve partisan gerrymandering claims. * * *

I

* * * [The] majority concedes (really, how could it not?) that gerrymandering is "incompatible with democratic principles." * * * That

recognition would seem to demand a response. The majority offers two ideas * * *. One is that the political process can deal with the problem— a proposition so dubious on its face that I feel secure in delaying my answer for some time. The other is that political gerrymanders have always been with us. To its credit, the majority does not frame that point as an originalist constitutional argument. After all (as the majority rightly notes), racial and residential gerrymanders were also once with us, but the Court has done something about that fact. The majority's idea instead seems to be that if we have lived with partisan gerrymanders so long, we will survive.

That complacency has no cause. * * * While bygone mapmakers may have drafted three or four alternative districting plans, today's mapmakers can generate thousands of possibilities at the touch of a key—and then choose the one giving their party maximum advantage (usually while still meeting traditional districting requirements). The effect is to make gerrymanders far more effective and durable than before, insulating politicians against all but the most titanic shifts in the political tides. * * *

Partisan gerrymandering of the kind before us not only subverts democracy (as if that weren't bad enough). It violates individuals' constitutional rights as well. * * * Th[e] practice implicates the Fourteenth Amendment's Equal Protection Clause. * * * And partisan gerrymandering implicates the First Amendment too. That Amendment gives its greatest protection to political beliefs, speech, and association. Yet partisan gerrymanders subject certain voters to "disfavored treatment"—again, counting their votes for less—precisely because of "their voting history [and] their expression of political views." Vieth, 541 U.S., at 314 (opinion of Kennedy, J.). * * *

[The] majority never disagrees; it appears to accept the "principle that each person must have an equal say in the election of representatives." And indeed, without this settled and shared understanding that cases like these inflict constitutional injury, the question of whether there are judicially manageable standards for resolving them would never come up.

II

So the only way to understand the majority's opinion is as follows: In the face of grievous harm to democratic governance and flagrant infringements on individuals' rights—in the face of escalating partisan manipulation whose compatibility with this Nation's values and law no one defends—the majority declines to provide any remedy. * * * I'll give the majority this one—and important—thing: It identifies some dangers everyone should want to avoid. Judges should not be apportioning political power based on their own vision of electoral fairness, whether proportional representation or any other. And judges should not be striking down maps left, right, and center, on the view that every smidgen of politics is a smidgen too much. Respect for state legislative processes—and restraint in the exercise of judicial authority—counsels intervention in only egregious cases.

But in throwing up its hands, the majority misses something under its nose: What it says can't be done *has* been done. Over the past several years, federal courts across the country—including, but not exclusively, in the decisions below—have largely converged on a standard for adjudicating partisan gerrymandering claims (striking down both Democratic and Republican districting plans in the process). * * *

A

Start with the standard the lower courts used. * * * [B]oth courts (like others around the country) used basically the same three-part test to decide whether the plaintiffs had made out a vote dilution claim. As many legal standards do, that test has three parts: (1) intent; (2) effects; and (3) causation. First, the plaintiffs challenging a districting plan must prove that state officials' "predominant purpose" in drawing a district's lines was to "entrench [their party] in power" by diluting the votes of citizens favoring its rival. [See Common Cause v. Rucho, 318 F. Supp. 3d 777, 805–806 (M.D.N.C. 2018).] Second, the plaintiffs must establish that the lines drawn in fact have the intended effect by "substantially" diluting their votes. [See Benisek v. Lamone, 348 F. Supp. 3d 493, 498 (D. Md. 2018).] And third, if the plaintiffs make those showings, the State must come up with a legitimate, non-partisan justification to save its map. If you are a lawyer, you know that this test looks utterly ordinary. It is the sort of thing courts work with every day. * * *

The majority's response to the District Courts' purpose analysis is discomfiting. The majority does not contest the lower courts' findings; how could it? Instead, the majority says that state officials' intent to entrench their party in power is perfectly "permissible," even when it is the predominant factor in drawing district lines. But that is wrong. * * * [W]hen political actors have a specific and predominant intent to entrench themselves in power by manipulating district lines, that goes too far. * * *

On to the second step of the analysis, where the plaintiffs must prove that the districting plan substantially dilutes their votes. * * * Consider the sort of evidence used in North Carolina first. There, the plaintiffs demonstrated the districting plan's effects mostly by relying on what might be called the "extreme outlier approach." * * * The approach—which also has recently been used in Michigan and Ohio litigation—begins by using advanced computing technology to randomly generate a large collection of districting plans that incorporate the State's physical and political geography and meet its declared districting criteria, *except for* partisan gain. * * * The further out on the tail, the more extreme the partisan distortion and the more significant the vote dilution.

Using that approach, the North Carolina plaintiffs offered a boatload of alternative districting plans—all showing that the State's map was an out-out-out-outlier. One expert produced 3,000 maps, adhering in the way described above to the districting criteria that the North Carolina redistricting committee had used, other than partisan advantage. To calculate the partisan outcome of those maps, the expert also used the same election data (a composite of seven elections) that [a North Carolina expert] had employed when devising the North Carolina plan in the first instance. * * * Every single one of the 3,000 maps would have produced at least one more Democratic House Member than the State's actual map, and 77% would have elected three or four more. * * * Based on those and other findings, the District Court determined that the North Carolina plan substantially dilutes the plaintiffs' votes.

Because the Maryland gerrymander involved just one district, the evidence in that case was far simpler—but no less powerful for that. * * * In the old Sixth [District], 47% of registered voters were Republicans and only 36% Democrats. But in the new Sixth, 44% of registered voters were Democrats and only 33% Republicans. That reversal of the district's partisan composition translated into four consecutive Democratic victories, including in a wave election year for Republicans (2014). In what was once a party stronghold, Republicans now have little or no chance to elect their preferred candidate. The District Court thus found that the gerrymandered Maryland map substantially dilutes Republicans' votes. * * *

By substantially diluting the votes of citizens favoring their rivals, the politicians of one party had succeeded in entrenching themselves in office. They had beat democracy.

B

The majority's broadest claim, as I've noted, is that this is a price we must pay because judicial oversight of partisan gerrymandering cannot be "politically neutral" or "manageable." * * * Consider neutrality first. Contrary to the majority's suggestion, the District Courts did not have to—and in fact did not—choose among competing visions of electoral fairness. That is because they did not try to compare the State's actual map to an "ideally fair" one (whether based on proportional representation or some other criterion). Instead, they looked at the difference between what the State did and what the State would have done if politicians hadn't been intent on partisan gain. Or put differently, the comparator (or baseline or touchstone) is the result not of a judge's philosophizing but of the State's own characteristics and judgments. * * *

The majority's sole response misses the point. According to the majority, "it does not make sense to use" a State's own (non-partisan) districting criteria as the baseline from which to measure partisan gerrymandering because those criteria "will vary from State to State and year to year." But that is a virtue, not a vice—a feature, not a bug. * * *

The majority's "how much is too much" critique fares no better than its neutrality argument. How about the following for a first-cut answer:

This much is too much. By any measure, a map that produces a greater partisan skew than any of 3,000 randomly generated maps (all with the State's political geography and districting criteria built in) reflects "too much" partisanship. Think about what I just said: The absolute worst of 3,001 possible maps. The *only one* that could produce a 10–3 partisan split even as Republicans got a bare majority of the statewide vote. And again: How much is too much? This much is too much: A map that without any evident non-partisan districting reason (to the contrary) shifted the composition of a district from 47% Republicans and 36% Democrats to 33% Republicans and 42% Democrats. A map that in 2011 was responsible for the largest partisan swing of a congressional district in the country.

And if the majority thought that approach too case-specific, it could have used the lower courts' general standard—focusing on "predominant" purpose and "substantial" effects—without fear of indeterminacy. I do not take even the majority to claim that courts are incapable of investigating whether legislators mainly intended to seek partisan advantage. * * * Nor is there any reason to doubt, as the majority does, the competence of courts to determine whether a district map "substantially" dilutes the votes of a rival party's supporters from the everything-but-partisanship baseline described above. * * * As this Court recently noted, "the law is full of instances" where a judge's decision rests on "estimating rightly . . . some matter of degree"— including the "substantial[ity]" of risk or harm. * * *

III

This Court has long understood that it has a special responsibility to remedy violations of constitutional rights resulting from politicians' districting decisions. * * * [T]he need for judicial review is at its most urgent in cases like these. "For here, politicians' incentives conflict with voters' interests, leaving citizens without any political remedy for their constitutional harms." [Gill v. Whitford, 138 S.Ct. 1916, 1941 (2018),] (Kagan, J., concurring). Those harms arise because politicians want to stay in office. No one can look to them for effective relief.

[Here Justice Kagan argued that Congress and state political processes were unlikely to provide an effective remedy. After noting that the majority had also recognized state courts as a possible source of relief—since the federal political question doctrine does not apply to claims brought under their states' constitutions—she asked:] But what do those courts know that this Court does not? If they can develop and apply neutral and manageable standards to identify unconstitutional gerrymanders, why couldn't we? * * *

The practices challenged in these cases imperil our system of government. Part of the Court's role in that system is to defend its foundations. None is more important than free and fair elections. With respect but deep sadness, I dissent.

NOTE ON NONJUSTICIABILITY DUE TO THE ABSENCE OF JUDICIALLY MANAGEABLE STANDARDS

(1) Varieties of Political Questions. In Nixon v. United States, Seventh Edition p. 237, the Supreme Court appeared to contemplate that the plaintiff had a right to be "tr[ied]" by the Senate before being convicted and removed from office, but ruled that the Impeachment Trial Clause, Art. I, § 3, cl. 6, constituted a "textually demonstrable constitutional commitment" of authority to the Senate to determine what "the word 'try'" required. In Rucho, by comparison, the Court does not appear to think that any branch, institution, or official other than the judiciary has constitutional responsibility for identifying and protecting the federal rights that the plaintiffs claimed, including under the Equal Protection Clause and the First Amendment.

The Court takes note of efforts by Congress and the states to restrict partisan vote dilution as a matter of federal statutory or state constitutional law. But suppose that Congress were to enact legislation specifically aimed at protecting constitutional rights under the Equal Protection Clause or the First Amendment. After Rucho, could such legislation pass muster as "enforcing" rather than "interpreting" the Constitution under City of Boerne v. Flores, Seventh Edition p. 188? Legislation enacted under the Elections Clause, Art. I, § 4, cl. 1, would not be subject to review under Boerne, but recall that the Court in Rucho specifically rejects a suggestion that that Clause constituted Congress as the authoritative arbiter of voting rights under the Equal Protection Clause in congressional districting cases.

If there are no judicially manageable standards for defining the constitutional right that the plaintiffs claim, and if the Constitution does not commit responsibility for defining and enforcing it to another branch, then in what sense does the Court recognize the existence of a constitutional right at all? Dissenting, Justice Kagan insists that the majority acknowledges that gerrymandering that goes "too far" violates rights: "[W]ithout this settled and shared understanding * * *, the question of whether there are judicially manageable standards for resolving [partisan gerrymandering cases] would never come up." Compare Chief Justice Roberts's framing of the question before the Court as whether the plaintiffs' claims "are claims of *legal* right, resolvable according to *legal* principles, or political questions that must find their resolution elsewhere" (emphasis in original). Is the majority as committed as Justice Kagan suggests to the proposition that the Constitution forbids gerrymanders that "go too far" and that the only problem is determining which gerrymanders violate that vague standard? Suppose the Court had ruled on the merits that the plaintiffs had not pleaded the violation of any rights cognizable under the Equal Protection Clause, the First Amendment, or any other provision of the Constitution. Would a ruling of that kind have practical consequences that differed in any way from those of the Court's actual ruling? See generally Harrison, *The Political Question Doctrines*, 67 Am.U.L.Rev. 457 (2017) (denying that the political question doctrine is jurisdictional in character).

(2) Judicially Manageable Standards. Consider the suggestion of Fallon, *Judicially Manageable Standards and Constitutional Meaning*, 119 Harv.L.Rev. 1274 (2006), that the term judicially manageable standards is ambiguous. In one usage, it refers to "inputs" to judicial deliberations, such as the First Amendment and the Equal Protection Clause. But when viewed as inputs, many constitutional provisions are too vague to serve as judicially manageable standards. To render them serviceable, the Supreme Court routinely devises tests and formulas of the kind that clutter the landscape of constitutional law, including strict scrutiny, rational basis review, the test for permissible restrictions on speech in a public forum, the test for forbidden racial gerrymanders (as discussed in Rucho), and so forth. In a second sense, the term judicially manageable standards thus refers to the *outputs* of constitutional adjudication or to the products of the Court's own efforts to devise tests or standards that pass muster as judicially manageable. In Rucho, the problem was that no one, in the view of the majority, had devised a constitutionally adequate judicially manageable standard in the output sense. When the Court says that it cannot find or discern judicially manageable standards (in the output sense) to gauge when gerrymanders go too far, does it confess a judicial failure (in comparison with the Court's success in devising tests to identify violations of other constitutional norms)?

(3) Standards for Judging the Judicial Manageability of Standards. Does the Supreme Court have a judicially manageable standard to guide its determinations about which proposed standards of constitutional validity— such as the tests proposed by the lower courts and the dissenting opinion in Rucho—are judicially manageable? At some point, the demand for further meta-standards must surely come to an end. But how would you reconstruct the Court's reasoning process in concluding that the standards proposed by the Rucho dissenters were not good enough? How would you reconstruct the Court's reasoning processes in concluding—as seems implicit in its conclusion that all challenges to partisan gerrymandering present nonjusticiable political questions—that no judicially manageable standard could possibly emerge in the future? Compare the position taken by Justice Kennedy, concurring in Vieth, finding no judicially manageable standard with which to resolve the case at bar but acknowledging that "in another case a standard might emerge."

In Zivotofsky v. Clinton, Seventh Edition p. 256, the Court determined that problems involving judicially manageable standards that would arise if the judiciary were asked to "decide the political status of Jerusalem" (as part of Israel or not) "dissipate when the issue is recognized to be the more focused one of the constitutionality of" a federal statute that identified Jerusalem as part of Israel. In elaboration, the Court summarized some of the parties' competing arguments of text, history, and precedent, then concluded: "Recitation of these arguments—which sound in familiar principles of constitutional interpretation—is enough to establish that this case does not 'turn on standards that defy judicial application'" (quoting Baker v. Carr, Seventh Edition p. 250). Based on that conclusion, the Court, in an opinion by Chief Justice Roberts, remanded the case to the lower court for decision of the constitutional question on the merits. It did so without pausing to specify the precise test of constitutional validity that the lower court should apply. Why was the Chief Justice so confident that the court could identify a judicially manageable standard in Zivotofsky but equally convinced that no judicially manageable standard could ever emerge in a constitutional challenge to a partisan gerrymander?

(4) Legitimacy. Part of the Court's explanation for its refusal to craft a test for identifying gerrymanders that go too far lies in a role-based aversion to entering what Justice Frankfurter, in Colegrove v. Green, Seventh Edition p. 250, described as a "political thicket." In a familiar articulation of this concern, the Supreme Court would put its legitimacy at risk, by raising questions about whether it is a neutral arbiter, if it were to seek to resolve politically charged disputes without clear criteria for decision. Compare this passage from Chief Justice Roberts' majority opinion, quoting an earlier opinion by Justice Kennedy: "With uncertain limits, intervening courts—even when proceeding with best intentions—would risk assuming political, not legal, responsibility for a process that often produces ill will and distrust." By contrast, Justice Kagan seems more concerned with what might be viewed as the legitimacy of American democratic institutions if incumbent politicians can virtually determine the outcome of future elections by gerrymandering voting districts.

The concept of legitimacy is an elusive one, which can mean different things in different contexts. Should the Justices have made calculations concerning legitimacy (in its various senses) a part of their decisionmaking process? If so, which kinds of legitimacy, and the legitimacy of which institutions, should they weigh most heavily? See generally Fallon, Law and Legitimacy in the Supreme Court (2018) (distinguishing among legal, sociological, and moral legitimacy).

(5) The Division of the Justices. In Rucho v. Common Cause, the five Justices in the majority were all appointed by Republican presidents. The four dissenters were all appointed by Democrats. Should a Justice who was troubled by the possible appearance of partisan division within the Court in a case with such obvious partisan political implications have considered changing his or her vote, otherwise contrary to his or her conscientious beliefs about proper constitutional adjudication, just to avoid that appearance? See Grove, *The Supreme Court's Legitimacy Dilemma*, 132 Harv.L.Rev. 2240 (2019) (discussing considerations that arise when Justices are urged to "vote[ ] in a way that they deem[ ] legally incorrect in order to safeguard the Court's public reputation"). See generally Charles & Fuentes-Rohwer, *Judicial Intervention as Judicial Restraint*, 132 Harv.L.Rev. 236, 271–75 (2018) (arguing that perceptions of the courts as political institutions are seeping from elites to the general public; that abstention from gerrymandering disputes will be viewed "through the lens of partisan polarization"; that gerrymandering is part of the dynamic that produces deepening partisan division and suspicion; and that the Court should intervene to break the cycle).

———

NOTE ON SPECIFIC SUBJECT MATTER AREAS IMPLICATING THE
POLITICAL QUESTION DOCTRINE

Page 259. Add at the end of Paragraph (2):

See also Williams, *The "Guarantee" Clause*, 132 Harv.L.Rev. 602 (2018)
(maintaining that the "guarantee" language echoed eighteenth-century
treaty formulations that would not have been judicially enforceable and
concluding that "available evidence regarding the [Guarantee Clause's]
original meaning strongly supports" treating disputes under the provision as
nonjusticiable).

CHAPTER III

THE ORIGINAL JURISDICTION OF THE SUPREME COURT

NOTE ON THE ORIGINAL JURISDICTION AS AN INAPPROPRIATE FORUM

Page 274. Add at the end of footnote 3:

In a dissent from the denial of motion for leave to file complaint in Nebraska v. Colorado, 136 S.Ct. 1034 (2016), Justice Thomas, joined by Justice Alito, reiterated the same view in somewhat more detail.

NOTE ON THE SCOPE OF JURISDICTION OVER CASES IN WHICH A STATE IS A PARTY: JURISDICTION ONLY WHEN INDEPENDENTLY CONFERRED BY STATE PARTY STATUS

Page 277. Add at the end of footnote 2:

For a defense and reconciliation of the Court's decisions, see Shelfer, *The Supreme Court's Original Jurisdiction Over Disputes Between the United States and a State*, 66 Buff.L.Rev. 193 (2018). Shelfer argues that Texas v. ICC correctly ruled that original jurisdiction over suits in which a State is a party is bounded by the party status heads of jurisdiction in the first paragraph of Article III, Section 2. But he further contends that disputes between the United States and a State fall within the Court's original jurisdiction because the constitutional framers and ratifiers understood the phrase "Controversies to which the United States shall be a Party" (in the first Paragraph of Section 2, which defines the judicial power generally) to entail "two separate provisions: one over controversies between the United States and a state, and one over other controversies between the United States and an individual or foreign state." The author squares this interpretation with United States v. Texas by arguing that it is best understood to base original jurisdiction not on the presence of a federal question but rather on the implicit grant of jurisdiction over a controversy between a State and the United States.

Page 278. Add a new footnote 3a at the end of the penultimate paragraph of Paragraph (5):

3a In Texas v. New Mexico, 138 S.Ct. 954 (2018), the Court allowed the United States to intervene in a case between states to assert a claim under an interstate compact even though the compact conferred on it no right to sue. Texas brought the original jurisdiction suit against New Mexico for alleged violations of the Rio Grande Compact, an agreement among Colorado, New Mexico, and Texas. In a unanimous opinion by Justice Gorsuch, the Court sustained the United States' exception to the Special Master's recommendation that its claim under the compact be dismissed. The Court reasoned that its "unique authority to mold original actions" enabled it to allow the United States to pursue claims that a "normal litigant might not be permitted to pursue in traditional litigation" at least when the government seeks to defend "distinctively federal interests." The United States could assert a claim under the compact, the Court concluded, because of its responsibilities closely related to the compact, because a breach of the compact could jeopardize treaty obligations with Mexico, and because the United States was intervening in an existing action and sought basically the same relief as Texas.

NOTE ON A STATE'S STANDING TO SUE AND ON PARENS PATRIAE STANDING

Page 279. Add a new footnote * at the end of the last paragraph of Section A:

* For a recent symposium on state standing that addresses many of the issues in this Note, see Symposium, *Federal Courts, Practice & Procedure: State Standing*, 94 Notre Dame L.Rev. 1883–2158 (2019). Grove, *Foreword: Some Puzzles of State Standing*, 94 Notre Dame L.Rev. 1883 (2019), is a good introduction to the literature on state standing. And Huq, *State Standing's Uncertain Stakes*, 94 Notre Dame L.Rev. 2127 (2019), analyzes the practical consequences of various resolutions of the doctrinal uncertainty in state standing outlined in this Note.

Page 286. Add at the end of footnote 5:

Professor Grove challenges this argument in *When Can a State Sue the United States?*, 101 Cornell L.Rev. 851 (2016). Grove maintains that states are entitled to "special solicitude" in standing analysis only when they "challenge federal action that preempts, or otherwise undermines the enforceability of, state law", but lack standing in cases that question the federal executive branch's compliance with federal law. Professor Nash responds that in areas where other actors lack standing to challenge Executive branch underenforcement, states should have standing under their *parens patriae* authority to protect their constituents. Nash, *Sovereign Preemption State Standing*, 112 Nw.U.L.Rev. 201 (2017). He argues for "sovereign preemption state standing", which would permit states to sue the federal government when it preempts state law in an area but the Executive branch allegedly underenforces the federal law that Congress enacted to address that area.

For other recent commentary on state standing in suits against the federal government, see Woolhandler & Collins, *Reining in State Standing*, 94 Notre Dame L.Rev. 2015 (2019) (arguing that state standing should presumptively be limited to suits involving the state as the object of federal regulation); Mikos, *Standing for Nothing*, 94 Notre Dame L.Rev. 2033 (2019) (arguing against "special solicitude" in standing analysis for states seeking to protect state law and warning that it risks making states "roving constitutional watchdogs" over the federal government); Crocker, *An Organizational Account of State Standing*, 94 Notre Dame L.Rev. 2057 (2019) (arguing for state standing by analogy to organizational plaintiffs); Hessick, *Quasi-Sovereign Standing*, 94 Notre Dame L.Rev. 1927 (2019) (explaining why states should be able to assert their quasi-sovereign interests against the U.S. government, but arguing that Congress should enact prudential limits on state standing); Young, *State Standing and Cooperative Federalism*, 94 Notre Dame L.Rev. 1893 (2019) (defending state standing in federal court lawsuits that challenge national policy as an attractive way for a competent and accountable party to aggregate diffuse claims); Mank & Solimine, *State Standing and National Injunctions*, 94 Notre Dame L.Rev. 1955 (2019) (arguing that state *parens patriae* standing to sue the federal government should be subject to "somewhat relaxed criteria" and proposing several factors that courts should account for before granting nationwide injunctions sought by states); Nash, *State Standing for Nationwide Injunctions Against the Federal Government*, 94 Notre Dame L.Rev. 1985 (2019) (arguing that if standing doctrine generally limits the availability of nationwide injunctions, states typically should not have "special solicitude" to seek such injunctions against the federal government); Davis, *The Private Rights of Public Governments*, 94 Notre Dame L.Rev. 2091 (2019) (mapping private rights model of standing onto state standing and arguing that courts should address questions about special solicitude only in cases where a state lacks standing under rules applicable to private parties); Davis, *The New Public Standing*, 71 Stan.L.Rev. 1229 (2019) (suggesting that courts should be wary of affording states special solicitude to sue the federal government based on financial injuries).

NOTE ON THE WAR CRIMES CASES

Page 294. Replace Paragraph (5) with the following:

(5) Review of Military Tribunals and of Other Non-Article III Federal Tribunals. The Supreme Court clarified some of these issues in *Ortiz v. United States*, 138 S.Ct. 2165 (2018), p. 56, *infra*, which held that

Article III permits direct Supreme Court review of the decisions of the United States Court of Appeals for the Armed Forces (CAAF). The CAAF is a "court of record" that reviews decisions of the four appellate courts for the armed services, which, in turn, review decisions by trial-level courts martial. The CAAF is not an Article III court because its members lack tenure and salary protections. Rather, it is located within the Executive branch.

In an opinion by Justice Kagan, the Court acknowledged that review of CAAF decisions cannot rest on its original jurisdiction because the CAAF does not resolve cases that affect ambassadors, public ministers or consuls, or that involve a State party, as Article III, § 2, cl. 2, requires. But the Court ruled that such review is an exercise of appellate jurisdiction because it involves a federal question and satisfies (in Marbury's words) the "essential criterion of appellate jurisdiction" since "it revises and corrects the proceedings in a cause already instituted, and does not create that cause." The Court rejected an argument by an amicus that courts located in the Executive branch are akin to Secretary of State James Madison, over whose decision the Court in Marbury held it lacked appellate jurisdiction. In contrast with Madison, the CAAF's "essential character" is "judicial" and thus is similar to the other non-Article III courts—state courts, territorial courts and District of Columbia courts—over which the Court has long exercised appellate jurisdiction. The Court distinguished Ex parte Vallandigham, 68 U.S. 243 (1864), which held that neither section 14 of the First Judiciary Act nor Article III permitted the Supreme Court to entertain a petition for a writ of certiorari directly from a military commission that had convicted a prisoner of disloyalty during the Civil War. In contrast with the CAAF, that commission lacked "judicial character" because it was created and controlled entirely by a Union general and thus was "more an adjunct to a general than a real court". Justice Alito, joined by Justice Gorsuch, dissented.

What are Ortiz's implications for the Supreme Court's appellate jurisdiction over other types of military courts? Does Ortiz provide a clearer rationale for Hirota, Seventh Edition p. 292, since the International Military Tribunal of the Far East, similar to the commission in Vallandigham but unlike the CAAF, was "set up by General MacArthur as the agent of the Allied Powers"? What if General MacArthur had established an appellate court independent of his command to review Tribunal decisions?

CHAPTER IV

CONGRESSIONAL CONTROL OF THE DISTRIBUTION OF JUDICIAL POWER AMONG FEDERAL AND STATE COURTS

1. CONGRESSIONAL REGULATION OF FEDERAL JURISDICTION

INTRODUCTORY NOTE ON CONGRESSIONAL POWER OVER THE JURISDICTION OF THE ARTICLE III COURTS

Page 298. Add at the end of footnote 9:

For further elaboration of this theme, see Grove, *The Origins (and Fragility) of Judicial Independence*, 71 Vand.L.Rev. 465 (2018), which argues that central conventions of judicial independence are historically contingent rather than structurally compelled.

Page 303. Add a new footnote 25 at the end of the carryover paragraph:

[25] Echoing some of these concerns about elected state judges, the Court in Williams-Yulee v. Florida Bar, 575 U.S. 433 (2015) (5–4), rejected a First Amendment challenge to Florida's ban on the solicitation of campaign funds by candidates for state judicial office. Distancing the Court from its earlier decision in Republican Party of Minnesota v. White, Seventh Edition p. 302, Chief Justice Roberts' opinion for the Court in Williams-Yulee applied strict scrutiny and held (a) that Florida has a compelling governmental interest in preserving public confidence in the neutrality of the state's judicial officers and (b) that the state's limit on personal solicitation is narrowly tailored to that interest.

In a separate opinion, Justice Ginsburg reiterated her position that, in light of the institutional differences between politicians and judges, states should generally have broader latitude to regulate judicial elections and that the Court should not apply strict scrutiny to such regulation. In a dissent joined by Justice Thomas, Justice Scalia assumed that the state had a compelling interest in the appearance of judicial neutrality but argued that the personal solicitation ban was insufficiently tailored to that interest. In a separate dissent, Justice Kennedy emphasized the dangers of treating a judicial election differently from other elections for First Amendment purposes. Justice Alito also dissented, arguing that the ban was not narrowly tailored.

NOTE ON THE POWER OF CONGRESS TO LIMIT THE JURISDICTION OF FEDERAL COURTS

Page 307. Add at the end of footnote 1:

See also Dow, *Is the "Arising Under" Jurisdictional Grant in Article III Self-Executing?*, 25 Wm. & Mary Bill Rts.J. 1, 10 (2016) (arguing that Professor Bator's argument is "perfectly question-begging" and that "such evidence as there is of original intent on this question reveals that the

Framers themselves did not believe Congress would enjoy the power Bator" ascribed to the Madisonian Compromise).

Page 314. Add at the end of the first paragraph in footnote 15:

Further, based on his survey of English constitutional practice, Professor Birk found that when Parliament made "exceptions" or "exemptions" to the jurisdiction of English and Scottish "supreme courts" at common law, it did not divest the courts of power to correct major interpretive errors, denials of due process, or transgressions of jurisdictional limits. Consistent with that history, Birk infers that the Founders' understanding of the power granted Congress by the Exceptions Clause would not readily have accommodated exceptions denying the Supreme Court of the United States power to exercise such supervisory authority over inferior courts. See Birk, *The Common-Law Exceptions Clause: Congressional Control of Supreme Court Appellate Jurisdiction in Light of British Precedent*, 63 Vill.L.Rev. 189 (2018).

Page 315. Add a new footnote 15a at the end of the penultimate paragraph on Page 315:

[15a] For another elaboration and defense of Hart's view, see Monaghan, *Jurisdiction Stripping Circa 2020: What the Dialogue (Still) Has to Teach Us*, 69 Duke L.J. 1 (2020). Monaghan proposes that the Court should "excise subject-matter limitations on its appellate jurisdiction when a substantial, undefended purpose of such jurisdiction-stripping legislation is to limit the Court's ability to consider a properly preserved constitutional claim." He grounds this conclusion in "Marbury v. Madison's emphasis on limited government and rule-of-law principles", arguing that "the line of our constitutional development" has given the Court a "unique and essential role in maintaining the idea of the limited government contemplated by the written 1789 Constitution."

Page 315. Add at the end of the second paragraph in footnote 16:

Grove, *Article III in the Political Branches*, 90 Notre Dame L.Rev. 1835 (2015), shows that, at least since McCardle, Congress and the President have fairly consistently rejected proposals under the Exceptions Clause to strip Supreme Court jurisdiction over specific subject areas. Professor Grove argues, however, that the political branches' decisions *not* to enact legislation may shed little light on the validity of jurisdiction stripping because it is difficult to know whether and to what extent such decisions reflect political rather than constitutional judgments about jurisdiction stripping. She adds that "the different institutional makeup and capacities of the courts" may position them better than the political branches to protect the "individual and minority rights" that jurisdiction stripping puts at risk. If constitutional text and history are as inconclusive as Frost and Grove suggest, would the judicial branch ever be justified in displacing a legislative judgment to strip Supreme Court jurisdiction? What role if any should accumulated historical gloss on the meaning of Article III or the development of uncodified constitutional conventions about judicial independence play in analyzing such questions? See, *e.g.*, Bradley & Neil Siegel, *Historical Gloss, Constitutional Conventions, and the Judicial Separation of Powers*, 105 Geo.L.J. 255 (2017) (arguing that such considerations have importantly influenced the political defeat or rejection of important jurisdiction-stripping proposals in the past century).

Page 318. Add a new footnote 20a at the end of the first sentence in Paragraph (5):

[20a] In contrast, Huq, *The Constitutional Law of Agenda Control*, 104 Cal.L.Rev. 1401 (2016), argues that, "in the absence of a definitive statement to the contrary from the Court, it would seem that the text of Article III vests the legislature with tolerably broad authority to determine which constitutional questions of national import end up on the judiciary's agenda."

Page 321. Add the following at the end of footnote 26:

Finally, Professor Walsh identifies yet another potentially significant gap in Section 25's coverage, arguing that the text of Section 25, read in its historical context, does not reach criminal cases. See Walsh, *In the Beginning There Was None: Supreme Court Review of State Criminal Prosecutions*, 90 Notre Dame L.Rev. 1867 (2015). How heavy is Professor Walsh's burden of persuasion, given the contrary view about Section 25 expressed by Chief Justice Marshall's opinion for the Court in Cohens v. Virginia, 19 U.S. (6 Wheat.) 264 (1821)?

Page 324. Add in place of the last paragraph in Paragraph D(2):

To similar effect is Bank Markazi v. Peterson, 136 S.Ct. 1310 (2016) (6–2), in which the Court rejected a challenge under United States v. Klein,

Seventh Edition p. 323, to a federal statute that sought to resolve a dispute over the availability of assets for the execution of certain judgments. Bank Markazi arose out of judgments entered against the Republic of Iran for terrorism-related harms under a "terrorism exception" to the Foreign Sovereign Immunities Act (FSIA). Sixteen groups of respondents, consisting of more than 1,000 plaintiffs, moved to enforce those judgments in consolidated proceedings in the U.S. District Court in the Southern District of New York. Pursuant to a 2002 statute that provides for the execution of judgments obtained under the terrorism exception, the enforcement proceedings focused on certain assets in a New York bank account that, according to respondents, was owned by Bank Markazi, Iran's central bank. Petitioners contested the claim that the assets in question belonged to the Bank. In light of that dispute, a provision in the Iran Threat Reduction and Syria Human Rights Act of 2012, 22 U.S.C. § 8772, provided that, if the district court made several specified findings, it could enforce respondents' underlying judgments against the financial assets "that are identified in and the subject of * * * Case No. 10 Civ. 4518 (BSJ) (GWG)."

Petitioners, invoking Klein, argued that § 8772 violated the separation of powers. They contended, in relevant part, that Congress invaded the judicial function by imposing a rule of decision on the district court in a pending case. Relying on Robertson v. Seattle Audubon Soc'y, Seventh Edition p. 324, Justice Ginsburg's opinion for the Court rejected petitioners' contention, drawing a distinction between prescribing rules of decision and " 'amend[ing] applicable law.' " The Court stressed that " 'congressional power to make valid statutes retroactively applicable to pending cases has often been recognized' " (quoting the Seventh Edition p. 324). In this case, the Court held, Congress had merely amended existing law. That conclusion, moreover, was unaffected by the fact that Congress specified the docket number of the proceedings to which its new policy applied.

In a dissent joined by Justice Sotomayor, Chief Justice Roberts argued that Congress rather than the judiciary had, in reality, decided the case. The dissent reasoned that if the legislature "targeted [the] specific case and eliminated [one party's] specific defenses so as to ensure [the other's] victory," then the judiciary "presided over [a] *fait accompli*" rather than actually deciding the case. To the dissent, § 8772 was not different from "a law saying 'respondents win.' " Such a statute, according to the Chief Justice, contradicted the historical context and purpose of the Founders' decision to establish an independent judiciary.

In Patchak v. Zinke, 138 S.Ct. 897 (2018), the Court divided (4–2–3) again over Klein's implications for statutory questions. The case arose out of Patchak's challenge to a decision by the Secretary of the Interior under the Indian Reorganization Act (IRA), 25 U.S.C. § 5108, to acquire a tract of land, known as the Bradley Property, to be held in trust for the Match-E-Be-Nash-She-Wish Band of Pottawatomi Indians. The Band had requested that the Secretary take into trust the Bradley Property so that the Band could build a casino on the site. In Match-E-Be-Nash-She-Wish Band of Pottawatomi Indians v. Patchak, 567 U.S. 209, 224–28 (2012), the Supreme Court had held that Patchak, who owns nearby land that would be affected by the use to which the land in question was to be put, had prudential standing to challenge the Secretary's decision under the Administrative Procedure Act.

Subsequently, Congress passed the Gun Lake Trust Land Reaffirmation Act (Gun Lake Act), Pub.L.No. 113–179, 128 Stat. 1913 (2014), to settle the status of the Bradley Property. Section 2(a) of the Act stated that the Bradley Property "is reaffirmed as trust land, and the actions of the Secretary of the Interior in taking that land into trust are ratified and confirmed." Section 2(b) stated that, "[n]otwithstanding any other provision of law, an action (including an action pending in a Federal court as of the date of enactment of this Act) relating to the land described [herein] shall not be filed or maintained in a Federal court and shall be promptly dismissed."

In a plurality opinion, Justice Thomas, joined by Justices Breyer, Alito, and Kagan, rejected Patchak's claim that the Gun Lake Act violated Article III. Invoking Robertson v. Seattle Audubon Society, Seventh Edition p. 324, the plurality concluded that jurisdiction-stripping statutes run afoul of Article III if they seek to "compel[ ] . . . findings or results under old law", but not if they create new law. The plurality ruled that the Gun Lake Act *changed* the law respecting federal jurisdiction, a permissible exercise of legislative power under Article I, § 8, and Article III, § 1. The plurality then distinguished United States v. Klein, Seventh Edition p. 323, on the ground that the statute at issue there had sought to use jurisdiction to produce an outcome indirectly that Congress could not produce directly. In Klein, the plurality explained, "Congress had no authority to declare that pardons are not evidence of loyalty, so it could not achieve the same result by stripping jurisdiction whenever claimants cited pardons as evidence of loyalty." The Gun Lake Act, by contrast, permissibly "create[d] new law for suits relating to the Bradley Property".

In an opinion concurring in the judgment, Justice Ginsburg, joined by Justice Sotomayor, reasoned that the Gun Lake Act reflected a permissible decision by Congress to retract a previously granted waiver of sovereign immunity by the United States.

In dissent, Chief Justice Roberts, joined by Justices Kennedy and Gorsuch, analogized the Gun Lake Act to a statute "directing that, in the hypothetical pending case of Smith v. Jones, 'Smith wins.' " Noting that the Framers designed Article III in reaction to the familiar state practice of legislative revision of judgments, the dissent deemed it dispositive that, in its view, Congress had enacted the Gun Lake Act in order to direct an outcome in the pending case. "Because the Legislature has no authority to direct entry of judgment for a party," the Chief Justice stated, "it cannot achieve the same result by stripping jurisdiction over a particular proceeding."

The plurality expressed doubt that the constitutionality of jurisdiction-stripping should turn upon the number of cases to which a statute applied when enacted or upon concerns about an "unexpressed [legislative] motive[ ]" to resolve a particular piece of litigation. In any case, the plurality found it sufficient that the Gun Lake Act applied to all potential suits relating to the Bradley Property, and not just the case before it.

Does Klein now stand largely (or only) for the proposition that Congress cannot use jurisdiction to achieve indirectly a disposition that it could not achieve directly under the Constitution?

Page 325. Add at the end of footnote 31:

For a somewhat different take on Klein, see Zoldan, *The Klein Rule of Decision Puzzle and the Self-Dealing Solution*, 74 Wash. & Lee L.Rev. 2133 (2017), which argues that Klein is best understood as the instantiation of the background constitutional principle that Congress may not engage in self-dealing—in this case, by gerrymandering jurisdiction to favor the government and disfavor a claimant against the public fisc.

———

NOTE ON PRECLUSION OF ALL JUDICIAL REVIEW AND ON THE RIGHT TO SEEK JUDICIAL REDRESS

Page 329. Add at the end of Paragraph (2):

Cf. Cuozzo Speed Technologies, LLC v. Lee, 136 S.Ct. 2131, 2141 (2016) (reserving the question whether a statute barring judicial review of certain decisions by the Director of the Patent Office applies to constitutional questions).

Page 335. Add a new footnote 8 at the end of Paragraph (6):

8   Bracketing the question of due process constraints, Professor Dorf suggests that the Necessary and Proper Clause may give Congress power to strip state and federal court jurisdiction over the constitutionality of federal but not state statutes. See Dorf, *Congressional Power to Strip State Courts of Jurisdiction*, 97 Tex.L.Rev. 1 (2018).

Page 335. Add at the end of Paragraph (7):

For the argument that Congress's greater power to forgo creating federal statutory rights altogether includes the lesser power to create such rights but omit a judicial enforcement mechanism, see Dorf, n. 8, *supra*, at 16–22.

———

FURTHER NOTE ON PRECLUSION OF ALL JUDICIAL REVIEW AND ON THE RIGHT TO SEEK JUDICIAL REDRESS: HABEAS CORPUS AND THE SUSPENSION CLAUSE

Page 337. Add at the end of footnote 2:

In response to the St. Cyr decision, Congress added a "limited review provision" to the INA that restricted judicial review of removal orders in certain cases to "constitutional claims or questions of law". 8 U.S.C. § 1252(a)(2)(D). In Guerrero-Lasprilla v. Barr, 140 S.Ct. 1062 (2020), the Court, per Justice Breyer, held that the phrase "questions of law" permits judicial review of "the application of a legal standard to undisputed or established facts." The Court reached this conclusion based on textual interpretation, the "strong presumption" favoring judicial review of administrative action, and legislative history suggesting that Congress intended to provide an adequate substitute for habeas review. This analysis elicited a strong dissent by Justice Thomas, joined in part by Justice Alito, who argued that "the majority effectively nullifies a jurisdiction-stripping statute, expanding the scope of judicial review well past the boundaries set by Congress."

Page 338. Strike the second paragraph of footnote 5.

Page 338. Add at the end of Paragraph (2):

In Department of Homeland Security v. Thuraissigiam, 140 S.Ct. 1959 (2020), the Supreme Court rejected Suspension Clause and due process challenges to restrictions on the ability of an asylum seeker to obtain review of expedited administrative removal proceedings. Petitioner crossed the border clandestinely and a border patrol agent apprehended him within 25 yards of the border. Once in government custody, petitioner sought asylum in the administrative proceedings that Congress prescribed, but failed to convince various immigration officials that he had a "credible fear of persecution" upon return to his native country. A different finding on the "credible fear" determination would have spared him "expedited removal" afforded him additional procedural opportunities to seek asylum in the United States. After an Immigration Judge approved petitioner's removal from the country, he sought a writ of habeas corpus in federal court, contending that he satisfied the credible fear test and that he had been denied a fair hearing. Challenging the various provisions in IIRIRA purporting to restrict federal court review of his case,[5a] petitioner requested a new opportunity to present his asylum claim before administrative officials.

Justice Alito's opinion for the Court (joined by Chief Justice Roberts and Justices Thomas, Gorsuch, and Kavanaugh) analyzed the Suspension Clause claim against the backdrop of the understanding of the Clause that existed in 1789. The Court reasoned that habeas at the time of the Founding was "a means to secure *release* from unlawful detention," and did not extend to an invocation of the writ, like petitioner's, "to achieve an entirely different end, namely, to obtain additional administrative review of his asylum claim and ultimately to obtain authorization to stay in this country."[5b] The Court explained that the principle embraced by St. Cyr—that "the writ could be invoked by aliens already in the country who were held in custody pending deportation"—could not help petitioner, who was seeking *entry* into the United States. As for petitioner's due process argument, the Court noted that "[w]hile aliens who have established connections in this country have due process rights in deportation proceedings, the Court long ago held that Congress is entitled to set the conditions for an alien's lawful entry into this country and that, as a result, an alien at the threshold of initial entry cannot

---

[5a] Section 1252(e)(2) provides for habeas review in limited circumstances: first, to ascertain "whether the petitioner is an alien"; second, "whether the petitioner was ordered removed"; and third, whether the petitioner has already been granted lawful entry to the United States. 8 U.S.C. §§ 1252(e)(2)(A)–(C). Section 1252(a)(2)(A)(iii) otherwise provides that "[n]otwithstanding any other provision of law (statutory or nonstatutory), including section 2241 of Title 28, or any other habeas corpus provision * * * no court shall have jurisdiction to review * * * [a] determination made [with respect to a credible fear claim]".

[5b] How does the Court's emphasis on the relief sought by Thuraissigiam compare to the Court's treatment of the remedy sought in Boumediene v. Bush, Seventh Edition pp. 338–341, 1224–36, 1249–58? There, the Court remanded the habeas cases to the lower courts for expanded proceedings within which detainees held at Guantanamo Bay could challenge their classifications as enemy combatants in the War on Terror. And how does the Court's methodology compare in the two cases? In Boumediene, the Court said that it "has been careful not to foreclose the possibility that the protections of the Suspension Clause have expanded along with post-1789 developments" (citing St. Cyr, 533 U.S. at 300–01). For further discussion, see pp. 113–114, *infra.*

claim any greater rights under the Due Process Clause (citing Nishimura Ekiu v. United States, 142 U.S. 651, 660 (1892))." Because petitioner had "attempted to enter the country illegally and was apprehended just 25 yards from the border", the Court held, he "has no entitlement to procedural rights other than those afforded by statute." That he was actually taken into custody on United States soil, accordingly, was of no moment to the Court's analysis in light of Congress's "plenary authority to decide which aliens to admit" (citing Nishimura Ekiu, 142 U. S. at 659), and earlier holdings providing that "even those paroled elsewhere in the country for years pending removal * * * are 'treated' for due process purposes 'as if stopped at the border' " (quoting Shaughnessy v. United States ex rel. Mezei, 345 U.S. 206, 215 (1953)).

Justice Thomas wrote a concurring opinion "to address the original meaning of the Suspension Clause". He argued that the expedited removal procedures bore "little resemblance to a suspension as that term was understood at the founding", since they did "not allow the executive to detain based on mere suspicion of a crime or dangerousness." Justice Breyer, joined by Justice Ginsburg, concurred in the judgment. The concurring Justices concluded that the statutory scheme was constitutional as applied to petitioner. They emphasized petitioner's "status" as akin to one stopped at the border and opined that "[t]o interpret the Suspension Clause as insisting upon habeas review of these claims would require, by constitutional command, that the habeas court make indeterminate and highly record-intensive judgments on matters of degree." Finding no precedent "suggesting that the Suspension Clause demands parsing procedural compliance at so granular a level", they concluded that the expedited removal procedures were constitutional as applied here.

Justice Sotomayor, joined by Justice Kagan, dissented. The dissent maintained that the Court had long heard "claims indistinguishable from those" raised by petitioner. Characterizing petitioner's claims as raising both mixed questions of law and fact and legal challenges to "procedural defects" in the administrative procedures Congress prescribed, the dissent argued that the Constitution required judicial review. More generally, the dissent took issue with the majority's fixation on 1789 to frame its analysis, pointing out that no analogous immigration restrictions were then in existence. Finally, in analyzing petitioner's claims under the Due Process Clause, Justice Sotomayor emphasized that he "was actually within the territorial limits of the United States" when captured, a fact that in her view raised a host of questions as to just how far the majority's holding would sweep in future cases.

For additional discussion of Thuraissigiam, see pp. 112–115, *infra*.

2. CONGRESSIONAL AUTHORITY TO ALLOCATE JUDICIAL POWER TO NON-ARTICLE III FEDERAL TRIBUNALS

NOTE ON CROWELL V. BENSON AND ADMINISTRATIVE ADJUDICATION

Page 357. Add at the end of footnote 6:

In recent years, moreover, several of the Justices have questioned whether the Chevron doctrine comports with the requirements of separation of powers and with the judiciary's law declaration function. See PDR Network, LLC v. Carlton & Harris Chiropractic, Inc., 139 S.Ct. 2051, 2057 (2019) (Thomas, J., concurring in the judgment); BNSF Railway Co. v. Loos, 139 S.Ct. 893, 908–09 (2019) (Gorsuch, J., dissenting); Pereira v. Sessions, 138 S.Ct. 2105, 2121 (2018) (Kennedy, J., concurring); Michigan v. EPA, 135 S.Ct. 2699, 2712–14 (2015) (Thomas, J., concurring).

Page 358. Add a new footnote 6a at the end of Paragraph (5)(c):

[6a] For the argument that due process and Article III considerations justify the judiciary's exercise of meaningful constitutional fact review of administrative decisions, see Redish & Gohl, *The Wandering Doctrine of Constitutional Fact*, 59 Ariz.L.Rev. 289 (2017).

INTRODUCTORY NOTE ON LEGISLATIVE COURTS

Page 362. Add at the end of Paragraph (2)(a):

For an article contending that Canter provides an inapt analogy for the historically and constitutionally unique status of the District of Columbia, see Durling, *The District of Columbia and Article III*, 107 Geo.L.J. 1205 (2019).

Page 362. Add at the end of footnote 3:

For an article questioning the textual and historical basis for the Court's broad acceptance of military tribunals, see Vladeck, Military Courts and Article III, 103 Geo.L.J. 933 (2015) (proposing a limiting principle that authorizes military courts only in contexts in which "established norms of foreign and international practice" justify their use).

Page 363. Add in place of Paragraph (3):

(3) The Constitutional Status of Non-Article III Courts. How court-like are legislative courts despite their lack of Article III status? Certainly, legislative courts sometimes handle Article III business. Territorial courts (and the D.C. local courts), for example, hear diversity and federal question cases, and American Ins. Co. v. Canter, Seventh Edition p. 362, was an admiralty case. Territorial courts, the D.C. local courts, and courts martial adjudicate criminal cases—matters that only a court, and not an administrative agency, could properly hear. Indeed, the Court has long acknowledged that, where historical exceptions to Article III govern, legislative courts can properly hear Article III business even though their judges do not have life tenure and salary protection. See Glidden Co. v. Zdanok, 370 U.S. 530, 549–51 (1962) (opinion of Harlan, J.).

In Ortiz v. United States, 138 S.Ct. 2165 (2018), the Court made clear that when legislative courts hear such cases, they operate as courts for purposes of Supreme Court review. At issue was whether the Supreme Court could exercise appellate jurisdiction over the final judgment of the Court of Appeals for the Armed Forces (CAAF)—a non-Article III tribunal that reviews the judgments of courts-martial in criminal cases. In Marbury v. Madison, Seventh Edition p. 59, Chief Justice Marshall's opinion for the Court established that "the essential criterion of appellate jurisdiction" is "that it revises and corrects the proceedings in a cause already instituted, and does not create that cause." In Ortiz, an amicus contended that, because the CAAF is in reality an adjudicative body within the Executive Branch— and not an Article III court—appellate jurisdiction did not lie under the criterion set forth in Marbury.

In an opinion for a divided (7–2) Court, Justice Kagan noted that courts-martial and military courts possess a judicial "character" that gives them a certain "*court*-likeness", even if they are not Article III courts. She reasoned that military courts exercise a "vast swath" of jurisdiction over criminal offenses that overlaps with the jurisdiction of federal and state courts; military courts impose "terms of imprisonment and capital punishment" upon service members; render judgments that carry res judicata effect; and feature an appellate process that functions much like that of ordinary courts. Although military judges lack life tenure and salary protection, Justice Kagan emphasized that the tradition of non-Article III courts-martial goes back to the beginning of the Republic. She noted, moreover, that in United States v. Coe, 155 U.S. 76 (1894), the Court upheld its appellate jurisdiction over the judgments of territorial courts, even though they are not Article III tribunals. In other cases, moreover, the Court had uncontroversially exercised appellate jurisdiction over judgments of the non-Article III D.C. local courts. In her view, the petition for a writ of certiorari to the CAAF was appellate because it asked the Court to revise the judgment in a case instituted "in a judicial system recognized since the founding as competent to render the most serious decisions."

In dissent, Justice Alito, joined by Justice Gorsuch, concluded that Article III authorized the Court to exercise appellate review only of an exercise of the judicial power. In the dissent's view, courts-martial "have always been understood to be Executive Branch entities that help the President, as Commander in Chief, to discipline the Armed Forces." According to Justice Alito, "Executive Branch adjudications . . . do not give rise to 'cases' that Article III grants us appellate jurisdiction to review, precisely because officers of the Executive Branch cannot lawfully be vested with judicial power." The dissent distinguished courts-martial from territorial and D.C. local courts on the ground that the latter reflect Congress's "unique authority to create governments for the Territories and the District of Columbia and to confer on the various branches of those governments powers that are distinct from the legislative, executive, and judicial power of the United States."[8]

If Congress restyled the NLRB as the National Labor Relations Court, could Congress provide for direct Supreme Court review of the resulting adjudications? And if the Supreme Court could review directly a decision of the NLRB, could it also review directly a decision made by a single federal official, as when Secretary of State Madison "adjudicated" Marbury's claim that he was entitled to his commission?

     [8]   Justice Alito's dissent finds support in Baude, *Adjudication Outside Article III*, 133 Harv.L.Rev. 1511 (2020). Baude argues that whether a tribunal's exercise of power is consistent with Article III's vesting of "judicial power" in the Supreme Court and lower federal courts should not turn on the form of adjudication, since adversary presentation of issues, and the application of law to fact, are not processes limited to Article III courts. Instead, the relevant inquiry should focus on the type of power the tribunal possesses, and whether it purports to exercise the "judicial Power of the United States". Applying this framework, Baude concludes that the majority in Ortiz was wrong, and Justice Alito was right, because "[m]ilitary tribunals may have judicial *character*," but they exercise executive rather than "judicial *power*."

———

FURTHER NOTE ON LEGISLATIVE COURTS

Page 384. Add at the end of footnote 4:

Baude, *Adjudication Outside Article III*, 133 Harv.L.Rev. 1511 (2020), argues that the public rights framework was inappropriate in Stern and Northern Pipeline for a different reason: "The public rights doctrine is a principle of executive power. But today's bankruptcy courts have not been vested with executive power. Their judges are appointed by Article III courts, supervised by Article III courts, and 'constitute[d]' as 'a unit of the district court.'" Baude concludes that bankruptcy courts must be sustained, if at all, as adjuncts to Article III courts.

Page 385. Add in place of the final paragraph of Paragraph (5):

Oil States Energy Servs., LLC v. Greene's Energy Group, LLC, 138 S.Ct. 1365 (2018), cast some light on the definition of a public right by suggesting that both the government's status as a party and the historical practice surrounding a particular type of claim remain relevant to determining whether a claim is a "public right." At issue was a procedure established by the Leahy-Smith America Invents Act, 125 Stat. 284, pursuant to which the Patent and Trademark Office (PTO) conducts "inter partes review" of a patent's validity. Under this procedure, a party other than the patent holder may petition the PTO to determine whether to cancel a patent on the ground that it fails the novelty or nonobviousness criteria for patentability.

Although the inter partes review arguably involves adjudication between private parties—the patent challenger and the patent holder—the Court held (7–2) that the adjudication concerned public rights properly assigned to a non-Article III tribunal. In his opinion for the Court, Justice Thomas explained that the PTO's granting a patent itself involves a public right—a matter between the government and a patent applicant seeking a public franchise. From that starting point, the Court reasoned that inter partes review merely seeks "reconsideration of that grant". Justice Thomas also relied on the fact that, under the common law of England, the Privy Council—an executive body—had concurrent jurisdiction with the courts to revoke a patent, suggesting that patent challenges would have been seen as a permissible executive function at the time of the founding. In a dissent joined by Chief Justice Roberts, Justice Gorsuch disagreed not with the Court's reliance on history, but rather with its reading of the historical record, which he took to establish that patent challenges had become an exclusive judicial function at common law prior to the founding and that they continued to be treated as such in subsequent U.S. practice.

Should the concept of public rights be limited to situations, like those in the Oil States case, in which the claim can be resolved exclusively by the executive—whether by reason of history or because sovereign immunity shields the government from judicial process in cases to which the government is a party (as, for example, when an agency denies an individual's claim for monetary benefits)?[5] Put another way, does the greater power to forgo judicial process include the lesser power to provide something less than the full Article III process? On such a view, much agency adjudication, including matters in which the government imposes a sanction against an individual, would have to be rerationalized on a different basis—perhaps on an adjunct theory or some variant of it. Indeed, note that Justice Breyer's dissent in Stern v. Marshall, Seventh Edition p. 364, fears that the Court's decision calls into question the validity of a range of longstanding administrative agencies like the NLRB, CFTC, and HUD, while the majority in Stern simply says that those tribunals are distinguishable without necessarily blessing them; and Justice Scalia injects a note of skepticism when he mentions "certain adjudications by federal administrative agencies, which are governed (for better or worse) by our landmark decision in Crowell v. Benson".

[5] Sovereign immunity would not necessarily bar a claim against a federal official involving the same matter in dispute, but that claim differs from one against the government itself.

Page 388. Add a new Subparagraph (c) at the end of Paragraph (7):

(c) The Implications of Consent. In Wellness International Network, Limited v. Sharif, 575 U.S. 665 (2015), Justice Sotomayor's opinion for the Court held that Article III permits bankruptcy judges to adjudicate Stern claims when both parties consent. Justice Sotomayor explained that, since the early days of the Republic, federal courts have often referred matters to special masters, arbitrators, and referees when the parties have given their consent. The Court added that consent played an important role in sustaining (a) agency adjudication of common law counterclaims in CFTC v. Schor, Seventh Edition p. 383, and (b) magistrates' authority to oversee jury selection in various cases. See Seventh Edition p. 393.

The Court in Wellness International held that a litigant may waive his or her "personal" right to an Article III tribunal. Citing Schor, the Court explained that, with such a waiver, the proper question was what " 'practical effect' " non-Article III adjudication would have on the " 'constitutionally assigned role of the federal judiciary.' " In the bankruptcy context, the Court found such effects to be minimal because bankruptcy judges are appointed and removable by Article III judges and function as judicial officers within the district court. In addition, the bankruptcy courts' jurisdiction over Stern claims encompasses only a " 'narrow class' " of common law matters that are incidental to the primary jurisdiction over bankruptcy. Finally, the Court concluded that Congress had no evident purpose "to aggrandize itself or humble the Judiciary" by assigning Stern claims to bankruptcy judges. Rather, Congress merely sought to "supplement[ ] the capacity of district courts through the able assistance of bankruptcy judges."

In a dissent joined by Justice Scalia and, in part, by Justice Thomas, Chief Justice Roberts criticized the majority for reviving a functionalist approach that put efficiency, convenience, and utility ahead of the prophylactic protections that an independent judiciary assures. Casting the right to an Article III forum as central to liberty and accountability, the dissent argued that "an individual may not consent away the institutional interest protected by the separation of powers." Justice Thomas also dissented separately.

Read together, do Stern and Wellness International suggest that the Court will apply (a) a strict, formalist approach to cases that do not involve party consent and (b) a more forgiving, functionalist approach when consent is present? If litigants cannot consent to the adjudication of non-Article III business heard in Article III courts, should they be able to consent to the adjudication of Article III business in non-Article III courts? For analysis questioning the relationship between party consent and the permissibility of non-Article III adjudication, see Dodge, *Reconceptualizing Non-Article III Tribunals*, 99 Minn.L.Rev. 905 (2015); Hessick, *Consenting to Adjudication Outside Article III Courts*, 71 Vand.L.Rev. 715 (2018).

––––––––

NOTE ON MAGISTRATE JUDGES

Page 393. Add in place of footnote 8:

[8]   At least four federal circuits have upheld § 636(c) consent jurisdiction in class actions, based on the consent of the class representative(s) and defendant(s), rejecting the view that unnamed class members are "parties" whose consent is required. See Koby v. ARS Nat'l Servs., Inc. 846 F.3d 1071, 1076 (9th Cir.2017); Day v. Persels & Associates, LLC, 729 F.3d 1309, 1324–25 (11th Cir.2013); Dewey v. Volkswagen Aktiengesellschaft, 681 F.3d 170, 180–81 (3d Cir.2012); Williams v. Gen. Elec. Capital Auto Lease, Inc. 159 F.3d 266, 268–70 (7th Cir.1998).

––––––––

NOTE ON MILITARY TRIBUNALS OR COMMISSIONS

Page 409. Add in place of footnote 10:

[10]   In Bahlul v. United States, 840 F.3d 757 (D.C.Cir.2016) (en banc), cert. denied, 138 S.Ct 313. (2017), a badly splintered en banc decision of the D.C. Circuit affirmed a military tribunal's conviction of Bahlul for conspiracy to commit war crimes. Bahlul, who was a Pakistani national, argued that, under Articles I and III, the government could invoke non-Article III military commissions only to try offenses against "the *international* law of war" and that conspiracy was not such an offense.

In a brief per curiam opinion, the court affirmed Bahlul's conviction. The nine participating judges, however, produced five separate opinions (two of which concluded that Bahlul's conviction could be affirmed without reaching the constitutional question). Judge Kavanaugh, joined by two other judges, concurred on the ground that nothing in the Constitution or the Court's precedents requires Congress to restrict military tribunals only to offenses against the international laws of war. In addition, he concluded, "Congress's longstanding practice strongly supports the conclusion that international law is not a constitutional constraint on Congress's authority to [invoke a] . . . military commission." (A separate concurrence by Judge Henderson took a similar position). In a joint dissent, Judges Rogers, Tatel, and Pillard argued that Article III establishes a strong default rule of adjudication by judges with life-tenure and salary protection and that military commissions represent a limited historical exception for cases involving (a) courts in areas under martial law, (b) courts in areas of temporary military occupation, and (c) cases involving enemy combatants charged with violations of the international laws of war.

In a case such as Bahlul, how conclusive should historical practice be in determining the constitutionality of Congress's decision to assign adjudication of an offense such as conspiracy to a military commission? For the view that judges have done a poor job of capturing the historical complexities that surround the use of military commissions over the course of more than two centuries, see Lederman, *The Law(?) of the Lincoln Assassination*, 118 Colum.L.Rev. 323 (2018) (suggesting that divisions of opinion among Civil War-era officials and the Court's post-war decision in Ex parte Milligan, Seventh Edition p. 405, complicate modern reliance on Civil War-era practices relating to military commissions); and Lederman, *Of Spies, Saboteurs, and Enemy Accomplices: History's Lessons for the Constitutionality of Wartime Military Tribunals*, 105 Geo.L.J. 1529 (2017) (arguing that, without deep immersion in prior common law practice, it is easy for judges to overread Revolutionary War-era and early congressional practices relating to the use of military tribunals to try spies and those accused of giving aid and comfort to the enemy).

Page 410. Add a new footnote 11 at the end of Paragraph (7):

[11] Based on a comprehensive historical analysis of the writ starting with its codification in England's Habeas Corpus Act of 1679, Professor Tyler argues that the privilege protects citizens and individuals in allegiance with the sovereign against being detained outside the formal criminal process, even in wartime, absent Congress's suspension of the writ for one of the reasons enumerated in the Suspension Clause. See Tyler, Habeas Corpus in Wartime: From the Tower of London to Guantanamo Bay (2018). To what extent should historical practice determine the present content of the habeas guarantee? Should it at least furnish a baseline below which the government may not go? For further discussion, see *infra* pp. 109–111.

———

3. FEDERAL AUTHORITY AND STATE COURT JURISDICTION

NOTE ON THE OBLIGATION OF STATE COURTS TO ENFORCE FEDERAL LAW

Page 445. Add a new footnote 6a at the end of Paragraph (4):

[6a] Though in a different context, Montgomery v. Louisiana, 136 S.Ct. 718 (2016), further suggests that state courts may have a duty to hear federal claims for reasons other than avoiding discrimination against such claims. At issue was whether a state court conducting collateral review of a state conviction may preclude retroactive application of a new rule of substantive federal constitutional law. In 1970, a Louisiana court sentenced Henry Montgomery to life without parole for a crime he committed while under the age of 18. More than four decades later, Miller v. Alabama, 567 U.S. 460 (2012), held that states may not, consistent with the Eighth Amendment, impose a life sentence without the possibility of parole for a crime committed by a juvenile. Montgomery brought a claim for relief under Miller through a state collateral review procedure that allows prisoners to challenge the legality of their sentences on Eighth Amendment grounds. As a matter of state practice, however, the state court held that Miller does not apply retroactively on state collateral review.

In a 6–3 decision, Justice Kennedy wrote for the Court that, as a matter of federal constitutional law, state collateral proceedings must give retroactive effect to new substantive constitutional rules—those "that place certain criminal laws and punishments altogether beyond the State's power to impose." The Court relied on the fact that while Teague v. Lane, Seventh Edition p. 1295, barred the retroactive application of new law in collateral federal habeas corpus proceedings, that same decision had made an exception for new substantive rules of constitutional law. Although Teague itself purported only to interpret the jurisdictional statutes governing collateral federal habeas review, Justice Kennedy's opinion in Montgomery held that the relevant Teague exception was "best understood as resting upon constitutional premises." In particular, Montgomery reasoned that "when a State enforces a proscription or penalty barred by the Constitution, the resulting conviction or sentence is, by definition, unlawful." To buttress its conclusion, the Court cited "a long tradition" of its giving retroactive effect to substantive constitutional rules on collateral review.

Justice Scalia, joined by Justices Thomas and Alito, dissented on the ground that the Teague exception for new rules of substantive constitutional law was not constitutionally compelled. In a separate dissent, Justice Thomas argued that nothing in the text of the

Constitution or historical practice creates a right to collateral relief, either in state or federal court. According to Justice Thomas, the retroactivity requirement would not apply if the state eliminated state collateral review of all federal claims or perhaps even just Eighth Amendment claims. "Only when state courts have chosen to entertain a federal claim," he wrote, "can the Supremacy Clause conceivably command a state court to apply federal law." This conclusion, he added, reflects the idea that "the Constitution leaves the initial choice to entertain federal claims up to state courts, which are 'tribunals over which the government of the Union has no adequate control, and which may be closed to any claim asserted under a law of the United States'" (quoting Osborn v. Bank of the United States, 22 U.S. (9 Wheat.) 738, 821 (1824)).

Can Justice Thomas's position about state courts be squared with the majority's reasoning? The majority seems to say that the U.S. Constitution prohibits a state court from keeping a prisoner in confinement when his or her conviction or sentence contravenes substantive constitutional rules limiting the state's power. Does that conclusion suggest that states have a constitutional duty to provide some form of collateral relief in such cases? Does your answer depend on whether federal habeas corpus relief is available to such a prisoner? For further discussion of Montgomery v. Louisiana, see pp. 78–79, 117, 121–133, *infra*.

Page 448. Add in place of Subparagraph (d):

(d) The Murphy Decision. In Murphy v. National Collegiate Athletic Ass'n, 138 S.Ct. 1461 (2018), the Court (6–3) reaffirmed and extended its anticommandeering doctrine. The Professional and Amateur Sports Protection Act of 1992 (PASPA), 106 Stat. 4227, in relevant part made it unlawful for states to "authorize by law or compact" various forms of gambling on competitive sporting events. In the Court's view, this statute precluded a state from partially repealing any existing state legislation that barred such gambling. In effect, therefore, PASPA put state legislatures "under the direct control of Congress"—"as if federal officers were installed in state legislative chambers and were armed with the authority to stop legislators from voting on any offending proposals." This result, the Court said, constituted a "direct affront to state sovereignty" under the system of dual sovereignty affirmed by the Tenth Amendment.

(e) The Import of the Decisions. Do concerns with state autonomy expressed in New York, Printz, and Murphy provide a basis for the Justices, in an appropriate case, to limit congressional power to require unwilling state courts to hear federal claims? For an affirmative answer, see Blackman, *State Judicial Sovereignty*, 2016 U.Ill.L.Rev. 2033.

CHAPTER V

REVIEW OF STATE COURT DECISIONS BY THE SUPREME COURT

------

1. THE ESTABLISHMENT OF THE JURISDICTION

NOTE ON THE ATTACKS UPON THE JURISDICTION

Page 475. Add a new footnote 4a at the end of the first sentence in Paragraph (2):

[4a] James v. City of Boise, 136 S.Ct. 685 (2016) (per curiam), summarily reversed a decision of the Idaho Supreme Court refusing to follow the Supreme Court's interpretation of a federal statute. In civil rights cases brought in state court pursuant to 42 U.S.C. § 1983, state court judges may "allow the prevailing party * * * a reasonable attorney's fee." *Id.* § 1988. Notwithstanding the fact that § 1988 refers to "the prevailing party" without qualification, the Court in Hughes v. Rowe, 449 U.S. 5 (1980) (per curiam), held that a prevailing *defendant* may recover fees only if the court finds that the plaintiff filed a frivolous lawsuit. In James, the Idaho Supreme Court held that the Supreme Court of the United States lacked " 'the authority to limit the discretion of state courts where such limitation is not contained in the statute.' " In a two-page per curiam, the Supreme Court reversed. Quoting Justice Story's opinion for the Court in Martin v. Hunter's Lessee, Seventh Edition p. 464, the Court wrote that "if state courts were permitted to disregard this Court's rulings on federal law, 'the laws, the treaties, and the constitution of the United States would be different in different states, and might, perhaps, never have precisely the same construction, obligation, or efficacy, in any two states. The public mischiefs that would attend such a state of things would be truly deplorable.' "

Did the Idaho Supreme Court technically contradict Martin when it refused to follow a precedent rather than a judgment of the Supreme Court? Given the modern Court's sharply limited capacity to review cases, would the refusal of state courts to acquiesce in the Court's interpretation of federal law compromise federal uniformity almost as much?

------

2. THE RELATION BETWEEN STATE AND FEDERAL LAW

A. SUBSTANTIVE LAW

NOTE ON REVIEW OF STATE DECISIONS UPHOLDING CLAIMS OF FEDERAL RIGHT

Page 503. Add a new Paragraph (5):

(5) The Debate Renewed. In Kansas v. Carr, 136 S.Ct. 633 (2016), the Court revisited the debate over whether it should hear cases in which state courts "overprotect" federal rights. In its modern incarnation, the debate takes the form of asking whether the Court should exercise its discretion to deny certiorari in such cases, and not whether there is an adequate and independent state ground per se. Petitioner sought review of a Kansas Supreme Court decision vacating respondents' capital sentences on the ground that the trial court violated the Eighth Amendment by (a) giving the jury unclear instructions about mitigating circumstances and (b) declining to sever sentencing proceedings for respondents, who had been jointly tried. In his final opinion for the Court, Justice Scalia held that the state supreme court's opinion left "no room for doubt that it was relying on the Federal Constitution."

In a dissent that echoed some of the concerns voiced by Justice Stevens in Michigan v. Long, Seventh Edition p. 499, Justice Sotomayor argued that the Court should grant certiorari only when "the benefits of hearing a case outweigh the costs of so doing." In her view, reviewing state court cases that grant relief to criminal defendants imposes several systemic costs: First, Supreme Court's review "may have little effect if a lower court is able to reinstate its holding as a matter of state law." Second, in cases involving "no suggestion" that the state court "violated any [individual's] federal constitutional right", federal review "intervene[s] in an intrastate dispute between the State's executive and its judiciary rather than entrusting the State's structure of government to sort it out." Third, granting review interferes with federalism interests in "state experimentation with how best to guarantee a fair trial." In this case, moreover, Justice Sotomayor saw few benefits to Supreme Court review because the key issues were hard to generalize beyond the particular state sentencing scheme or even the facts of the case. Finally, Justice Sotomayor stressed that the state court's rulings neither "indicate[d] a hostility to applying federal precedents" nor granted relief that was "particularly likely to destabilize or significantly interfere with federal policy." In that light, she concluded that "the Court should not have granted certiorari".

Justice Scalia's opinion for the Court responded that Supreme Court review was appropriate because the state court held that "the Federal Constitution *requires*" vacation of the state sentences. The Court emphasized that "state courts may experiment all they want with their own constitutions, and often do in the wake of this Court's decisions." The Court added that "what a state court cannot do is experiment with our federal Constitution and expect to elude this Court's review so long as victory goes to the criminal defendant." Such an approach, in Justice Scalia's view, undermined uniformity while "enabl[ing] state courts to blame the unpopular death-sentence reprieve of the most horrible criminals upon the Federal Constitution when it is in fact their own doing."

Does shifting the debate to one about the appropriateness of granting certiorari alter the competing interests at stake? When, if ever, should the Court allow the posture of the parties to influence its decisions to grant or deny certiorari?

———————

NOTE ON AMBIGUOUS STATE DECISIONS AND TECHNIQUES FOR
CLARIFYING THEM

Page 507. Add at the end of the penultimate paragraph of Paragraph (5):

See also Wilson v. Sellers, 138 S.Ct. 1188 (2018) (holding that for purposes of assessing whether an unexplained state court decision "unreasonabl[y]" applied federal law or determined questions of fact, a federal habeas court should presume that the decision rested on the same grounds as the last reasoned state court decision in the case); Foster v. Chatman, 136 S.Ct. 1737, 1746 n.3 (2016) (affirming the Court's practice of reviewing "a lower [state] court decision * * * in order to ascertain whether a federal question may be implicated in an unreasoned summary order from a higher court").

Page 509. Add at the end of the penultimate paragraph of Paragraph (7):

Shapiro, *An Incomplete Discussion of "Arising Under" Jurisdiction*, 91 Notre Dame L.Rev. 5 (2016) (contribution to symposium in honor of Dan Meltzer), elaborates thoughtfully on the evolution of doctrinal and scholarly positions concerning the Supreme Court's authority to hear cases that turn on state incorporation of federal law.

B. PROCEDURAL REQUIREMENTS

NOTE ON THE ADEQUACY OF STATE PROCEDURAL GROUNDS

Page 539. Add at the end of Paragraph (5)(b):

Should the federal courts analyze the adequacy of state procedural grounds one by one, as in the previous cases, or focus more systematically on the fairness of the complex procedural mazes that criminal defendants must often clear before they can assert their federal claims in state court? See Primus, *Federal Review of State Criminal Convictions: A Structural Approach to Adequacy Doctrine*, 116 Mich.L.Rev. 75 (2017) (advancing the latter view).

Page 542. Add in place of the final sentence of the penultimate paragraph of Paragraph (6):

For decisions reaffirming Kindler's approach to discretion and procedural default in habeas, see Johnson v. Lee, 136 S.Ct. 1802 (2016) (per curiam); Walker v. Martin, 562 U.S. 307 (2011).

Page 546. Add in place of the final sentence of Paragraph (10):

Subsequent decisions have tried more nuanced approaches to deciphering unreasoned state court decisions. See Wilson v. Sellers, 138 S.Ct. 1188 (2018) (applying the presumption, in the context of federal habeas corpus, that an unexplained state court decision rests on the same grounds as the last reasoned state court decision in the same case); Foster v. Chatman, 136 S.Ct. 1737, 1746 n.3 (2016) (employing a similar framework); Ylst v. Nunemaker,

Seventh Edition p. 507 (same); Coleman v. Thompson, Seventh Edition p. 507 (relying in part on the content of the motion to dismiss as a means to decode an ambiguous state court decision). *Cf.* Capital Cities Media, Inc. v. Toole, Seventh Edition p. 506 (instead of presuming one way or the other, vacating and remanding to the state court for clarification).

————

3.   FINAL JUDGMENTS AND THE HIGHEST STATE COURT

NOTE ON THE FINAL JUDGMENT RULE AND THE HIGHEST STATE COURT REQUIREMENT

Page 557. Add at the end of Paragraph (8):

In Atlantic Richfield Co. v. Christian, 140 S.Ct. 1335 (2020), the Supreme Court reviewed a state supreme court's determination that a federal environmental statute did not displace various common law claims notwithstanding the state's highest court having remanded the case to proceed to trial. The state supreme court had exercised review through a writ of supervisory control, which under state law presents "a self-contained case, not an interlocutory appeal" and "initiates a separate lawsuit." Under such circumstances, the Court held, "[i]t is the nature of the [state] proceeding, not the issues the state court reviewed, that establishes our jurisdiction."

CHAPTER VI

THE LAW APPLIED IN CIVIL ACTIONS IN THE DISTRICT COURTS

————

1. PROCEDURE

NOTE ON THE HISTORICAL DEVELOPMENT OF THE STATUTES AND RULES OF COURT

Page 565. Add at the end of the first paragraph of Paragraph (2):

In a few words appearing in Rule 2 of the new rules (which, slightly changed, now reads "There is one form of action—the civil action"), the rulemakers both specifically rejected use of the common-law forms of action (then still operative in a number of states) and effectuated, with respect to the rules of procedure, the merger of law and equity referred to at Seventh Edition p. 560."[7a]

[7a] Bray, *The System of Equitable Remedies*, 63 UCLA L.Rev. 530 (2016), argues that despite the merger of procedural rules eight decades ago, "there has been remarkably little merger of law and equity" for remedies. Challenging the "reigning view in the American legal academy" that the separation of legal and equitable remedies is irrational, the author argues that the "surviving equitable remedies and related doctrines work together as a system" to give courts the capacity to manage ongoing relief when damages at law are inadequate. The system, Bray maintains, has three components: (1) the equitable remedies themselves, which serve the need of compelling action or inaction; (2) equitable managerial devices, such as contempt, which enable courts to "manag[e] the parties and ensur[e] compliance"; and (3) equitable constraints, such as equitable ripeness requirements and equitable defenses, that serve as "frictions against the abuse of equitable remedies and managerial devices." Assuming the soundness of Bray's thesis, is there any reason for a court in a merged system not to resort to "equitable" methods or techniques when they would be of use in an action that would have been purely one "at law" before merger?

————

NOTE ON CHALLENGES TO THE VALIDITY OF THE FEDERAL RULES

Page 573. Add at the end of footnote 1:

For additional reflection on the relationship between Rule 4 and amenability to suit, see Spencer, *The Territorial Reach of Federal Courts*, 71 Fla.L.Rev. 979 (2019) (arguing that Rule 4(k) exceeds the rulemaking authority conferred by the Rules Enabling Act and should be revised to permit nationwide service of process); Woolley, *Rediscovering the Limited Role of the Federal Rules in Regulating Personal Jurisdiction*, 56 Hous.L.Rev. 565 (2019) (arguing that the Rules Enabling Act generally does not permit the Court to regulate amenability to suit and that Murphree is not to the contrary, but that Rule 4(k) is valid because it merely restates otherwise applicable law).

Page 575. Add the following at the end of footnote 5:

See also Spencer, *Substance, Procedure, and the Rules Enabling Act*, 66 UCLA L.Rev. 654 (2019) (reading the Rules Enabling Act's authorization to prescribe "rules of practice and procedure" to be an independent constraint on rulemaking beyond the prohibition on rules that "abridge, enlarge or modify any substantive right", and explaining implications).

---

2. THE POWERS OF THE FEDERAL COURTS IN DEFINING PRIMARY LEGAL OBLIGATIONS THAT FALL WITHIN THE LEGISLATIVE COMPETENCE OF THE STATES

NOTE ON THE RATIONALE OF THE ERIE DECISION

Page 591. Add at the end of footnote 4:

For more recent views, see Sherry, *Normalizing Erie*, 69 Vand.L.Rev. 1161 (2016) (arguing that the Court has exaggerated Erie's constitutional concerns and should apply "ordinary federalism" principles found in doctrines like the dormant commerce clause and implied preemption to vertical choice-of-law questions); Young, *Erie as a Way of Life*, 10 ConLawNOW 175 (2018–2019) (maintaining that Erie appropriately "enlisted the national separation of powers in the cause of federalism" by affirming the "interstitial" character of federal law without categorically limiting federal legislative power).

Page 591. Add at the end of footnote 5:

In *Finding Law*, 107 Cal.L.Rev. 527 (2019), Professor Sachs seeks to revive the view, supposedly rejected in Erie, "that unwritten law can be found, rather than made." He argues that judges might plausibly "find" customary rules of law by analogizing them to "dictionary authors" who identify customary rules of language. He further argues that court decisions might carry precedential effect without becoming instances of judicial lawmaking; a legal system might use prior precedents to resolve particular cases "as if" they were the law, much the way preclusion doctrines treat prior judgments as resolving disputes without altering the underlying law on which the judgments are based. Sachs describes Erie as a "blunder" that distorted states' efforts to adopt a general common law as their own law, and that unduly encouraged federal courts to recognize a category of "so-called" federal common law.

NOTE ON THE KLAXON DECISION AND PROBLEMS OF HORIZONTAL CHOICE OF LAW IN CASES INVOLVING STATE-CREATED RIGHTS

Page 594. Add at the end of footnote 2:

Wolff, *Choice of Law and Jurisdictional Policy in the Federal Courts*, 165 U.Pa.L.Rev. 1847 (2017), offers a concise but rich historical analysis of the "multiple lines of doctrine that intersect" in Klaxon in order to emphasize the narrowness of its holding and to argue that it "does not foreclose the development of a federal rule of decision in resolving conflicts between the local policies of interested states".

Page 596. Replace footnote 6 with the following:

⁶ In Atlantic Marine Constr. Co. v. United States Dist. Court, 571 U.S. 49 (2013), the Court recognized a significant exception to the Van Dusen choice-of-law principle. Atlantic Marine held that when a transfer of venue under § 1404 is made on the basis of a valid forum selection clause, the transferee court should apply the choice-of-law rules of the state in which it sits. The Court explained that the "policies motivating our exception [in Van Dusen] to the Klaxon rule for § 1404(a) transfers" did not apply because, in contrast with Van Dusen, a plaintiff who files suit in violation of a valid forum selection clause enjoys no "venue privilege" and thus is not entitled to concomitant "state-law advantages." Atlantic Marine assumed that the forum selection clause was valid and thus left open what law governs that question when the underlying claim is based on state law. Most courts of appeals have concluded that federal

common law should govern, see, *e.g.*, Albemarle Corp. v. AstraZeneca UK Ltd., 628 F.3d 643, 650 (4th Cir.2010), though one has held that state law controls, see Jackson v. Payday Fin., LLC, 764 F.3d 765, 774–75 (7th Cir.2014). For academic treatments of the issue, compare Adam Steinman, *Atlantic Marine Through the Lens of Erie*, 66 Hastings L.J. 795, 804–19 (2015) (suggesting that Erie and Klaxon compel application of state law), with Sachs, *The Forum Selection Defense*, 10 Duke J.Const.L. & Pub.Pol'y 1, 14–26 (2014) (arguing that a range of federal interests justifies development of federal common law). For an argument that courts administering multidistrict litigation proceedings under 28 U.S.C. § 1407 should apply the choice-of-law rules of transferor courts notwithstanding the presence of a forum selection clause and the holding of Atlantic Marine, see Bock, *All Disputes Must Be Brought Here: Atlantic Marine and the Future of Multidistrict Litigation*, 106 Cal.L.Rev. 1657 (2018).

———

3. ENFORCING STATE-CREATED OBLIGATIONS— EQUITABLE REMEDIES AND PROCEDURE

NOTE ON STATE LAW AND FEDERAL EQUITY

Page 604. Add at the end of footnote 2:

Morley, *The Federal Equity Power*, 59 B.C.L.Rev. 217 (2018), comprehensively analyzes Erie's application to equity and concludes that "the equitable principles a court must apply to a claim arise from the source of law giving rise to that cause of action." On this view, federal equitable principles govern federal claims but federal courts must look to the equitable principles of the state in deciding whether to grant equitable relief for claims arising under state law. Is it a bug or a feature of this elegant proposal that when a plaintiff presents multiple claims in a diversity or supplemental jurisdiction case, "a plaintiff may be able to obtain an injunction for her federal claims, but not her state ones, or vice versa"?

Page 605. Replace the last sentence of footnote 3 with the following:

The Court held, in the context of a contracting party's effort to compel arbitration, that the FAA preempts a California state rule that treats class action waivers as unconscionable in certain consumer contracts of adhesion. The Court subsequently explained that Concepcion establishes an "equal-treatment principle" that requires preemption of "any state rule discriminating on its face against arbitration". Kindred Nursing Centers Ltd. v. Clark, 137 S.Ct. 1421 (2017) (holding that the FAA preempts a Kentucky judge-made rule that a power of attorney does not entitle a representative to enter into an arbitration agreement unless the power of attorney expressly grants that authority); see also DIRECTV, Inc. v. Imburgia, 136 S.Ct. 463 (2015) (applying equal-treatment principle in a case where parties had conditionally chosen pre-Concepcion California law to govern waiver of class arbitration, reasoning that construction of parties' choice to allow waiver would not put arbitration contracts on an "equal footing with all other contracts" under California law).

Page 606. Add at the end of footnote 4:

Bray, *The Supreme Court and the New Equity*, 68 Vand.L.Rev. 997 (2015), argues that Grupo Mexicano and Great-West were the first of a line of eleven recent Supreme Court decisions that together establish a "new equity" jurisprudence. The defining features of this jurisprudence, Bray maintains, include a focus on history and tradition to define the scope of equitable relief, a reaffirmation of the "no adequate remedy at law" prerequisite for such relief, and an insistence that equitable remedies are exceptional and discretionary. After acknowledging the historical and doctrinal errors in many of the "new equity" decisions (including Grupo Mexicano and Great-West), the author offers a qualified defense of the jurisprudence that emerges from the decisions on the grounds that it (a) is "well suited to judicial decisionmaking", and (b) constitutes a reasonable response to the challenge of making sense of equitable doctrines in a world without courts of equity. Do you agree with the author that the Court's historical analysis in the "new equity" decisions, though "not good as historians' history", can be "good as history for legal purposes because its very artificiality makes it more suited to the judicial resolution of cases", at least so long as this "artificial history" is a "sensible interpretation" of statutes that authorize "equitable relief" and is "largely consistent with traditional equitable principles"?

CHAPTER VII

FEDERAL COMMON LAW

———

1. DEFINING PRIMARY OBLIGATIONS

A. CRIMINAL PROSECUTIONS

NOTE ON FEDERAL COMMON LAW CRIMES

Page 640. Add a new footnote 2a at the end of Paragraph (1):

²ᵃ For cautionary notes about relying on the early history of federal courts law, see Fallon, *The Many and Varied Roles of History in Constitutional Adjudication*, 90 Notre Dame L.Rev. 1753, 1775 (2015) ("[P]erhaps the safest conclusion is that all agree that historical inquiries are necessary and appropriate to determine whether historical practice has 'liquidated' the meaning of otherwise vague or ambiguous constitutional provisions, and if so how, but that a number of questions about the nature and conditions of liquidation remain unsettled."); Tyler, *Assessing the Role of History in the Federal Courts Canon: A Word of Caution*, 90 Notre Dame L.Rev. 1739, 1741–42 (2015) (noting that in the history of "the early years following ratification of the Constitution, one tends to find both examples of major principles that remained the subject of disagreement as well as examples of early legislation and practices that today we would reject as plainly inconsistent with the constitutional separation of powers").

———

B. CIVIL ACTIONS

NOTE ON THE EXISTENCE, SOURCES, AND SCOPE OF FEDERAL COMMON LAW

Page 652. Add a new footnote 7a at the end of the penultimate paragraph of Paragraph (6):

⁷ᵃ In recent years, the Court has moved away from the broad implied delegation theory epitomized by Justice Jackson's D'Oench Duhme concurrence. Consider Rodriguez v. Federal Deposit Insurance Corporation, 140 S.Ct. 713 (2020), where the unanimous Court declined to adopt a federal common law rule that several circuits had used to resolve disputes over the distribution of joint tax refunds among affiliated corporations, and held instead that state law should govern. The Court explained that "[j]udicial lawmaking in the form of federal common law plays a necessarily modest role under a Constitution that vests the federal government's 'legislative Powers' in Congress and reserves most other regulatory authority to the States." It recognized "limited areas" (such as admiralty and interstate disputes) where judges "may appropriately craft the rule of decision", but emphasized that "strict conditions must be satisfied" before "federal judges may claim a new area for common lawmaking". One of the "most basic" conditions, the need "to protect uniquely federal interests," was missing in the case. Federal regulations specified a government interest in receiving taxes from corporate groups and in delivering refunds to such groups, but were silent on the issue at hand: the distribution of such refunds among group members. That was enough for the Court to conclude that it lacked the authority to make federal common law even though the issue arose in the context of a federal tax dispute in a federal bankruptcy proceeding.

Page 652. Add in place of the last sentence in Paragraph (6):

If, in some cases "in which no state's law controls, and to which no federal statute or treaty provides an answer," federal judges can and do "find law" that is grounded in settled principles of common law, equity, or the law of nations, why must the resulting rule of decision be understood as *federal* common law? For the argument that it should not be so understood, see Sachs, *Finding Law*, 107 Cal.L.Rev. 527, 578 (2019).

Page 656. Add a new footnote 12 at the end of Paragraph (7)(c):

[12] Professor Pojanowski argues that those who claim that American judges should exercise common law powers in the interpretation of statutes underestimate the historical similarities between the common law and legislative traditions from which the U.S. legal system emerged. See Pojanowski, *Reading Statutes in the Common Law Tradition*, 101 Va.L.Rev. 1357 (2015). He argues, in particular, that "classical common lawyers saw legislation as a central component in a common law *system* that sought to internalize the general customs and ways of the realm." To the extent that the common law itself originated in custom, moreover, it was also "possible to claim that this positive law grew up from the community." And, much like the process of common law adjudication, English parliamentary procedures were designed to arrive at a community judgment about disputed matters. Hence, Professor Pojanowski concludes that those who today invoke (or resist) common law reasoning as a model for interpreting legislation do so based on an ahistorical view of the distinctions between the two. Assuming that Professor Pojanowski correctly identifies overlooked historical similarities between the common law and legislation, how does that insight affect the role of the courts in a constitutional system that departs in important ways from its common law antecedents?

_____

NOTE ON FEDERAL PREEMPTION OF STATE LAW

Pages 680–81. Substitute the following for Paragraph (5):

(5) Express Preemption Clauses. In theory, an express preemption clause presents a standard question of statutory interpretation. Recent decisions interpreting such clauses, however, have suggested that they do not preclude consideration of implied preemption as well, and some decisions find implied preemption without even reaching the question of express preemption. See generally Geier v. American Honda Motor Co., 529 U.S. 861, 869–74 (2000); Jordan, *The Shifting Preemption Paradigm: Conceptual and Interpretive Issues*, 51 Vand.L.Rev. 1149 (1998). Compare, *e.g.*, Boggs v. Boggs, 520 U.S. 833 (1997) (ignoring ERISA's broad and explicit preemption clause and holding instead that applying Louisiana community property law to determine the disposition of a decedent's ex-spouse's undistributed pension benefits would conflict with the purpose of particular substantive ERISA provisions), with Egelhoff v. Egelhoff, 532 U.S. 141 (2001) (holding that ERISA's express preemption clause displaced state law establishing a default provision that the designation of a spouse as the beneficiary of a pension and life insurance policy was automatically revoked upon divorce). If Congress takes the trouble to enact an express preemption clause, does the Court threaten to disrupt the balance that Congress struck if it invokes implied preemption principles as well? *Cf.* Gobeille v. Liberty Mut. Ins. Co., 136 S.Ct. 936, 948 (2016) (Thomas, J., concurring) (approvingly noting that in some "cases involving express pre-emption provisions, the [statutory] text has been the beginning and often the end of our analysis").

In interpreting express preemption clauses, the Court has articulated two competing views about whether the presumption against preemption applies. In one line of authority, the Court has said that "when the text of a pre-emption clause is susceptible of more than one plausible reading, courts ordinarily 'accept the reading that disfavors pre-emption.'" See Altria Group, Inc. v. Good, 555 U.S. 70, 77 (2008) (quoting Bates v. Dow Agrosciences LLC, 544 U.S. 431, 449 (2005)). In another, the Court has said that when a "statute 'contains an express pre-emption clause,' we do not invoke any presumption against pre-emption but instead 'focus on the plain wording of the clause, which necessarily contains the best evidence of Congress' pre-emptive intent.'" Puerto Rico v. Franklin California Tax-Free Trust, 136 S.Ct. 938, 946 (2016) (quoting Chamber of Commerce v. Whiting, 563 U.S. 582, 594 (2011)).[7] Does the Court have sound reasons to apply the presumption against preemption, rather than ordinary rules of construction, when Congress has expressed an explicit intention to preempt, leaving only the question of scope to be decided by the courts? If principles of federalism counsel against preemption in cases of doubt, should the same federalism policies govern in cases in which Congress has spoken unclearly about its intention to preempt?

[7]　For a decision in which the Court broadly interpreted an awkwardly worded preemption clause without any mention of the presumption against preemption, see Bruesewitz v. Wyeth LLC, 562 U.S. 223 (2011). See also Coventry Health Care of Mo., Inc. v. Nevils, 137 S.Ct. 1190, 1197 (2017) (holding that an express preemption clause of the Federal Employees Health Benefits Act preempts a given state law despite the availability of a "plausible" nonpreemptive interpretation).

Pages 681–82. Add in place of the final paragraph of Paragraph (6):

Several of the Court's most textually inclined Justices have sharply questioned "obstacle" preemption. For example, describing the Court's "entire body of 'purposes and objectives' pre-emption jurisprudence [as] inherently flawed", Justice Thomas' separate opinion in Wyeth v. Levine, 555 U.S. 555, 594 (2009) (Thomas, J., concurring in the judgment), argued that obstacle preemption cases "improperly rely on legislative history, broad atextual notions of congressional purpose, and even congressional inaction in order to pre-empt state law." To find preemption based on those indicia of unenacted statutory purpose, he reasoned, contradicts the safeguards of federalism found in the Supremacy Clause, U.S. Const. Art. VI, cl. 2, which "gives 'supreme' status only to those [laws] that are 'made in Pursuance' of '[t]his Constitution.'" To respect that condition, he said, the Court may find preemption only when a state law conflicts with a statutory text (or a regulation authorized by such a text) that has cleared the hurdles of bicameralism and presentment set forth by Article I, § 7. How convincing is Justice Thomas' reading of the Supremacy Clause?

Expressing similar concerns, a recent plurality opinion by Justice Gorsuch, joined by Justices Thomas and Kavanaugh, concluded that finding preemption based on asserted interference with the "purposes and objectives" of a federal statute "risk[s] displacing the legislative compromises actually reflected in the statutory text—compromises that sometimes may seem irrational to an outsider coming to the statute cold, but whose genius lies in having won the broad support our Constitution demands of any new law." Virginia Uranium, Inc. v. Warren, 139 S.Ct. 1894, 1908 (2019); see also AT & T Mobility LLC v. Concepcion, 563 U.S. 333, 353 (2011) (Thomas, J., concurring) (reiterating his concerns about "purposes-and-objectives preemption"); Williamson v. Mazda Motor of America, Inc., 562 U.S. 323, 341–43 (2011) (Thomas, J., concurring in the judgment) (same).[8] This position aligns with views about legislative compromise and bicameralism that the Court has embraced in some of its recent opinions. See Seventh Edition pp. 654–655, *supra*.[9]

In view of the challenges Congress would face if it were to try to anticipate, specify, and accurately express the proper resolution to all of the preemption questions that would arise in the lifetime of even a moderately complex regulatory statute, can textualism plausibly supply a workable approach to preemption questions? *See* Meltzer, *Textualism and Preemption*, 112 Mich.L.Rev. 1 (2013) (arguing that the answer is no). For an essay situating Professor Meltzer's critique in a broader theory of purposive interpretation, see Fallon, *On Viewing the Courts as Junior Partners of Congress in Statutory Interpretation Cases: An Essay Celebrating the Scholarship of Daniel J. Meltzer*, 91 Notre Dame L.Rev. 1743 (2016) (contribution to symposium in honor of Dan Meltzer).

[8] Williamson highlights the judicial lawmaking discretion inherent in obstacle preemption. In that case, the Court held that a Department of Transportation regulation giving auto manufacturers the choice to install lap or shoulder belts in certain rear positions in a vehicle did not preempt a state tort action alleging that Mazda acted negligently by using a shoulder rather than a lap belt in such a position. By contrast, the Court in Geier v. American Honda Motor Co., *supra*, had previously held that, by giving manufacturers the choice between airbags or passive restraints, a prior version of the same regulation *did* preempt a state tort action alleging that an auto manufacturer had negligently failed to equip its vehicles with airbags. In Williamson, the majority distinguished Geier on the ground that both the drafting history and subsequent agency interpretations of the amended regulation revealed no agency intent to give manufacturers an *affirmative* choice between shoulder and lap belts. In his opinion concurring in the judgment in Williamson, Justice Thomas argued that the Court's reasoning, which he described as free-ranging "psychoanalysis" of the agency's goals, confirmed that "[p]urposes-and-objectives pre-emption" necessarily "roams beyond statutory or regulatory text" and "is thus wholly illegitimate."

[9] In contrast with his views on "obstacle" preemption, Justice Thomas would not hesitate to find preemption in a case resting on a true conflict—one in which a party cannot simultaneously comply with state and federal law. See Seventh Edition pp. 679–680. In a plurality opinion in PLIVA, Inc. v. Mensing, 564 U.S. 604 (2011), Justice Thomas (joined by Chief Justice Roberts and Justices Scalia and Alito) relied on historical analysis found in Nelson, *supra*, to conclude that the Supremacy Clause was modeled on *non obstante* clauses that eighteenth century legislatures had inserted into statutes to signal their intention to repeal earlier statutes on the same subject. In particular, legislatures used *non obstante* clauses to signal the inapplicability of the traditional strong presumption against implied repeal—a presumption that required interpreters to strain to read potentially conflicting statutes as being in harmony. From that starting point, the plurality concluded that the *non obstante* language in the Supremacy Clause meant that courts should not strain to find ways to avoid an evident conflict between state and federal law. See also Merck Sharp & Dohme Corp. v. Albrecht, 139 S.Ct. 1668, 1681 (2019) (Thomas, J., concurring) (arguing that founding-era evidence suggests that a federal law preempts a state law when "the two are in logical contradiction").

Page 685. Add a new footnote 10a at the end of the penultimate paragraph of Paragraph (9):

[10a] One commentator has suggested that the Court's readiness to find field or obstacle preemption in a case like Arizona v. United States, Seventh Edition p. 685, compromises the states' ability to address perceived underenforcement of federal law by the Executive Branch of the federal government. See Morley, *Reverse Nullification and Executive Discretion*, 17 U.Pa.J.Const.L. 1283 (2015). How should the Court balance the executive's interest in exercising

prosecutorial discretion against the states' interests in enforcing federal norms they think important? Does it depend on whether the question at issue implicates an area of special national concern such as foreign relations? On a perceived need for federal uniformity?

Page 685. Add a new footnote 13 at the end of the last paragraph of Paragraph (9):

[13] In Kansas v. Garcia, 140 S.Ct. 791 (2020), the Court considered whether the Immigration Reform and Control Act (IRCA) preempted Kansas from using information on an alien's fraudulent W-4 and K-4 forms as the basis for a state law identity theft prosecution. The four-Justice dissent, written by Justice Breyer, argued that Arizona v. United States "demonstrates that IRCA impliedly preempts state laws that trench on Congress's detailed and delicate design" for policing fraud committed in the process of demonstrating federal work authorization. The majority, however, per Justice Alito, distinguished Arizona on the ground that "federal law does not create a comprehensive and unified system regarding the information that a State may require employees to provide." The Court emphasized that "[f]rom the beginning of our country, criminal law enforcement has been primarily a responsibility of the States," and it argued that the "federal system would be turned upside down if we were to hold that federal criminal law preempts state law whenever they overlap".

NOTE ON FEDERAL COMMON LAW IMPLIED BY JURISDICTIONAL GRANTS

Page 694. Add at the end of footnote 10:

See also Air & Liquid Sys. Corp. v. DeVries, 139 S.Ct. 986, 992 (2019) ("In maritime tort cases, we act as a common-law court, subject to any controlling statutes enacted by Congress.").

Page 694. Add in place of footnote 11:

[11] In some tension with its earlier position in Moragne, the Court in Atlantic Sounding Co. v. Townsend, 557 U.S. 404 (2009), held that the common law of admiralty authorizes the recovery of punitive damages when a shipowner willfully denies a crew member maintenance and cure after an injury. See Seventh Edition p. 686 n.*, *supra* (defining maintenance and cure). In so holding, the Court (5–4, per Justice Thomas) concluded that the punitive damages remedy traditionally available in maintenance and cure actions remained so despite the fact that such damages would *not* be recoverable in an action brought pursuant to the Jones Act, 46 U.S.C. § 30104, which allows someone in the plaintiff's position to elect between a common law and statutory remedy. In contrast with its approach in Moragne, the Court in Townsend did not use the policy reflected in a federal statute to define a parallel common law admiralty claim. A dissent written by Justice Alito and joined by the Chief Justice and Justices Scalia and Kennedy would have followed the Jones Act's policy in determining the availability of punitive damages under the common law of admiralty.

In contrast, in The Dutra Group v. Batterton, 139 S.Ct. 2275 (2019), the Court (6–3, per Justice Alito) followed the Jones Act's policy to hold that a seaman could not recover punitive damages on a claim of unseaworthiness. In so doing, the Court reaffirmed its position that " 'an admiralty court should look primarily to ... legislative enactments for policy guidance' " (quoting Miles v. Apex Marine Corp., Seventh Edition p. 693). While acknowledging that Atlantic Sounding had deviated from the policy of the Jones Act based on established maritime law tradition, the Court in Dutra found that, "unlike maintenance and cure, [the maritime law of] unseaworthiness did not traditionally allow recovery of punitive damages." In light of that history, the Court thought it inappropriate to recognize a novel remedy that would create disuniformity between the common law of unseaworthiness and the statutory remedy for personal injury available under the Jones Act.

Why should the Court apply the "policy" of a statute to common law cases that the statute does not govern directly? For an argument that courts possessing common law authority may properly use that power to broaden a statute's reach to new cases that text itself does not reach, see Pojanowski, *Statutes in Common Law Courts*, 91 Tex.L.Rev. 479 (2013).

Page 697. Add before the penultimate sentence of Paragraph (2):

The Supreme Court now seems to have accepted, at least in dicta, the structural reading of Hinderlider, concluding that "implicit alterations to the

States' relationships with each other" at the time of the founding opened the door for application of a federal rule of decision to interstate disputes. Franchise Tax Bd. v. Hyatt, 139 S.Ct. 1485, 1497–98 (2019).

────────

NOTE ON FEDERAL COMMON LAW RELATING TO FOREIGN AFFAIRS

Page 709. Add a new footnote 1a at the end of the first paragraph of Paragraph (2)(a):

[1a] Harrison, *The American Act of State Doctrine*, 47 Geo.J.Int'l L. 507, 533–37 (2016), argues that the act of state doctrine, properly understood, originally served a choice of law function directing American courts to accept as binding the legal judgments of a foreign sovereign. Does that understanding of the act of state doctrine, if correct, clarify the source of the Supreme Court's authority to develop and apply that doctrine?

Page 715. Add at the end of footnote 11:

For a history of the debate and an argument that modern technological and economic changes support the revisionist position, see Stephan, *One Voice in Foreign Relations and Federal Common Law*, 60 Va.J.Int'l L. 1 (2019).

Page 716. Add at the end of the penultimate paragraph in Paragraph (5)(c):

See generally Bellia & Clark, The Law of Nations and the United States Constitution (2017) (elaborating on the ways in which the law of nations informs the allocation of U.S. constitutional power respecting relations with foreign sovereigns). For further analysis of Bellia & Clark's structural and historical contentions, see Symposium, *The Law of Nations and the United States Constitution*, 106 Geo.L.J. 1558 (2019).

Page 716. Add at the end of footnote 13:

Born, *Customary International Law in United States Courts*, 92 Wash.L.Rev. 1641 (2017), purports to "reject[ ] central elements of both the modernist and revisionist positions" in the course of arguing that CIL should be treated as federal law but "will be directly applicable in U.S. courts only when the federal political branches have expressly or impliedly provided for judicial application of a particular rule." Compare Howard, *A Revised Revisionist Position in the Law of Nations Debate*, 15 Duke J.Const.L. & Pub.Pol'y 53 (2020), who concludes that "the traditional law of nations is exclusively within the domain of federal law, while modern CIL can be adopted by either the federal or state political branches", and that "the law of nations only becomes domestic law if either (a) the Constitution permits or requires the law of nations in interpretation of its provisions; or (b) the political branches adopt a certain custom or give the judiciary jurisdiction to decide questions regarding the law of nations." How, if at all, do these positions differ from the revisionist position?

────────

NOTE ON THE ALIEN TORT STATUTE AND CUSTOMARY INTERNATIONAL LAW

Page 720. Add a new footnote 8a at the end of Paragraph (2):

[8a] The Court moved sharply in the direction of Justice Scalia's Sosa dissent in Jesner v. Arab Bank, PLC, 138 S.Ct. 1386 (2018), a suit by foreign nationals against a Jordanian financial institution for its alleged financing of terrorist attacks on them or their families in the Middle East. In an opinion written by Justice Kennedy, the Court held, 5–4, that a cause of action is not available under the ATS in a suit against a foreign corporation. The Court relied on precedents that "cast doubt on the authority of courts to extend or create private causes of action even in the realm of domestic law." Those precedents included two decisions that refused to

imply constitutional causes of action: Ziglar v. Abbasi, 137 S.Ct. 1843 (2017), also discussed on p. 79–81, 95, 140–140, *infra*, which emphasized that " 'the Legislature is in the better position to consider if the public interest would be served by imposing a new substantive legal liability' "; and Correctional Services Corp. v. Malesko, Seventh Edition p. 774, which extended the Court's reluctance to imply constitutional causes of action to the question of corporate liability. The Court in Jesner concluded that "[n]either the language of the ATS nor the precedents interpreting it support an exception to these general principles". It further noted that lower-court ATS litigation against foreign corporate defendants had sparked diplomatic tensions that disserved the aims of the ATS and that underscored the wisdom of declining to imply a cause of action here. In a portion of the opinion that garnered only a plurality, Justice Kennedy, joined by Chief Justice Roberts and Justice Thomas, expressed doubt whether corporate liability for human rights violations was well enough established in international law to satisfy Sosa's requirement "of a norm that is specific, universal, and obligatory."

Justices Alito and Gorsuch joined the parts of the opinion that garnered a majority but filed separate concurring opinions. Justice Gorsuch emphasized that when the ATS was enacted in 1789, a federal court case between aliens would have been impermissible because alien-alien suits in non-federal question cases were (and remain) inconsistent with Article III, see Mossman v. Higginson, 4 Dall. 12 (1800), and because a suit under the law of nations did not arise under federal law in 1789 since the law of nations was then part of general law.

In a dissenting opinion joined by Justices Ginsburg, Breyer, and Kagan, Justice Sotomayor contended that the Sosa test went only to the question of what tort "violations" were well enough recognized under the law of nations, and not to which defendants might be called to account in a civil action to remedy recognized violations. The dissent also questioned whether Justice Gorsuch's separate opinion sufficiently accounted for the broad and dynamic language of the ATS, which in the dissent's view authorized the recognition of federal rights of action under the Sosa test. Finally, the dissent concluded that categorically rejecting corporate liability was too overinclusive and underinclusive an instrument for addressing diplomatic concerns arising out of the ATS's application.

Can Jesner's strict approach to implying causes of action, which led the Court to note that "a proper application of Sosa" might "preclude courts from ever recognizing any new causes of action under the ATS", be squared with the approach in Sosa itself, which refused to "close the door to further independent judicial recognition of actionable international norms"? Jesner's holding was limited to suits against alien corporate defendants, but is there any reason to think that actions against U.S. corporate defendants will fare any differently under Jesner's test for implying ATS causes of action?

Page 722. Add a new footnote 10 at the end of Paragraph (5):

[10] Legal scholars have expressed a range of views on Kiobel. See, *e.g.*, Vázquez, *Things We Do With Presumptions: Reflections on Kiobel v. Royal Dutch Petroleum*, 89 Notre Dame L.Rev. 1719 (2014) (arguing, *inter alia*, that the presumption against extraterritoriality does not apply to a jurisdictional statute purporting to give courts power to adjudicate universal norms); Weinberg, *What We Don't Talk About When We Talk About Extraterritoriality: Kiobel and the Conflict of Laws*, 99 Cornell L.Rev. 1471 (2014) (contending that Kiobel's facts fall within the literal terms of the ATS's jurisdictional grant and that the national interest in having U.S. courts hear a case like Kiobel lies in the "mutual, reciprocal interest" of all nations in "protecting human rights"); Young, *Universal Jurisdiction, the Alien Tort Statute, and Transnational Public-Law Litigation After Kiobel*, 64 Duke L.J. 1023, 1100 (2015) (arguing that Kiobel "was a particularly appropriate case for judicial caution about the extraterritorial reach of American law" because of the foreign relations implications of recognizing an implied right of action in wholly extraterritorial cases).

2. ENFORCING PRIMARY OBLIGATIONS

A. CIVIL ACTIONS

NOTE ON IMPLIED RIGHTS OF ACTION

Page 739. Add a new footnote 1a at the end of the first sentence in Paragraph (1):

[1a] Bellia & Clark, *The Original Source of the Cause of Action in Federal Courts: The Example of the Alien Tort Statute*, 101 Va.L.Rev. 609 (2015), argues that the issue of implied rights of action is a relatively modern one because federal courts had little reason, prior to the twentieth century, to consider the question. The reason, according to Bellia and Clark, is that the Process Acts of 1789 and 1792 and the Conformity Acts enacted beginning in 1872 authorized federal courts to apply state forms of proceeding in actions at law. Because federal courts could therefore apply state "forms of action," as appropriate, to address federal statutory violations, the question whether federal courts had inherent power to recognize implied rights of action simply did not arise. Conceptual and statutory developments in the twentieth century—including the Rules Enabling Act's elimination of the use of state forms of action—did away with off-the-rack rights of action and put into play the federal judiciary's inherent power to provide a remedy when Congress has not done so expressly. See Bellia, *Article III and the Cause of Action*, 89 Iowa L.Rev. 777 (2004).

Page 746. Add the following in place of the last sentence of footnote 12:

Should the Court presume, in the absence of specification to the contrary, that traditional principles of equity are generally available to remedy violations of federal statutes? See Morley, *The Federal Equity Power*, 59 B.C.L.Rev. 217 (2018).

For further discussion of Armstrong, see Seventh Edition pp. 845, 934, & 1012–13.

———

B. REMEDIES FOR CONSTITUTIONAL VIOLATIONS

NOTE ON REMEDIES FOR FEDERAL CONSTITUTIONAL RIGHTS

Page 757. Add a new footnote 4a at the end of Paragraph (3)(c):

[4a] In Nelson v. Colorado, 137 S.Ct. 1249 (2017), the Court held that it violated due process for a state law to require a defendant who is acquitted on appeal to prove his innocence by "clear and convincing" evidence in order to recover costs, fees, and restitution paid by virtue of the subsequently vacated conviction. In so holding, the Court in Nelson invoked the due process balancing test prescribed by Matthews v. Eldridge, 424 U.S. 219 (1976). Does that approach implicitly underlie the frameworks used to require meaningful tax refund remedies in Ward, McKesson, and Reich?

Page 759. Add at the end of Paragraph (4):

The Court's decision in Montgomery v. Louisiana, 136 S.Ct. 718 (2016), confirms that there is a constitutional law of retroactivity that stands apart from and, in some cases, limits courts' remedial discretion. At issue was whether, and in what circumstances, a state court must apply a new rule of constitutional law on state collateral review of a state court criminal conviction. The Court's reasoning was framed by earlier decisions governing the retroactive application of new rules of law in collateral federal habeas proceedings. When the plurality in Teague v. Lane, Seventh Edition p. 1295, announced a general proscription against applying a new rule of federal law retroactively in collateral federal habeas proceedings, it also articulated an exception allowing a federal habeas court to provide relief if a new rule imposes a substantive limitation on the state's very authority to criminalize the conduct at issue. Subsequent decisions held that this "first exception" to Teague "cover[s] not only rules forbidding criminal punishment but also rules prohibiting a certain category of punishment of certain primary conduct for a class of defendants because of their status or offense." Penry v. Lynaugh, 492 U.S. 302, 330 (1989).

Nothing in Teague suggested that its rules governing retroactivity were constitutionally required. Indeed, the plurality had made clear that its framework was an interpretation of the jurisdictional statutes governing collateral federal habeas proceedings. In a subsequent case, the Court further held that state courts may apply retroactivity rules that differ from those prescribed by Teague. See Danforth v. Minnesota, 552 U.S. 264, 266 (2008). In Montgomery, however, the Court held that state courts exercising collateral review may not deny retroactive application of new rules involving substantive limitations that would fall under Teague's first exception. The Court thus explained: "Substantive rules[ ] * * * set forth categorical constitutional guarantees that place certain criminal laws and punishments altogether beyond the State's power to impose. It follows that when a State enforces a proscription or penalty barred by the Constitution, the resulting conviction or sentence is, by definition, unlawful." From that starting point, the Court derived "a general principle" that a state court "has no authority to leave in place a conviction or sentence that violates a substantive rule, regardless of whether the conviction or sentence became final before the rule was announced."

Since the Court imposed this new rule of retroactivity in the teeth of contrary state remedial law, the Court's position on retroactivity must be one of constitutional dimension. What is the source of the constitutional law of retroactivity? Is there one? See Montgomery v. Louisiana, 136 S.Ct. at 741 (Scalia, J., dissenting) (calling the Court's decision an "ipse dixit" and ruling out due process and equal protection as the sources of the principle). For further discussion of Montgomery v. Louisiana, see pp. 61, *supra*; p. 117, 121–133 *infra*.

────────

NOTE ON BIVENS AND THE FORMULATION OF REMEDIES IN CONSTITUTIONAL CASES

Page 773. Add a new Paragraph (6)(c):

(c)   The Court in Ziglar v. Abbasi, 137 S.Ct. 1843 (2017), gave new emphasis to the "special factors" analysis developed in prior cases. The case arose out of the post-9/11 detention of six individuals who were arrested on immigration charges and then held without bail in a maximum security facility under a "hold-until-cleared policy"—a policy that applied to detainees whom the FBI deemed of potential interest to the investigation of terrorism. Respondents—all of whom were of Arab or South Asian descent and five of whom were Muslim—filed a Bivens action against three officials of the U.S. Department of Justice and two wardens of the federal facility at which respondents had been held. Respondents sought damages on that grounds that the petitioners had (1) held them in "harsh pretrial conditions for a punitive purpose," in violation of substantive due process; (2) singled them out because of their "race, religion, or national origin," contrary to the equal protection component of the Fifth Amendment; (3) subjected them to strip searches "without any legitimate penological interest," in contravention of the Fourth and Fifth Amendments; and (4) knowingly permitted the guards to abuse them, again in violation of due process.

In an opinion for the Court (joined by Chief Justice Roberts and Justices Thomas and Alito),[3a] Justice Kennedy concluded that a Bivens action did not lie for respondents' claims. Noting that Bivens was the product of a time in which the Court more freely recognized implied rights of action, Justice Kennedy deemed it "a significant step under separation-of-powers principles for a court" to create an implied damages action against federal officials for a constitutional violation. While not overruling Bivens in the contexts to which it already applied, the Court held that when asked to extend Bivens to a new context, it would ask "whether the Judiciary is well suited, absent congressional action or instruction, to consider and weigh the costs and benefits of allowing a damages action to proceed." In this case, even though the claims were at some level related to those recognized under Bivens and its progeny, the Court reasoned that the challenged actions—undertaken "pursuant to a high-level executive policy created in the wake of a major terrorist attack on American soil"—in fact bore "little resemblance" to previously recognized Bivens claims. More generally, the Court concluded that "special factors" counseled hesitation against extending Bivens to respondents' claims against large-scale executive policy concerning "sensitive issues of national security."[3b] Indeed, the Court found it "telling" that Congress has not prescribed liability for post-9/11 detention policy even though the USA PATRIOT Act required the Department of Justice to provide Congress with periodic reports on civil rights and civil liberties abuses in the fight against terrorism.

In dissent, Justice Breyer (joined by Justice Ginsburg) reasoned that respondents' claims were not novel because Bivens, Davis v. Passman, Seventh Edition p. 770, and Carlson v. Green, Seventh Edition p. 771, had recognized implied rights of action, respectively, for unlawful searches and seizures, invidious discrimination, and unconstitutional conditions of confinement. Justice Breyer further argued that, although the Constitution vests "primary power" over national security in the political branches, it "also delegates to the Judiciary the duty to protect an individual's fundamental constitutional rights." It followed, in his view, that the judiciary had a proper

---

[3a] Justices Sotomayor, Kagan, and Gorsuch took no part in the consideration or decision of the case.

[3b] Justices Sotomayor, Kagan, and Gorsuch took no part in the consideration or decision of the case.

respondents' claims, it remanded the case to the court of appeals to apply the "special factors" analysis to the particular allegation that one of the wardens had allowed the guards to abuse respondents. That claim, in the Court's view, involved a more "modest extension" of Bivens and thus warranted its own analysis. In a separate concurrence, Justice Thomas explained that he would apply Bivens only to the "precise circumstances" of that case.

"role to play" in crafting remedies when national security interests and individual rights conflict. The Court, he added, could rely on doctrines of qualified immunity, heightened pleading, and tailored discovery to mitigate potential intrusions upon national security interests.

In Hernandez v. Mesa, 140 S.Ct. 735 (2020), the Court continued its long-term trend of reading Bivens very narrowly. The Bivens claim in that case arose out of a cross-border shooting incident in which a U.S. border patrol agent fired two shots across the U.S.-Mexico border that killed a Mexican national on Mexican soil. In an opinion by Justice Alito (joined by Chief Justice Roberts and Justices Thomas, Gorsuch, and Kavanaugh), the Court ruled that a cross-border shooting presented a "new context, *i.e.*, one that is meaningfully different", and it identified three "special factors" that counseled hesitation in extending Bivens to that context. First, a Bivens remedy for cross-border shootings could affect foreign relations and undermine the executive branch's "lead role in foreign policy". Second, "the risk of undermining border security provides reason to hesitate before extending Bivens into this field." Finally, the Court took guidance from "what Congress has done in statutes addressing related matters." Examining 42 U.S.C. § 1983, the Westfall Act, and the Torture Victim Protection Act, the Court noted that "Congress has repeatedly declined to authorize the award of damages for injury inflicted outside our borders".[3c]

Justice Ginsburg dissented, joined by Justices Breyer, Sotomayor, and Kagan. Justice Ginsburg disputed the Court's view that a cross-border shooting presented a "new context". Because "the purpose of Bivens is to deter the *officer*" from using unjustified force, "the fortuity that the bullet happened to strike Hernandez on the Mexican side of the embankment . . . should not matter one whit." She further argued that the Bivens remedy should be available even if the cross-border shooting did present a new context. In contrast to the plaintiffs in Abassi, the plaintiffs here have no access to alternative remedies, and they challenge "the rogue action of a rank-and-file law enforcement officer" rather than government policies or policymakers. Moreover, the Court "does not home in on how a Bivens suit for an unjustified killing would in fact undermine security at the border", and recognizing Bivens liability here would aid, not impair, foreign relations.

For a thoughtful account of the role Bivens has played in the post-9/11 environment, see James E. Pfander, Constitutional Torts and the War on Terror (2017). See also Kent, *Are Damages Different?: Bivens and National Security*, 87 S.Cal.L.Rev. 1123 (2014); Litman, *Remedial Convergence and Collapse*, 106 Cal.L.Rev. 1477 (2018) (discussing Bivens' application to national security cases); Marguiles, *Curbing Remedies for Official Wrongs:*

[3c] Justice Thomas, joined by Justice Gorsuch, concurred but wrote separately to argue that Bivens should be overruled. In light of the Court's sharp retrenchment in implying both constitutional and statutory causes of action, its refusal to extend Bivens liability for nearly four decades, and the majority's recognition that "it is doubtful" that the Court would reach the same result if Bivens were decided today, he concluded that the Court had repudiated Bivens' foundation and that "continued adherence to even a limited form of the Bivens doctrine appears to 'perpetuate a usurpation of the legislative power' ". (Citation omitted.)

The Need for Bivens Suits in National Security Cases, 68 Case W.Res.L.Rev. 1153 (2018) (same).

Page 777. Add a new Paragraph (10):

(10) Bivens, Erie, and Federalism. In Hernandez v. Mesa, 140 S.Ct. 735, 742 (2020), the Court invoked Erie to argue that "federal courts today cannot fashion new claims in the way that they could before 1938. With the demise of federal general common law, a federal court's authority to recognize a damages remedy must rest at bottom on a statute enacted by Congress, and no statute expressly creates a Bivens remedy." Is Bivens at odds with Erie? Compare Fallon, *Bidding Farewell to Constitutional Torts*, 107 Calif.L.Rev. 933, 987–88 (2019): "Bivens lay well within the federal judiciary's traditional, common lawmaking power. The analogy to Ex Parte Young is strong, as are analogies to the exclusionary rule and other judge-made remedies for constitutional violations, including mandates to state courts to entertain damages actions against state officials. Insistence that separation-of-powers concerns preclude federal judicial lawmaking also ignores, and would leave unjustified, the role the Court has assumed in shaping official immunity law."

Note also that the Westfall Act, passed in 1988, precludes state-law tort actions against federal officers for actions taken in the scope of their employment. Thus, in a case like Hernandez, the "traditional" route to damages—a state-law tort suit where the constitutional issue is litigated as part of the officer's defense—is now unavailable. Should the absence of a state court remedy change the way federal courts approach Bivens claims? For affirmative answers, see Fallon, *supra*, at 989 ("With the Westfall Act creating a substantially broadened category of victims of constitutional lawbreaking for whom it is Bivens actions or nothing, the historically well-grounded principle that damages remedies should normally be available to victims of constitutional misconduct ought to control."); Vladeck, *Constitutional Remedies in Federalism's Forgotten Shadow*, 107 Calif.L.Rev. 1043 (2019) (similar).

CHAPTER VIII

THE FEDERAL QUESTION JURISDICTION OF THE DISTRICT COURTS

---

1. INTRODUCTION

NOTE ON THE STATUTORY DEVELOPMENT OF THE JURISDICTION

Page 783. Replace footnote 38 with the following:

³⁸ In Merrill Lynch, Pierce, Fenner & Smith Inc. v. Manning, 136 S.Ct. 1562 (2016), the Court held that interpretive doctrines governing subject matter jurisdiction under § 1331 also apply to § 27 of the Securities Exchange Act of 1934, which grants federal district courts exclusive jurisdiction "of all suits in equity and actions at law brought to enforce any liability or duty created by [the Exchange Act] or the rules or regulations thereunder." 15 U.S.C. § 78aa(a). The Court further noted that wording similar to § 27 "appears in nine other federal jurisdictional provisions—mostly enacted, like § 27, as part of New Deal-era regulatory statutes."

---

2. THE SCOPE OF THE CONSTITUTIONAL GRANT OF FEDERAL QUESTION JURISDICTION

NOTE ON THE SCOPE OF THE CONSTITUTIONAL GRANT

Page 800. Add at the end of Paragraph (7):

The Court recently clarified the Red Cross rule. The federal corporate charter of the Federal National Mortgage Association (Fannie Mae) grants Fannie Mae the power "to sue and to be sued, and to complain and to defend, in any court of competent jurisdiction, State or Federal." 12 U.S.C. § 1723(a). In Lightfoot v. Cendant Mortgage Corp., 137 S.Ct. 553 (2017), the Court held that this provision established Fannie Mae's capacity to bring suit and be sued but did not grant federal jurisdiction over cases involving Fannie Mae. The Court acknowledged that the specific reference to federal court, taken alone, pointed toward federal jurisdiction. But the Court further reasoned that the phrase "any court of competent jurisdiction" required an extant, independent source of subject-matter jurisdiction. The Court concluded that Fannie Mae's corporate charter permits suit by or against Fannie Mae only in a "state or federal court already endowed with subject-matter jurisdiction over the suit."

The Court has now interpreted a "sue and be sued" clause in six federal corporate charters stretching back to the charter of the first Bank of the

United States at issue in Deveaux. While members of Congress may not have been aware of the jurisdictional consequences of the specific language on which they voted in all of these charters, does Lightfoot imply that future legislators drafting a "sue and be sued" clause should be guided by the following interpretive principle?: A specific reference in the clause to federal court will confer federal jurisdiction unless some other provision in the clause indicates a need for an independent basis of jurisdiction.

———

3. THE SCOPE OF THE STATUTORY GRANT OF FEDERAL QUESTION JURISDICTION

A. THE STRUCTURE OF "ARISING UNDER" JURISDICTION UNDER THE FEDERAL QUESTION STATUTE

NOTE ON "ARISING UNDER" JURISDICTION AND THE CAUSE OF ACTION TEST

Page 819. Replace footnote 2 with the following:

   [2]   For decisions taking a narrow view of when a federal question is so insubstantial as to provide a basis for federal question jurisdiction, see Shapiro v. McManus, 136 S.Ct. 450 (2015); Hagans v. Lavine, 415 U.S. 528 (1974). The Court has indicated that the Bell v. Hood "nonfrivolous-argument" pleading standard for statutory federal question jurisdiction does not necessarily apply to other bases of statutory federal jurisdiction. In Bolivarian Republic of Venezuela v. Helmerich & Payne International Drilling Co., 137 S.Ct. 1312 (2017), the Court considered what averments must be made in a case asserting jurisdiction under 28 U.S.C. § 1605(a)(3). This provision creates an exception to foreign sovereign immunity, and thus statutory federal jurisdiction, in a "case * * * in which rights in property taken in violation of international law are in issue." Relying on the language and purpose of § 1605(a)(3), the Court rejected the Bell v. Hood standard and instead required the plaintiff to make out and maintain a legally valid claim that property rights are in issue and that the relevant property was taken in violation of international law. The Court also noted that under the diversity jurisdiction statute, 28 U.S.C. § 1332, parties must in fact be diverse, and not merely arguably so. Are there good reasons to have a relatively lenient pleading standard for statutory federal question jurisdiction but not for other forms of statutory federal jurisdiction?

———

NOTE ON THE SCOPE OF "ARISING UNDER" JURISDICTION UNDER 28 U.S.C. § 1331

Page 836. Add a new Paragraph (3)(c) just before Paragraph (4):

   (c)   In Merrill Lynch, Pierce, Fenner & Smith Inc. v. Manning, 136 S.Ct. 1562 (2016), the Court held that the "arising under" test of 28 U.S.C. § 1331 applies to § 27 of the Securities Exchange Act of 1934, which grants federal district courts exclusive jurisdiction "of all suits in equity and actions at law brought to enforce any liability or duty created by [the Exchange Act] or the rules or regulations thereunder." Manning sued several financial institutions in New Jersey state court under New Jersey law for allegedly illegal "naked short sales" of stock that, according to the complaint, also violated a Securities and Exchange Commission regulation. The defendants removed the case to federal court but the court of appeals remanded. It ruled that the district court lacked subject matter jurisdiction under § 1331 because Manning's claims were "brought under state law" and none "necessarily raised" a federal issue. This ruling decided the question of subject matter jurisdiction under § 27, which, the court held, was co-extensive with § 1331. The Supreme Court reviewed only the § 27 issue, and affirmed.

In explaining why it was appropriate for § 27 to include the "federal element" component of § 1331's jurisdictional test, the Court noted that a state-law action could be brought in federal court to enforce an Exchange Act duty under § 27 if it "necessarily depends on a showing that the defendant breached the Exchange Act". The Court offered this hypothetical:

"Suppose, for example, that a state statute simply makes illegal 'any violation of the Exchange Act involving naked short selling.' A plaintiff seeking relief under that state law must undertake to prove, as the cornerstone of his suit, that the defendant infringed a requirement of the federal statute. (Indeed, in this hypothetical, that is the plaintiff's *only* project.) Accordingly, his suit, even though asserting a state-created claim, is also 'brought to enforce' a duty created by the Exchange Act."

The Court then noted that such a claim, whose "very success depends on giving effect to a federal requirement", is like a claim for federal jurisdiction under § 1331 when the state-law claim " 'necessarily raise[s] a stated federal issue, actually disputed and substantial, which a federal forum may entertain without disturbing any congressionally approved balance' of federal and state power" (quoting Grable, 545 U.S., at 314).

Justice Thomas, in a concurrence in the judgment joined by Justice Sotomayor, rejected the assimilation of the "federal element" prong of the § 1331 test to § 27. He argued that the better reading of § 27 would be to allow federal jurisdiction over all state-law claims that necessarily raise an Exchange Act issue without importing the "arising under" test's additional inquiries about substantiality, disputedness, and the federal-state balance. The Court responded:

"[T]his Court has not construed any jurisdictional statute, whether using the words 'brought to enforce' or 'arising under' (or for that matter, any other), to draw the concurrence's line. For as long as we have contemplated exercising federal jurisdiction over state-law claims necessarily raising federal issues, we have inquired as well into whether those issues are 'really and substantially' disputed. See, e.g., Hopkins v. Walker, 244 U.S. 486, 489 (1917); Shulthis v. McDougal, 225 U.S. 561, 569 (1912). And similarly, we have long emphasized the need in such circumstances to make 'sensitive judgments about congressional intent, judicial power, and the federal system.' Merrell Dow Pharmaceuticals Inc. v. Thompson, 478 U.S. 804, 810 (1986). At this late juncture, we see no virtue in trying to pull apart these interconnected strands of necessity and substantiality-plus. Indeed, doing so here—and thus creating a gap between our 'brought to enforce' and 'arising under' standards—would conflict with this Court's precedent and undermine important goals of interpreting jurisdictional statutes."

The Court acknowledged the oddity of construing the very different language in § 1331 and § 27 to mean the same thing. But it said that the test for "arising under" jurisdiction has never been based on the statute's "particular phrasing", and noted that that § 1331 was given a narrower construction than the identical words in Article III due to the statute's "history[,] the demands of reason and coherence, and the dictates of sound judicial policy" (quoting Romero v. Int'l Terminal Operating Co., 358 U.S. 354, 379 (1959)). Because the "arising under" test does not turn on § 1331's text, "there is nothing remarkable in its fitting as, or even more, neatly a differently worded statutory provision."

The Court insisted that the extension of the scope of § 1331's "arising under" jurisprudence to § 27 promoted administrative simplicity because "judges and litigants are familiar with the 'arising under' standard and how it works", the test "[f]or the most part * * * provides ready answers to jurisdictional questions", and "an existing body of precedent gives guidance whenever borderline cases crop up." Do the decisions studied in this Section support this happy assessment? Or is it more accurate to say, with Justice Thomas, that the "arising under" standard "is anything but clear" and "involves numerous judgments about matters of degree that are not readily susceptible to bright lines"?

Page 837. Add the following at the end of Paragraph (4):

For further reflections in this context on the virtues and vices of clear and determinate rules versus refined but less determinate ones, and on how this casebook and two of its authors have approached this issue over the years, see Shapiro, *An Incomplete Discussion of "Arising Under" Jurisdiction*, 91 Notre Dame L.Rev. 1931 (2016) (contribution to symposium in honor of Dan Meltzer).

———

5. SUPPLEMENTAL (PENDENT) JURISDICTION

NOTE ON SUPPLEMENTAL JURISDICTION IN FEDERAL QUESTION AND OTHER NONDIVERSITY CASES

Pages 870–71. Replace the text of Paragraph (7)(b) with the following:

(b) Tolling the Statute of Limitations. Section 1367(d) specifies the time period in which an asserted supplemental claim that is later dismissed may be refiled in state court. It provides that the state-law period of limitations for any such claim "shall be tolled while the claim is pending [in federal court] and for a period of 30 days after it is dismissed unless State law provides for a longer tolling period." In Artis v. District of Columbia, 138 S.Ct. 594 (2018), the Court, in an opinion by Justice Ginsburg for five Justices, rejected the view that Section 1367(d) permits the state limitation period to run during the pendency of the supplemental claim but imposes a 30-day grace period to refile. It instead held that Section 1367(d) "stops the clock" on the state limitations period during the claim's pendency in federal court, thus giving the plaintiff whatever time remained under state law on the stopped clock, plus 30 days, to refile. The Court reasoned that this conclusion best comported with the language of subsection (d) and the dominant usage of the term "tolled".

The Court rejected the argument that Section 1367(d), so interpreted, exceeds Congress' enumerated powers. Relying on Jinks v. Richland County, 538 U.S. 456 (2003) (rejecting constitutional objections to Section 1367(d)'s 30-day grace period for claim refiled in state court and otherwise time-barred there), it ruled that the subsection was "necessary and proper" for carrying out Congress' power to establish inferior federal courts in a fair and efficient manner because it provides an alternative to the unsatisfactory options that federal courts otherwise faced when deciding whether to retain jurisdiction over supplemental claims that might be time barred in state court. The Court further ruled that the provision does not unduly infringe state sovereignty. It acknowledged that the rejected "grace period" interpretation of Section 1367(d) might be less intrusive on state authority, but ruled that the Constitution did not limit Congress' discretion to that degree. Justice Gorsuch, joined by Justices Kennedy, Thomas, and Alito, dissented. He disagreed with the Court's interpretation of Section 1367(d) and expressed particular concern about its impact on state authority to define time limitations on state-law claims.

CHAPTER IX

SUITS CHALLENGING OFFICIAL ACTION

1. SUITS CHALLENGING FEDERAL OFFICIAL ACTION

PRELIMINARY NOTE ON THE SOVEREIGN IMMUNITY OF THE UNITED STATES AND THE ENFORCEMENT OF THE LAW AGAINST FEDERAL OFFICIALS AND FEDERAL AGENCIES

Page 879. Add to footnote 6:

See also Brettschneider & McNamee, *Sovereign and State: A Democratic Theory of Sovereign Immunity,* 93 Tex.L.Rev. 1229 (2015) (arguing that the state is rightly immune from suit when it acts with democratic legitimacy, but insisting that it ceases to act with democratic legitimacy, and that sovereign immunity should not apply, in cases involving violations of "fundamental" rights)

Page 880. Add a footnote 6a at the end of Paragraph (2)(d):

6a For contending views about whether sovereign immunity applies in actions under the Takings Clause, compare Brauneis, *The First Constitutional Tort: The Remedial Revolution in Nineteenth-Century State Just Compensation Law,* 52 Vand.L.Rev. 57, 135–40 (1999) (yes), with Berger, *The Collision of the Takings and State Sovereign Immunity Doctrines,* 63 Wash. & Lee L.Rev. 493 (2006) (no).

Page 880. Add at the end of Paragraph (2):

Note, 129 Harv.L.Rev. 1068 (2016), argues that if the Constitution creates a cause of action against the states in takings and tax refund cases, then the Fourteenth Amendment alters any element of the constitutional plan that otherwise would have afforded the states sovereign immunity in such cases.

Page 881. Add a footnote 7a at the end of the first full paragraph:

7a For praise of the nineteenth-century framework that subjected government officials to the same common-law liability rules as private individuals, even for actions taken in wartime, see Pfander, *Dicey's Nightmare: An Essay on the Rule of Law,* 107 Calif.L.Rev. 737 (2019). According to Professor Pfander, that strategy better realized rule-of-law ideals than does modern law that creates distinctive liabilities but also establishes special immunity rules for officials sued for constitutional violations. But see Fallon, *Bidding Farewell to Constitutional Torts,* 107 Cal.L.Rev. 933 (2019), maintaining that "[e]ven if we could return to a common law regime in which governmental officials were subject to the same liability rules as ordinary citizens, we should not." On the one hand, Professor Fallon argues, officials cloaked with public authority pose distinctive threats, including to interests that the common law did not protect. On the other hand, public interests might sometimes require recognition of distinctive official immunities from damages liability.

NOTE ON STATUTORILY AUTHORIZED REVIEW OF FEDERAL OFFICIAL ACTION AND ON LEGISLATION WAIVING THE SOVEREIGN IMMUNITY OF THE UNITED STATES

Page 901. Add at the end of Paragraph (2)(c)(ii):

See also Daniel v. United States, 139 S.Ct. 1713 (2019) (Thomas, J., dissenting from denial of certiorari) (calling for reconsideration of Feres). (Justice Ginsburg also noted that she would grant the petition, but did not expressly join Justice Thomas's opinion.)

Page 902. Substitute for the first sentence of Paragraph (3)(a):

According to Kovacs, *Scalia's Bargain*, 77 Ohio St.L.J. 1155 (2016), the circuits are split over whether the waiver of sovereign immunity is limited to suits under the APA and is constrained by its "final agency action" requirement. The majority position is no: though codified in the APA, the waiver applies to any suit, whether or not brought under the APA.

---

2. SUITS CHALLENGING STATE OFFICIAL ACTION

A. THE ELEVENTH AMENDMENT AND STATE SOVEREIGN IMMUNITY

INTRODUCTORY NOTE ON STATE SOVEREIGN IMMUNITY AND THE ELEVENTH AMENDMENT

Page 905. Add a new footnote * at the end of Paragraph (1):

*   Clark & Bellia, *The International Law Origins of American Federalism*, 120 Colum.L.Rev. 835 (2020), argue that the term "State" as it appears in Article III was a "term of art," drawn from international law, and presupposed that the states retained all of the powers and prerogatives of international law sovereigns—including immunity from unconsented suit—unless they "clearly and expressly" surrendered their sovereign rights. According to the authors, early debates about state sovereign immunity are best understood against this international law background.

NOTE ON THE ORIGIN, MEANING, AND SCOPE OF THE ELEVENTH AMENDMENT

Page 920. Add to footnote 15:

Note, *Waiver by Removal? An Analysis of State Sovereign Immunity*, 102 Va.L.Rev. 549 (2016), reports that the circuits are split on whether a state's removal of a suit from state to federal court waives its immunity from claims against which it would have possessed sovereign immunity in state court.

NOTE ON EX PARTE YOUNG AND SUITS AGAINST STATE OFFICERS

Page 927. Add to footnote 3:

For a valuable study of Ex parte Young's historical and doctrinal context, including its situation in the Lochner era and its subsequent embrace by jurists and commentators "of all political stripes", see Barry Friedman, *The Story of Ex parte Young: Once Controversial, Now Canon*, in Federal Courts Stories (Jackson & Resnik eds. 2010), at 247.

Page 933. Add at the end of the first paragraph of Paragraph (5)(a):

In response to Professor Harrison, Pfander & Dwinell, *A Declaratory Theory of State Accountability*, 102 Va.L.Rev. 153 (2016), argue that "[e]quity did not recognize routine antisuit injunctions" (although it did authorize some) and, in particular, that equity "had no jurisdiction over criminal matters, a gap that explains the frequent dictum that equity has no power to stay criminal proceedings." Accordingly, the authors conclude, "[t]he Court * * * broke new ground in Ex parte Young, authorizing a new kind of injunction that was untethered to established antisuit forms", and was recognized by commentators at the time as having done so.

————

NOTE ON CONGRESSIONAL POWER TO ABROGATE STATE IMMUNITY

Page 958. Add to footnote 4:

Jackson & Resnik, *Sovereignties—Federal, State and Tribal: The Story of Seminole Tribe of Florida v. Florida*, in Federal Courts Stories (Jackson & Resnik eds. 2010), at 329, locates the decision in its evolving doctrinal context and provides interesting background on the litigation itself, including its origins in tension between state and tribal sovereigns.

Page 960. Add a new footnote 8a at the end of Paragraph (4)(a):

[8a] In Allen v. Cooper, 140 S.Ct. 994 (2020), the Court relied on Florida Prepaid to hold that Congress lacked authority to abrogate the states' sovereign immunity from suit for patent infringement.

Page 966. Add at the end of footnote 12:

The Court unanimously rebuffed an invitation to extend Central Virginia Community College v. Katz beyond the bankruptcy power in Allen v. Cooper, 140 S.Ct. 994 (2020), which involved a suit against a state for copyright infringement. Justice Breyer, joined by Justice Ginsburg, concurred in the judgment. Although he continued to believe that the Court "went astray in Seminole Tribe of Fla. v. Florida," Seventh Edition p. 940, he "recognize[ed] that my longstanding view has not carried the day, and that the Court's decision in Florida Prepaid [Postsecondary Educ. Expense Bd. v. College Savings Bank, Seventh Edition p. 959, from which he had also dissented,] controls this case."

————

NOTE ON ALDEN V. MAINE AND STATE IMMUNITY FROM SUIT ON FEDERAL CLAIMS IN STATE COURT

Page 976. Add at the end of Paragraph (6):

The prediction that the Court would overrule Nevada v. Hall came to fruition (by 5 to 4) in Franchise Tax Board of California v. Hyatt, 139 S.Ct. 1485 (2019). In an opinion by Justice Thomas, the Court ruled that "Hall's determination that the Constitution does not contemplate sovereign immunity for each State in a sister State's courts misreads the historical record and misapprehends the 'implicit ordering of relationships within the federal system necessary to make the Constitution a workable governing charter' " (quoting Hall, 440 U.S. 410, 433 (1979) (Rehnquist, J., dissenting)). Hall had rested on the premise that the interstate sovereign immunity that prevailed at the time of the Founding existed as a matter of "comity", not legal obligation. According to Justice Thomas, even if comity provided the basis for interstate sovereign immunity, abundant evidence showed that "the Founders believed that both 'common law sovereign immunity' and 'law-of-nations sovereign immunity' prevented States from being amenable to process in any court without their consent". In addition, he argued, "the Constitution affirmatively altered the relationships between the States, so that they no longer relate to each other solely as foreign sovereigns", and "embeds interstate sovereign immunity within the constitutional design." Dissenting, Justice Breyer found Hall's reading of the historical record more persuasive than the majority's: "[W]here the Constitution alters the authority of States vis-à-vis other States, it tends to do so explicitly." Justice Breyer also emphasized that "stare decisis requires us to follow Hall" in the absence of a "special justification" that the majority had not identified: "While reasonable jurists might disagree about whether Hall was correct, that very fact—that Hall is not obviously wrong—shows that today's majority is obviously wrong to overrule it." The majority found support for its ruling in Hall's status as "an outlier in our sovereign-immunity jurisprudence, particularly when compared to more recent decisions", including Alden v. Maine. How relevant should it have been that Alden found Nevada v. Hall to be distinguishable?

Page 976. Add to footnote 2:

Baude, *Sovereign Immunity and the Constitutional Text*, 103 Va.L.Rev. 1 (2017), argues that Nevada v. Hall, Seventh Edition p. 975, was rightly decided under a theory that sovereign immunity is a kind of common law doctrine that is constitutionally protected against most federal, but not state, efforts to override it. Baude maintains that his theory fits both the text of the Constitution and most of the leading Supreme Court decisions. But he offers little historical or explicitly normative support beyond the constitutional text. Compare Hoffheimer, *The New Sister-State Sovereign Immunity*, 92 Wash.L.Rev. 1771 (2017) (arguing largely on original historical grounds that a state should enjoy sovereign immunity in the courts of other states only for acts committed within its own territory).

Page 981. Add at the end of Paragraph (9):

Pfander & Dwinell, *A Declaratory Theory of State Accountability*, 102 Va.L.Rev. 153 (2016), call upon states to adopt a "cooperative approach" to constitutional accountability by authorizing plaintiffs who have secured federal injunctions or declaratory judgments in suits against state officials to follow up with suits for damages against the states themselves pursuant to "the ordinary processes of state law." The earlier federal judgments would have issue preclusive effect in subsequent state law actions, but the authors emphasize that states that otherwise waived their sovereign immunity could protect their coffers by imposing damages caps or other limitations on monetary relief. How likely are the states to accept the authors' proposal? Are there any good reasons for a state not to accept it?

————

C. FEDERAL STATUTORY PROTECTION AGAINST STATE OFFICIAL ACTION: HEREIN OF 42 U.S.C. § 1983

NOTE ON 42 U.S.C. § 1983: AN OVERVIEW

Page 996. Add a new footnote 8a at the end of the first paragraph of Paragraph (2):

[8a] Lewis v. Clarke, 137 S.Ct. 1285 (2017), similarly held that in a suit against an employee of a Native American tribe in his individual capacity, tribal sovereign immunity does not apply, even if the tribe has agreed to indemnify the employee.

Page 997. Add at the end of Paragraph (2)(b):

According to Evans, *Supervisory Liability in the Fallout of Iqbal*, 65 Syracuse L.Rev. 103 (2014), the courts of appeals are confused and divided in their interpretation of Iqbal, with most refusing to accept that it has abolished supervisory liability entirely and with some circuits either limiting Iqbal to its facts or essentially ignoring it.

Page 1001. Add at the end of Paragraph (5):

In a subsequent article, *How Governments Pay: Lawsuits, Budgets, and Police Reform*, 63 UCLA L.Rev. 1144 (2016), Professor Schwartz finds the evidence inconclusive on whether liability for officials' misconduct led police departments to alter their supervisory or training practices. Her survey of 100 law enforcement agencies reveals that well over half felt no direct budgetary implications from judgments and settlements (because the costs were absorbed, for example, by insurance or by jurisdiction-wide risk-management funds). In addition, interviews with a small sample of officials in agencies that do bear financial costs out of their own budgets elicited mixed messages, with some reporting that liability "does not influence their risk management efforts because they are already highly motivated to train and supervise their officers and reduce risk whenever possible."

Another empirical study, Rappaport, *How Private Insurers Regulate Public Police*, 130 Harv.L.Rev. 1539 (2017), advances partly divergent findings. Based largely on interviews with thirty-three people connected with the police liability insurance industry, Professor Rappaport reports that insurers frequently impose training and oversight obligations on police departments as conditions of coverage or pricing. He concludes unequivocally that "insurance companies can and do shape police behavior" in jurisdictions that purchase liability insurance (rather than self-insuring, as cities and counties with populations larger than 500,000 commonly do).

Page 1003. Add to footnote 15:

Smith, *Local Sovereign Immunity*, 116 Colum.L.Rev. 409 (2016), argues that current barriers to suits against municipalities, including the causation requirement, endow municipalities with a de facto form of sovereign immunity. To narrow the resulting right-remedy gap while simultaneously respecting some of the values that underlie sovereign immunity, Professor Smith proposes making municipalities more readily suable, but permitting damages caps or limitations on the execution of judgments against them. Does the desirability of these suggested reforms depend on whether current obstacles to suing municipalities should be viewed as forms of sovereign immunity?

Page 1005. Add at the end of Paragraph (2):

The Supreme Court decided two cases involving procedural doctrine in § 1983 actions during its 2018 Term. Nieves v. Bartlett, 139 S.Ct. 1715 (2019), held that a plaintiff asserting a First Amendment retaliatory-arrest claim must ordinarily prove absence of probable cause. (The Court recognized an exception for cases in which a plaintiff can prove that other people engaging in similar speech or conduct were not arrested). Parts of Chief Justice Roberts's opinion suggested that the Court's ruling addressed the problems of "causation" that, as prior decisions had recognized, can arise in determining when a First Amendment violation has occurred: a plaintiff must ordinarily prove absence of probable cause in order to establish that retaliation for speech was the but-for cause of an arrest. But the Chief Justice also drew on § 1983: "When defining the contours of a claim under § 1983, we look to 'common-law principles that were well settled at the time of its enactment.'" At common law, the Chief Justice found, the most analogous precedents—involving false imprisonment and malicious prosecution— either required proof of the absence of probable cause or made probable cause a complete defense. Justice Gorsuch, concurring in part and dissenting in part, and Justice Sotomayor, dissenting, both argued that the decisive question should be whether the plaintiff had adequately alleged a violation of his First Amendment rights. If so, then neither thought that the common-law background to the enactment of § 1983 could justify denying him a remedy. (Justice Thomas concurred in part and concurred in the judgment. Justice Ginsburg concurred in the judgment in part and dissented in part.)

Are issues involving the pleading and proof of constitutional violations in § 1983 actions for damages better analyzed as pure constitutional questions, or as ones involving statutory requirements for recovery that the common law might illuminate? With neither § 1983 nor the First Amendment making specific reference to probable cause, should any practical consequences hinge on how the Court answers that question?

McDonough v. Smith, 139 S.Ct. 2149 (2019), presented a question about when the statute of limitations for § 1983 claims alleging the fabrication of evidence begins to run. In an opinion joined by five other Justices, Justice Sotomayor began by stating the generally governing rule: "Although courts look to state law for the length of the limitations period, the time at which a § 1983 claim accrues 'is a question of federal law,' 'conforming in general to common-law tort principles'" (quoting Wallace v. Kato, 549 U.S. 384, 388 (2007)). Pursuant to that rule, Justice Sotomayor concluded that "the most natural common-law analogy" was the tort of malicious prosecution. Based on that analogy and on "practical considerations that have previously led this Court to defer accrual of claims that would otherwise constitute an untenable collateral attack on a criminal judgment," the Court concluded that the statute of limitations for fabricated evidence claims did not "begin to run until the criminal proceedings against the defendant (*i.e.*, the § 1983 plaintiff) have terminated in his favor." Justice Thomas, joined by Justices Kagan and Gorsuch, dissented. The petitioner McDonough had "declined to take a definitive position on" the particular constitutional provision on which his fabricated-evidence claim was based. Believing this to be a necessary antecedent question to the statute-of-limitations issue, the dissenters would have dismissed the petition as improvidently granted.

_____

NOTE ON THE PARRATT DOCTRINE: ITS RATIONALE, IMPLICATIONS, AND AFTERMATH

Page 1027. Add to footnote 2:

Kingsley v. Hendrickson, 576 U.S. 389 (2015), held, by 5 to 4, that a pretrial detainee asserting a Fourteenth Amendment due process claim for use of excessive force by jail officers need only show that the force was objectively unreasonable, not that the officers were subjectively aware of its unreasonableness.

_____

3. OFFICIAL IMMUNITY

NOTE ON OFFICERS' ACCOUNTABILITY IN DAMAGES FOR OFFICIAL MISCONDUCT

Page 1040. Add a new footnote * at the end of the second paragraph of Paragraph (2)(b):

* Ziglar v. Abbasi, 137 S.Ct. 1843 (2017), also discussed at pp. 79–81, _supra_, and p. 140, _infra_, held that officials sued for conspiracy to violate equal protection rights under 42 U.S.C. and § 1985(3) were entitled to qualified immunity under the same formula that applies to Bivens and § 1983 cases.

Page 1041. Add at the end of Paragraph (2)(d):

See generally Crocker, _Qualified Immunity and Constitutional Structure_, 117 Mich.L.Rev. 1405 (2019) (offering a historical explanation of Harlow's qualified immunity framework as an attempted corrective for the perceived excesses of Bivens, and maintaining that the Court extended the Harlow rule to section 1983 actions for federalism-related reasons, but concluding that the resulting doctrine lacks normative justification).

Page 1041. Add at the end of Paragraph (2)(e):

In Ziglar v. Abbasi, 137 S.Ct. 1843 (2017), Justice Thomas concurred in the Court's judgment granting qualified immunity under the standard of Harlow v. Fitzgerald, Seventh Edition p. 1030, but he called for reconsidering "our qualified immunity jurisprudence" in "an appropriate case": "We apply this 'clearly established' standard 'across the board' and without regard to 'the precise nature of the various officials' duties or the precise character of the particular rights alleged to have been violated' " [quoting Anderson v. Creighton, Seventh Edition p. 1048]. * * * Because our analysis is no longer grounded in the common-law backdrop against which Congress enacted the 1871 Act, we are no longer engaged in 'interpret[ing] the intent of Congress' * * *. Our qualified immunity precedents instead represent precisely the sort of 'free-wheeling policy choice[s]' that we have previously disclaimed the power to make."

Baude, *Is Qualified Immunity Unlawful?*, 106 Calif.L.Rev. 45 (2018), marshals formidable arguments that modern qualified immunity doctrine "is so far removed from ordinary principles of legal interpretation" that it "lacks legal justification." With regard to suggestions that the Court begins its modern inquiries by looking at the traditional common law of immunity as it existed in 1871, Baude demonstrates that: (1) "[T]here was no well-established good-faith defense in suits about constitutional violations when Section 1983 was enacted, nor in Section 1983 suits early after its enactment"; (2) "the good faith defense that did exist in some common law suits" arose from the elements of some common law torts, "not a general immunity"; and (3) the qualified immunity standard formulated in Harlow v. Fitzgerald "is much broader than a good faith defense." Baude concludes: "If qualified immunity is unlawful it can be overruled. And even if the Court does not overrule it, it can stop expanding the legal error."

Near the end of the 2019 Term, the Supreme Court denied certiorari in Baxter v. Bracey, 140 S.Ct. 1862 (2020), in which the petitioner asked the Court to reconsider its qualified immunity precedents as applied to § 1983 actions. Only Justice Thomas recorded a dissent from the denial of certiorari.[1a]

[1a] For a reply to Professor Baude and a defense of qualified immunity on stare decisis grounds, see Nielson & Walker, *A Qualified Defense of Qualified Immunity*, 93 Notre Dame L.Rev. 1853 (2018) (noting, inter alia, that Congress amended section 1983 in 1996 without questioning qualified immunity and has provided for immunity in other modern-era statutes). For a more general defense of the Harlow standard as initially articulated (but with criticism of its recent, more defendant-protective reformulation), see Fallon, *Bidding Farewell to Constitutional Torts*, 107 Calif.L.Rev. 933 (2019).

If the Supreme Court's qualified immunity cases have paid little heed to "ordinary principles of legal interpretation", could the same be said of the Court's decisions developing forum non conveniens and abstention doctrines and interpreting a number of other federal jurisdictional statutes, including those conferring "arising under" jurisdiction and Supreme Court appellate jurisdiction over state court judgments? See generally Fallon *Why Abstention Is Not Illegitimate: An Essay on the Distinction Between 'Legitimate' and 'Illegitimate' Statutory Interpretation and Judicial Lawmaking*, 107 Nw.U.L.Rev. 847 (2013). Can a longstanding pattern of free-wheeling interpretive decisions provide legally adequate justification for extensions of the pattern? Do the Court's recent expansions of qualified immunity pose issues of legal justification that purposivist interpretation in earlier eras did not?

Page 1042. Substitute the following for the first two sentences of footnote 3:

By contrast, Schwartz, *After Qualified Immunity*, 120 Colum.L.Rev. 309 (2020), predicts that the abolition of qualified immunity would have at most a "modest" effect on the scope of recognized constitutional rights. Moreover, any such loss would be offset, Professor Schwartz anticipates, by the swifter clarification of substantive constitutional rights that the abolition of qualified immunity defenses would promote.

Page 1047. Add at the end of footnote 9:

Trump v. Vance, 140 S.Ct. 2412 (2020), held that a sitting President has no absolute immunity from state court subpoenas issued in conjunction with a criminal investigation. Chief Justice Roberts' majority opinion emphasized, however, that the President, "like any other citizen", can "raise subpoena-specific constitutional challenges," including objections "that compliance with a particular challenge would impede his constitutional duties", "in either a state or federal forum." See also Trump v. Mazars USA, LLP, 140 S.Ct. 2019 (2020) (holding that courts must weigh separation-of-powers principles in assessing whether a congressional subpoena "directed at the President's personal information" is valid and enforceable).

Page 1048. Substitute for the last sentence of the third paragraph of Paragraph (7)(a):

Cf. City of Escondido v. Emmons, 139 S.Ct. 500 (2019) (per curiam), in which the Court "[a]ssum[ed] without deciding that a court of appeals decision may constitute clearly established law for purposes of qualified immunity".

Page 1049. Add at the end of Paragraph (7)(b):

The Court quoted and applied Reichle v. Howard's broad formulation of the qualified immunity standard in Taylor v. Barkes, 575 U.S. 822 (2015) (per curiam). It similarly continued the trend of emphasizing qualified immunity's protective sweep in City and County of San Francisco, California v. Sheehan, 575 U.S. 600 (2015), in Mullenix v. Luna, 136 S.Ct. 305 (2015) (*per curiam*), and in a unanimous per curiam opinion in White v. Pauly, 137 S.Ct. 548 (2017), a case involving allegations that a police officer unreasonably used deadly force. Pointedly noting that "[i]n the last five years, this Court has issued a number of opinions reversing federal courts in qualified immunity cases", the opinion reiterated the importance of qualified immunity to "society as a whole" and emphasized that its prior cases on deadly force "do not by themselves create clearly established law outside an obvious case" (internal quotations omitted).

The trend continued into the 2017 Term with a per curiam reversal in Kisela v. Hughes, 138 S.Ct. 1148 (2018), yet another police-shooting case involving the allegedly unreasonable use of potentially lethal force in a fact situation that the majority deemed distinguishable from those in cited precedents: "This Court has repeatedly told courts—and the Ninth Circuit in particular—not to define clearly established law at a high level of generality" (internal quotations omitted). The Court quoted that language from Kisela in City of Escondido v. Emmons, 139 S.Ct. 500 (2019) (per curiam), in which it unanimously reversed the Ninth Circuit for denying a qualified immunity defense against a claim that police officers used excessive force. Although many of the recent decisions overturning denials of qualified immunity have been unanimous, in Kisela, Justice Sotomayor, joined by Justice Ginsburg, dissented, objecting that "this Court routinely displays an unflinching willingness 'to summarily reverse courts for wrongly denying officers the protection of qualified immunity' but 'rarely intervene[s] where courts wrongly afford officers the benefit of qualified immunity in these same cases.'" She added: "Such a one-sided approach to qualified immunity transforms the doctrine into an absolute shield for law enforcement officers. . . . It tells officers that they can shoot first and think later, and it tells the public that palpably unreasonable conduct will go unpunished."

See also Baude, *Is Qualified Immunity Unlawful?*, 106 Calif.L.Rev. 45, 82 (2018) (reporting that the Supreme Court has found a violation of clearly established law in just two of thirty qualified immunity cases since 1982); Blum, *Section 1983 Litigation: The Maze, the Mud, and the Madness,* 23 Wm. & Mary Bill Rts.J. 913 (2015) (surveying and critiquing the mounting obstacles confronting plaintiffs who seek to overcome qualified immunity defenses.

Notwithstanding the Supreme Court's efforts to enhance qualified immunity's protective force and to facilitate dismissals of insubstantial claims prior to trial and discovery, Schwartz, *How Qualified Immunity Fails*, 127 Yale L.J. 2 (2017), maintains that district courts rarely terminate Section 1983 cases on motions to dismiss. After reviewing 1,183 suits against state and local law enforcement defendants in five federal district courts over a two-year period, Professor Schwartz found that "defendants raised qualified immunity in motions to dismiss in [only] 13.9% of the cases in which they could raise the defense"; that these motions to dismiss were granted in whole or in part on qualified immunity grounds only 13.6% of the time; and that, overall, just 0.6% of the cases in her sample were dismissed on qualified immunity grounds at the motion to dismiss stage and just 2.6% on summary judgment. Professor Schwartz speculates that qualified immunity disposes of so few police misconduct cases on motions to dismiss because it frequently takes fact-finding to determine whether clearly established law applies.

In a subsequent article, *Qualified Immunity's Selection Effects*, 114 Nw.U.L.Rev. 1101 (2020), Professor Schwartz concludes, "[b]ased on a study of almost 1,200 federal court dockets, and surveys and interviews of plaintiffs' attorneys * * * that qualified immunity doctrine * * * likely dampens attorneys' willingness to bring" section 1983 actions. But she further finds that the deterrent effect applies to both meritorious and non-meritorious claims and "does not effectively weed out insubstantial cases at the prefiling stage." In yet another article, Schwartz maintains that because most officials are indemnified by their employers when sued for constitutional violations, qualified immunity is unnecessary to avoid overdeterrence of public-spirited action. Schwartz, *After Qualified Immunity*, 120 Colum.L.Rev. 309 (2020). Her bottom line: "If we take the Supreme Court at its word—that its qualified immunity jurisprudence is motivated by an interest in shielding government officials from the burdens of suit in insubstantial cases, and avoiding overdeterrence of officers and officials—the Court need not fear doing away with qualified immunity."

For a range of (mostly critical) comments on qualified immunity and the policy justifications most frequently advanced to support it, see Symposium, *Federal Courts, Practice & Procedure: The Future of Qualified Immunity*, 93 Notre Dame L.Rev. 1793 (2018). Prominent criticisms, as summarized in Schwartz, *The Case Against Qualified Immunity*, *id.* at 1797, include the following: (1) qualified immunity has no basis in the common law background to the enactment of § 1983; (2) qualified immunity is unnecessary to protect officials from liability or fear of liability because they are mostly indemnified by their employers anyway; (3) qualified immunity fails to lead to early dismissal of frivolous lawsuits with the frequency anticipated by the Supreme Court, perhaps in part because plaintiffs can plead around it; (4) qualified immunity "hollows out" constitutional rights; and (5) there is little evidence that qualified immunity encourages courts to expand rights that they would hesitate to expand if the consequence were an immediate imposition of liability. Additional contributions to the Symposium include Blum, *Qualified Immunity: Time to Change the Message* (citing rampant confusion in § 1983 immunity decisions and calling for the establishment of respondeat superior liability, which would " 'fix' the doctrine of qualified immunity by making it largely irrelevant"); Bray, *Foreword: The Future of Qualified Immunity* (highlighting leading questions about the justifiability of qualified immunity doctrine); Chen, *The Intractability of Qualified Immunity* (characterizing qualified immunity doctrine as racked by "tensions," including "the conceptual challenge of distinguishing pure questions of law from mixed questions of law and fact" and identifying "the appropriate level of generality at which 'clearly established constitutional rights' are articulated"); Michelman, *The Branch Best Qualified to Abolish Immunity* (maintaining that qualified immunity is a mistaken and unworkable doctrine that should not be sustained on stare decisis grounds); Nielson & Walker, *A Qualified Defense of Qualified Immunity* (countering assertions that qualified immunity is unlawful because not contemplated by § 1983 and that qualified immunity fails to advance its policy objectives); Preis, *Qualified Immunity and Fault* (arguing that qualified immunity "does not reliably differentiate between * * * faulty and faultless" defendants); Reinert, *Qualified Immunity at Trial* (concluding that although "qualified immunity rarely is the subject of jury deliberations," it can often be "outcome determinative" when judges do charge juries with qualified immunity issues); Shapiro & Hogle, *The Horror Chamber: Unqualified Impunity in Prison* (tracing how qualified immunity interacts with other doctrines to create nearly insuperable barriers to suits by prisoners); and Smith, *Formalism, Ferguson, and the Future of Qualified Immunity* (arguing that qualified immunity is ripe for reconsideration because it is out of step with both the Court's interpretive approach in other relevant areas of the law and "post-Ferguson" demands for "greater accountability for violations of rights").

Page 1051. Add a new footnote 12a at the end of the carryover paragraph:

[12a] Dawson, *Qualified Immunity for Officers' Reasonable Reliance on Lawyers' Advice*, 110 Nw.U.L.Rev. 525 (2016), reports that the circuits are divided on how, if at all, reliance on lawyers' advice matters to the qualified immunity inquiry. He argues that qualified immunity should depend on the reasonableness of a defendant's trusting in a lawyer's opinion under particular circumstances, not an "extraordinary circumstances" test. How often would those two tests be likely to yield different results?

Page 1053. Add at the end of Paragraph (8)(b):

A study that looked at all court of appeals cases that cited Pearson v. Callahan, Seventh Edition p. 1052, in the years 2009–12 found that the court exercised its discretion to reach the merits only roughly 45% of the time. Nielson & Walker, *The New Qualified Immunity*, 89 S.Cal.L.Rev. 1 (2015). The courts of appeals ruled for the defendants based on the absence of any clearly established right without reaching the merits in regard to 27% of qualified immunity claims and rejected qualified immunity defenses in 28%. When courts of appeals exercised their discretion to reach the merits, in only 8% of their rulings did they find a constitutional violation.

Page 1055. Add at the end of footnote 17:

See also Wells, *Constitutional Remedies: Reconciling Official Immunity with the Vindication of Rights*, 88 St.John's L.Rev. 713 (2014) (emphasizing plaintiffs' interests in "vindicating" their constitutional rights as a basis for tort remedies independent of compensation and deterrence rationales and arguing that, in light of the interest in vindicating constitutional rights, official immunity should not bar suits for nominal damages).

CHAPTER X

JUDICIAL FEDERALISM: LIMITATIONS ON DISTRICT COURT JURISDICTION OR ITS EXERCISE

---

2. STATUTORY LIMITATIONS ON FEDERAL COURT JURISDICTION

B. OTHER STATUTORY RESTRICTIONS ON FEDERAL COURT JURISDICTION

NOTE ON THREE-JUDGE DISTRICT COURTS, THE JOHNSON ACT OF 1934, AND THE TAX INJUNCTION ACT OF 1937

Page 1090. Add at the end of footnote 5:

Solimine, *The Fall and Rise of Specialized Constitutional Courts,* 17 U.Pa.J.Const.L. 115 (2014), identifies instances in which post-1976 Congresses have included provisions in substantive statutes prescribing exclusive review of constitutional challenges by three-judge district courts, often in the D.C. Circuit, and typically with a right of direct appeal to the Supreme Court. Professor Solimine criticizes such statutes on the grounds that they deny the Supreme Court the benefit of "percolation" of issues through a variety of courts, expedite constitutional review and therefore promote decision on an underdeveloped record. He also contends that by vesting the D.C. Circuit with exclusive jurisdiction over significant questions, these statutes contribute to a politicized process of nomination and confirmation to judgeships in that circuit.

Page 1091. Add a new paragraph between the two paragraphs in Paragraph (1):

The Tax Injunction Act is modeled in part upon the Anti-Injunction Act specific to the federal Tax Code, 26 U.S.C. § 7421(a), which provides that "no suit for the purpose of restraining the assessment or collection of any tax shall be maintained in any court by any person," thereby precluding certain challenges to federal tax collection practices. See Hibbs v. Winn, 542 U.S. 88, 100 (2004) (using federal tax law as a guide to defining the terms of the Tax Injunction Act).[5a]

[5a] For an overview of the history of the Federal Tax Code's Anti-Injunction Act and an argument that it should be construed narrowly to permit pre-enforcement review of Treasury regulations and IRS guidance documents, consult Hickman & Kerska, *Restoring the Lost Anti-Injunction Act*, 103 Va.L.Rev. 1683 (2017). For a skeptical take on their argument, see Hemel, *The Living Anti-Injunction Act*, 104 Va.L.Rev. Online 74 (2018).

Page 1091. Add a new Paragraph (1)(a):

(a) The Reach of the Prohibition. In Direct Marketing Association v. Brohl, 575 U.S. 1 (2015), the Supreme Court addressed whether injunctive relief sought in a federal court action challenging the constitutionality of a state sales and use tax notice and reporting scheme could be said to "enjoin, suspend or restrain the assessment, levy or collection of any tax under State law" within the scope of the Tax Injunction Act. In an attempt to capture sales and use taxes that would otherwise be lost to e-commerce transactions,[7a] Colorado required out-of-state retailers, under threat of financial penalties: (1) to inform in-state consumers of their obligations to pay state sales and use taxes; (2) to send annual reports to all Colorado customers who purchased more than $500 worth of products from a retailer in the prior year informing the customers of their obligation to pay the relevant taxes; and (3) to send year-end statements to the Colorado Department of Revenue listing the retailers' Colorado customers along with their known addresses and total amount of purchases in the prior year.

The Supreme Court unanimously concluded that nothing in the Tax Injunction Act precludes a district court from enjoining the enforcement of notice and reporting requirements by state tax officials. The Court reasoned that enforcement of the notice and reporting requirements could not be deemed an act of "assessment, levy or collection" within the meaning of the Act. Drawing upon analogies to the federal Tax Code Anti-Injunction Act,[7b] Justice Thomas posited that the notice and reporting requirements merely constituted "information gathering" that preceded any formal steps of "assessment" and "collection" of taxes by the state. In the Court's view, the Tax Injunction Act should be read narrowly to draw a clear jurisdictional line that asks "whether the relief [sought in the federal court action] to some degree stops 'assessment, levy or collection,' not whether it merely inhibits them."[7c] However powerful the justifications for the ruling, it seems certain to encourage pre-enforcement challenges to new state tax laws in order to avoid the reach of the Tax Injunction Act.

[7a] Quill Corp. v. North Dakota, 504 U.S. 298 (1992), reaffirmed an earlier decision holding that the dormant Commerce Clause prohibits states from requiring a retailer lacking a physical presence within a state to collect sales and use taxes. The Supreme Court overruled Quill Corp. in South Dakota v. Wayfair, Inc., 138 S.Ct. 2080 (2018).

[7b] Justice Thomas's opinion for the Court noted that the Tax Injunction Act was modeled upon the Anti-Injunction Act in the federal Tax Code, 26 U.S.C. § 7421(a), positing that "words used in both Acts are generally used in the same way, and we discern the meaning of the terms in the AIA by reference to the broader Tax Code."

[7c] The Court declined to address whether principles of comity counseled in favor of dismissal of the case.

———————

3. JUDICIALLY DEVELOPED LIMITATIONS ON FEDERAL COURT JURISDICTION: DOCTRINES OF EQUITY, COMITY, AND FEDERALISM

A. EXHAUSTION OF STATE NONJUDICIAL REMEDIES

NOTE ON EXHAUSTION OF STATE NONJUDICIAL REMEDIES

Page 1099. Add at the end of Paragraph (b):

More recently, in Ross v. Blake, 136 S.Ct. 1850 (2016), the Court rejected the rule adopted by some circuits that the exhaustion requirement of the Prison Litigation Reform Act (PLRA) is not absolute and need not be satisfied in cases involving "special circumstances." The case arose when a prisoner brought suit under 42 U.S.C. § 1983 against two corrections officers claiming that they had used excessive force while transferring him from his cell to a segregation unit. The district court dismissed claims against one defendant when he raised the affirmative defense of failure to exhaust. The Fourth Circuit reversed, concluding that it was reasonable for the prisoner to believe that he had exhausted all administrative remedies before filing his federal action, even though he had not done so.

Writing for the Court, Justice Kagan first rejected the Fourth Circuit's "freewheeling approach to exhaustion as inconsistent with the PLRA." Statutory exhaustion provisions are different from judge-made exhaustion requirements, Justice Kagan noted, with the former "foreclosing judicial discretion." This is because "Congress sets the rules—and courts have a role in creating exceptions only if Congress wants them to."[5a] The Court emphasized, however, that the PLRA's exhaustion requirement "hinges" on administrative remedies being " 'available' ", 42 U.S.C. § 1997e(a), a term that should not be understood to encompass administrative procedures that are a mere "dead end"; a scheme that is "so opaque that it becomes, practically speaking, incapable of use"; or a situation in which "prison administrators thwart inmates from taking advantage of a grievance process through machination, misrepresentation, or intimidation."[5b] Under the Court's understanding of congressionally-mandated exhaustion, is there any room left for application of judge-made abstention doctrines in such circumstances?[5c] As a separate matter, is it possible that the Court's framework for assessing availability of administrative procedures often will collapse with the Fourth Circuit's "special circumstances" exception to the PLRA's exhaustion requirement?

[5a] Justice Kagan added that the PLRA's exhaustion requirement contrasted "markedly" from its much " 'weak[er]' " predecessor provision that made exhaustion largely a matter " 'left to the discretion of the district court' " (quoting Woodford v. Ngo, 548 U.S. 81, 84, 85 (2006)).

[5b] More recently, Justice Sotomayor suggested that the extraordinary circumstances presented by the Covid-19 pandemic could implicate "the PLRA's textual exception" and therefore "open the courthouse doors where they would otherwise stay closed." Valentine v. Collier, 140 S.Ct. 1598 (2020) (statement of Sotomayor, J.) (suggesting that "if a plaintiff has established that the prison grievance procedures at issue are utterly incapable of responding to a rapidly spreading pandemic like Covid-19, the procedures may be 'unavailable' to meet the plaintiff's purposes, much in the way they would be if prison officials ignored the grievances entirely").

^{5c} Justice Breyer wrote separately to reiterate his earlier view that although he agreed that the PLRA does not permit " 'freewheeling' exceptions" of the kind adopted by the Fourth Circuit, the statute should be read to encompass "administrative law's 'well-established exceptions to exhaustion.' " Woodford v. Ngo, 548 U.S. 81, 103 (2006) (opinion of Breyer, J.).

Page 1099. Add a new paragraph after the first paragraph of Paragraph (5)(c):

A closely divided Court partially overruled Williamson County in Knick v. Township of Scott, Pennsylvania, 139 S.Ct. 2162 (2019), concluding that Williamson County had "effectively established an exhaustion requirement for § 1983 takings claims" by requiring litigants seeking just compensation to pursue available state proceedings in the first instance. Deeming Williamson County poorly reasoned, in tension with the Court's "longstanding position that a property owner has a constitutional claim to compensation at the time the government deprives him of his property", and at odds with Patsy and related decisions, the majority found the arguments favoring respecting *stare decisis* wanting. Instead, consistent with Patsy, the Court held that litigants should have the possibility of pursuing § 1983 takings claims in the first instance in a federal forum. Writing for four dissenters, Justice Kagan complained that the Court's decision "betrays judicial federalism" insofar as it will have the effect of "send[ing] a flood of complex state-law issues to federal courts", thereby rendering "federal courts a principal player in local and state land-use disputes." See also p. 28–29, *supra*.

———

B. ABSTENTION: PULLMAN AND RELATED DOCTRINES

NOTE ON ABSTENTION IN CASES INVOLVING A FEDERAL QUESTION

Page 1104. Add a new footnote 1a at the end of Paragraph (1)(a):

^{1a} Sutton, 51 Imperfect Solutions: States and the Making of American Constitutional Law (2018), urges federal courts to consider these two paths as well as certification when confronted with cases involving a critical question of state constitutional law. In Judge Sutton's view, federal courts should eschew "intruding on sensitive and complicated issues of state law without giving the state courts a chance to review, and perhaps resolve, the matter first." Further, he suggests that where a federal court maintains jurisdiction over a case involving arguably parallel state and federal claims, it should resolve the state claim first and even consider pointing out "the relevance of state constitutional guarantees to certain disputes" to foster greater development of state constitutional law. Doing so, he writes, marries well with Chief Justice Burger's admonition to state courts in one of his year-end reports that they "first . . . resolv[e] issues arising under their constitutions and statutes [before] passing on matters concerning federal law." Do you agree with this analogy? Why should a federal court resolve a (possibly more difficult) state claim before addressing a federal claim that it may be more qualified to decide and that may moot the state claim?

Page 1105. Insert the following at the end of the penultimate paragraph of Paragraph (1)(d):

For a detailed explication of the context in which the Pullman case arose and the proceedings in the case, see Robel, *Riding the Color Line: The Story of Railroad Commission of Texas v. Pullman Co.*, in Federal Courts Stories (Jackson & Resnik eds. 2010), at 163. Among other problems with Pullman abstention, Robel highlights the delays inherent in the procedures, noting that Pullman abstention frustrated efforts by the NAACP to enforce the mandate of Brown v. Board of Education, 347 U.S. 483 (1954). See also Harrison v. NAACP, 360 U.S. 167 (1959) (abstaining from deciding civil rights challenges to a host of Virginia statutes). As Professor Robel notes, only one month after handing down the decision in Pullman, the Supreme Court resisted calls to abstain from determining whether the Interstate Commerce Act mandated equal accommodations for passengers regardless of race, holding that the Act required equal accommodations. See Mitchell v. United States, 313 U.S. 80 (1941).

Page 1108. Add to the end of footnote 11:

See also Gardner, *Abstention at the Border*, 105 U.Va.L.Rev. 63 (2019) (contending that in the international context, federal judges today should generally decline to invoke forum non conveniens or abstention based on notions of comity).

Page 1109. Add a new footnote 11a at the end of Paragraph (e):

[11a] Woolhandler, *Between the Acts: Federal Court Abstention in the 1940s and '50s*, 59 N.Y.L.Sch.L.Rev. 211 (2014–15), argues that abstention became the norm in challenges to state legislation in the 1940s and 1950s but declined in the 1960s as the Supreme Court's deferential stance of the immediate post-Lochner era gave way to less deferential substantive doctrines expanding judicial protection of civil rights.

Page 1112. Add a new footnote 14a at the end of the last paragraph of Paragraph (6):

[14a] For additional discussion, see Sutton, note 1a, *supra*, at 80.

C. EQUITABLE RESTRAINT

NOTE ON YOUNGER V. HARRIS AND THE DOCTRINE OF EQUITABLE RESTRAINT

Page 1139. Insert the following in place of the first two sentences of Paragraph (2)(b):

(b)   Whatever may have been the case in other eras, perhaps by 1971 there was less reason to think state courts generally untrustworthy in cases involving claimed federal rights.[8] During this period, moreover, federal habeas corpus review was both available and robust, see, *e.g.*, Brown v. Allen, Seventh Edition p. 1275, and Supreme Court review of state court criminal decisions was available, see, *e.g.*, Friedman, *A Revisionist Theory of Abstention*, 88 Mich.L.Rev. 530, 561–63 (1989).

[8]   But cf. Bright, Can Judicial Independence Be Attained in the South? Overcoming History, Elections, and Misperceptions About the Role of the Judiciary, 14 Ga.St.U.L.Rev. 817 (1998) (arguing that southern state courts, in particular, have continued to reflect legacies of racism and have remained subject to political pressures, including those stemming from judicial elections).

Page 1141. Add a new footnote 11a at the end of Paragraph (6):

[11a] Along similar lines, Smith, *Abstention in the Time of Ferguson*, 131 Harv.L.Rev. 2283 (2018), argues that Younger abstention is inappropriate in cases challenging systemic or structural flaws in local or state criminal justice systems, such as suits challenging policies governing fines, fees, collection practices, and bail.

NOTE ON STEFFEL V. THOMPSON AND ANTICIPATORY RELIEF

Page 1153. Add a new footnote 1a at the end of Paragraph (1):

[1a] Seinfeld, *At the Frontier of the Younger Doctrine: Reflections on Google v. Hood*, 101 Va.L.Rev. Online 14 (2015), notes that the lower courts are divided over when enforcement proceedings should be deemed pending for purposes of Younger. As Professor Seinfeld notes, some courts view issuance of a subpoena as having initiated state proceedings while other courts view such steps as merely "preliminary" to a subsequent proceeding. See, *e.g.*, Guillemard-Ginorio v. Contreras-Gómez, 585 F.3d 508 (1st Cir. 2009). He argues that the larger principles behind Younger, Steffel, and cases elaborating upon the reach of Younger discussed later in this Note (*Huffman v. Pursue*, 420 U.S. 592 (1975), *Middlesex County Ethics Comm. v. Garden State Bar Ass'n*, 457 U.S. 423 (1982), and *Ohio Civil Rights Comm'n v. Dayton Christian Schools, Inc.*, 477 U.S. 619 (1986)), stand for the larger proposition that "a proceeding is not 'ongoing' for Younger purposes until such time as it has been turned over to an impartial state official or, at least, an impartial state actor is able to exercise meaningful oversight authority" of the case. Under this test, Professor Seinfeld concludes, issuance of an administrative subpoena alone does not warrant Younger abstention.

E. MATTERS OF DOMESTIC RELATIONS AND PROBATE

NOTE ON FEDERAL JURISDICTION IN MATTERS OF DOMESTIC RELATIONS

Page 1189. Add at the end of Paragraph (4):

Pfander & Damrau, *A Non-Contentious Account of Article III's Domestic Relations Exception*, 92 Notre Dame L.Rev. 117 (2016), argues that the domestic relations exception is best grounded in Article III's distinction between "cases" and "controversies." Building on earlier work of one of the authors, see Pfander & Birk, pp. 6–7, *supra*, the authors argue that the term "cases" encompasses "both disputes over federal law between adverse parties and a range of ex parte or non-contentious federal matters" while the term "controversy" extends to "only disputes between the opposing parties identified in Article III." Accordingly, the authors contend that the jurisdictional grant over "controversies" does not permit federal courts to entertain uncontested administrative or ex parte proceedings predicated upon state law, an omission that they argue explains and justifies narrow versions of both the domestic relations and probate exceptions to federal jurisdiction. (For discussion of application of the theory to the probate exception, see p. 107, *infra*.) Applying their framework, the authors conclude that Article III would permit federal question jurisdiction over non-contentious federal law cases in the domestic realm and that diversity jurisdiction could be extended to contested domestic relations matters involving diverse parties, including surrogacy agreements and divorce proceedings, while also encompassing ancillary matters, such as alimony and child custody.

Page 1189. Add at the end of Paragraph (6)(b):

This view draws support from the fact that in recent Terms, the Court has decided a number of federal question cases implicating marriage and child custody matters. See, *e.g.*, Obergefell v. Hodges, 135 S.Ct. 2584 (2015) (holding that the Fourteenth Amendment requires states to recognize same-sex marriages); V.L. v. E.L., 136 S.Ct. 1017 (2016) (per curiam) (summarily reversing one state's refusal to give full faith and credit to an adoption decree awarded in another state); Pavan v. Smith, 137 S.Ct. 2075 (2017) (holding that state law must recognize same-sex spouse of biological mother as second parent on birth certificate where it would otherwise by default recognize opposite-sex spouse on birth certificate); Monasky v. Taglieri, 140 S.Ct. 719 (2020) (detailing the appropriate inquiry governing habitual residence determinations for purposes of child custody disputes falling under the Hague Convention on the Civil Aspects of International Child Abduction, as implemented in the United States by the International Child Abduction Remedies Act); see also Troxel v. Granville, 530 U.S. 57 (2000) (holding that state court order granting visitation rights to paternal grandparents impermissibly infringed upon mother's due process rights to make decisions concerning the raising of her children); Michael H. v. Gerald D., 491 U.S. 110 (1989) (assessing due process rights of biological father and child in custody dispute with another man to whom she was married at time of child's birth).

———

NOTE ON FEDERAL JURISDICTION IN MATTERS OF PROBATE AND ADMINISTRATION

Page 1190. Add at the end of Paragraph (1):

Pfander & Downey, *In Search of the Probate Exception,* 67 Vand.L.Rev. 1533 (2014), offer a complex explanation, including both statutory and constitutional elements, of the historical origins and scope of the probate exception. As a statutory matter, the authors maintain that the 1789 Judiciary Act and other early enactments presupposed English conceptions of the scope of equity practice, which conferred no probate authority. But they also argue that Article III "extends judicial power only to 'controversies' or 'disputes' between adversaries on state law matters" and would therefore bar Congress from conferring federal jurisdiction over much of the ex parte work involved in probate proceedings conducted under state law. Despite highlighting that limitation, Pfander & Downey understand the historical record to suggest that Article III does not foreclose federal jurisdiction over "cases" under federal law (as distinguished from "controversies" under state law) that encompass ex parte proceedings. (Here, their examples include applications for naturalization and for warrants.) The authors conclude that Congress "could assign probate administration to the federal courts in connection with otherwise constitutionally proper federal legislation that regulated, say, the commercial implications of estates with ties to more than one state". They similarly contend that because nothing in Article III excludes adversary proceedings between diverse parties that involve probate-related matters under state law, Congress could authorize federal court diversity jurisdiction over such matters.

CHAPTER XI

FEDERAL HABEAS CORPUS

————

2. HABEAS CORPUS AND EXECUTIVE DETENTION

NOTE ON THE SUSPENSION CLAUSE OF THE CONSTITUTION

Page 1201. Add a new footnote 1a at the end of the first paragraph of Section A:

¹ᵃ Tyler, Habeas Corpus in Wartime: From the Tower of London to Guantanamo Bay (2017), surveys the Convention and ratification debates and concludes that "a wealth of evidence from this period demonstrates that in the Suspension Clause, the Founding generation sought to constitutionalize the protections associated with the seventh section of the English Habeas Corpus Act and import the English suspension model, while also severely limiting the circumstances when the suspension power could be invoked." For additional discussion, see pp. 110–111, *infra*.

————

NOTE ON HAMDI V. RUMSFELD AND THE SCOPE OF HABEAS INQUIRY OVER PETITIONS FILED BY ALLEGED ENEMY COMBATANTS

Page 1220. Add a new footnote * at the end of the first sentence of Paragraph (1):

* More recently, Justice Thomas opined that "[t]he Founders * * * enshrined" the English suspension model "in the Suspension Clause, which they understood to protect a substantive right"—specifically, "freedom from discretionary detention" at the hands of the executive. Department of Homeland Security v. Thuraissigiam, 140 S.Ct. 1959 (2020) (Thomas, J., concurring). Suspension, Justice Thomas added, "likely meant a statute granting the executive the power to detain without bail or trial based on mere suspicion of a crime or dangerousness," referencing, among other examples, Revolutionary War suspensions adopted in the states to authorize detention without charges of persons supporting the crown. Do these statements suggest that Justice Thomas's position has evolved since Hamdi? For additional discussion of Thuraissigiam, see pp. 54–55, *supra*, and pp. 113–114, 115, *infra*.

Page 1221. Add a new footnote 1a at the end of the first paragraph of Paragraph (2):

¹ᵃ In subsequent work, Bradley and Goldsmith detail the expansion of the reach of the AUMF to encompass military operations against the Islamic State and argue that one of the legacies of the Obama Administration is its interpretation of the AUMF to "support presidential discretion and flexibility." Bradley & Goldsmith, *Obama's AUMF Legacy*, 110 Am.J.Int'l.L. 628 (2016).

Page 1221. Substitute the following for the last sentence of Paragraph (2):

Defending the plurality's approach in Hamdi, Fallon and Meltzer argue that "a common law approach to habeas corpus issues has been not only historically dominant," but also that "[m]uch of the most important jurisdictional and substantive doctrine [in the habeas context] has been and remains judge-made." Fallon & Meltzer, Seventh Edition p. 1221 at 2044.[1b] Tyler, *A "Second Magna Carta": The English Habeas Corpus Act and the Statutory Origins of the Habeas Privilege*, 91 Notre Dame L.Rev. 1949 (2016) (from a Symposium honoring Daniel Meltzer), suggests a more complicated picture. She posits that the English Habeas Corpus Act of 1679 "was enormously significant in the development of English law's habeas jurisprudence." Going further, she observes that "extensive evidence of the Act's influence across the Atlantic dating from well before, during, and after the Revolutionary War demonstrates that much of early American habeas law was premised upon efforts to incorporate the Act's key protections rather than developed through judicial innovation."

In separate work, Tyler details the role that the English Habeas Corpus Act played in the Revolutionary War legal framework, noting that "determinations regarding the reach and application of the English Habeas Corpus Act of 1679 were of tremendous consequence" during this important period in American history. Tyler, *Habeas Corpus and the American Revolution*, 103 Calif.L.Rev. 635 (2015). As she notes, when asked for guidance as to the legal status of American prisoners brought to English soil for detention during the war, Lord Mansfield advised the North Administration that "in England, where the Habeas Corpus Act was unquestionably in force, it promised a timely criminal trial to those who could and did claim the protection of domestic law—a category of persons long understood to encompass traitors." It was against this backdrop that the Administration requested a suspension from Parliament "to legalize the detention in England of American rebels—considered traitors by the Crown—in the absence of criminal charges." By its terms, the Revolutionary War suspension applied to American colonists captured outside the geographic reach of the Habeas Corpus Act who were then brought within the realm, where the Act would have otherwise been in full force and theirs to claim as British subjects. As Tyler also explains, it was not until independence became a foregone conclusion that Parliament allowed the suspension legislation to lapse and declared Americans remaining in custody to be prisoners of war subject to exchange under the laws of war. Taking the story forward, Tyler, p. 109, *supra*, surveys the Convention and ratification debates and concludes that the Founding generation sought to constitutionalize the English suspension model and with it the protections long associated with the English Habeas Corpus Act. Moving beyond the Founding period, Tyler posits that this understanding of the constraints that the Clause imposed on executive detention largely controlled through Reconstruction, and it was only during World War II, with the forced detention of Japanese Americans in so-called "Relocation Centers" under Executive Order 9066 and resulting military regulations, that this model

[1b] For a detailed historical account of how English and British courts employed the common law writ in the period leading up to United States independence, see Halliday, Seventh Edition p. 1193. For elaboration of the arguments favoring a common law model in this context, see Fallon, *On Viewing the Courts as Junior Partners of Congress in Statutory Interpretation Cases: An Essay Celebrating the Scholarship of Daniel J. Meltzer*, 91 Notre Dame L.Rev. 1743 (2016) (from a Symposium honoring Daniel Meltzer). See also Vladeck, *Constitutional Remedies in Federalism's Forgotten Shadow*, 107 Calif.L.Rev. 1043 (2019); Freedman, Making Habeas Work: A Legal History (2018).

broke down. See Tyler, p. 109, *supra*, at 222–43 (detailing how senior government officials initially opposed detention proposals during this period on Suspension Clause grounds). See also Ex parte Endo, 323 U.S. 283 (1944) (declining to address the Suspension Clause issues raised by the detention of Japanese Americans during World War II and instead deciding a habeas petition brought by a detained citizen on narrower grounds).[1c]

Assessing this same history, White, *Looking Backward and Forward at the Suspension Clause*, 117 Mich.L.Rev. 1313 (2019), focuses on the Civil War as a turning point in the story of the privilege, observing that President Lincoln effectively defended "the outbreak of war [as] justifying suspension of the privilege, and as a result the privilege really did not exist in wartime." This, White suggests, established a new model for the operation of the privilege in wartime pursuant to which one now witnesses "limited executive 'suspensions,' " as occurred during World War II under Executive Order 9066. This shift, in turn, established the foundation for a case like Hamdi, with the result that together, each of these "strategic decisions of the Executive, and their legitimation by the Court, suggest that, at least since World War II, the Suspension Clause has not so much been 'forgotten' as deliberately bypassed."

Assuming that the English model provided the foundation of the Suspension Clause in the United States Constitution, what bearing, if any, should this history have on questions such as those raised in Hamdi?[1d] And if Professor White's conclusion about the function of the privilege in the wake of the Civil War is accurate, what bearing, if any, should that have on the interpretation of the Suspension Clause today?[1e]

[1c] In subsequent work, Tyler explores the contrasting positions of Prime Minister Churchill and President Roosevelt with respect to the domestic citizen internment programs implemented in Great Britain and the United States during the war, highlighting that Churchill pointed to the role of habeas corpus in the English legal tradition as teaching that the British program was unconstitutional and should be ended. Tyler, *Courts and the Executive in Wartime: A Comparative Study of the American and British Approaches to the Internment of Citizens during World War II and Their Lessons for Today*, 107 Calif.L.Rev. 789 (2019). For a different view contending that the habeas privilege should be understood as " 'only' a procedural remedy and * * * not the source of distinct substantive anti-detention rules," see Kovarsky, *Citizenship, National Security Detention, and the Habeas Remedy*, 107 Calif.L.Rev. 867 (2019).

[1d] Meyler, *Originalism and a Forgotten Conflict over Martial Law*, 113 Nw.U.L.Rev. 1335 (2019), explores the intersection of habeas corpus with martial law in the century leading up to ratification, explaining that in the colonies during this period, "the legal framework of England represented not simply a static backdrop for the development of the Constitution but a contested and dynamic space in which military commanders' imperial justifications vied with the arguments of colonial subjects based on English law. . . ." Thus, she concludes, martial law "furnished part of the context out of which the Suspension Clause emerged" and is therefore relevant to understanding the operation of the Clause as an original matter.

[1e] Pfander, *Constructive Constitutional History and Habeas Corpus Today*, 107 Calif.L.Rev. 1005 (2019), poses a similar question this way: "With habeas sidelined, how should we restore the rule of law in light of Lincoln's action?" He responds by proposing that the law permit persons subject to detention to bring suits for damages against responsible officers. Doing so, Pfander argues, "would preserve the Constitution and the rule of law, while signaling to future presidents that actions taken in the name of military necessity must ultimately face a test of legality."

Page 1222. Add at the beginning of footnote 2:

Potential support for the relevance of the distinction between a citizen and alien to the application of the Suspension Clause may be found in Department of Homeland Security v. Thuraissigiam, 140 S.Ct. 1959 (2020). In Thuraissigiam, after holding that the Suspension

Clause does not apply to an asylum seeker who was apprehended shortly after crossing the border challenging his removal following expedited administrative proceedings, the Court distinguished the situation of a citizen who is detained for deportation, clarifying that "today's opinion would not prevent the citizen from petitioning for release." For additional discussion of Thuraissigiam, see pp. 54–55, *supra*, and pp. 113–114, 115, *infra*.

Page 1222. Add to the end of Paragraph (3)(a):

When Padilla sought review in the Supreme Court a second time, the government indicted him on various criminal charges and transferred him to the control of civilian authorities. The Court then declined to take up his case anew. Padilla v. Hanft, 547 U.S. 1062 (2006).

––––––––

NOTE ON THE SCOPE OF REVIEW IN IMMIGRATION CASES

Page 1242. Add to the end of Paragraph (2):

The difficulty in drawing a clear distinction between questions of law and fact arose anew in Department of Homeland Security v. Thuraissigiam, 140 S.Ct. 1959 (2020). Petitioner argued (1) that in removal proceedings he had satisfied the "credible fear of persecution" test such that he should be afforded a fuller opportunity to apply for asylum in this country; and (2) that he had been denied a full and fair opportunity to demonstrate that he satisfied the relevant standard in the administrative proceedings. Concurring in the Court's judgment that petitioner was not constitutionally entitled to judicial review of his claims under the Suspension Clause or the Due Process Clause, Justice Breyer, joined by Justice Ginsburg, characterized petitioner's primary claims as "at their core, challenges to factual findings." As for petitioner's additional claims challenging the asylum officer's application of the relevant legal standard, Justice Breyer observed that "[a]t the heart of [what are] purportedly legal contentions * * * lies a disagreement with immigration officials' findings" relating to the underlying facts. Accordingly, he viewed the latter "claims as factual in nature, notwithstanding respondent's contrary characterization," concluding that the Suspension Clause does not require that a "habeas court make indeterminate and highly record-intensive judgments on matters of degree." Justices Sotomayor, joined by Justice Kagan, dissented and disagreed. Deeming petitioner's claims as raising both mixed questions of law and fact and legal challenges to "procedural defects" in the administrative procedures Congress prescribed, the dissent argued that the Constitution required judicial review. Sidestepping the debate, the majority in Thuraissigiam said that it had no occasion to address whatever distinctions existed between petitioner's claims, which the government had labeled as raising "at best a mixed question of law," and the those advanced in St. Cyr. The Court instead relied upon the distinction that St. Cyr was already within the United States when he sought review of his claims. For additional discussion of Thuraissigiam, see pp. 54–55, *supra*, and pp. 113–114, 115, *infra*.

––––––––

NOTE ON EXHAUSTION OF NON-HABEAS REMEDIES

Page 1245. Add at the end of footnote 5:

Cf. In re Al-Nashiri, 791 F.3d 71 (D.C.Cir. 2015) (declining to review, on petition for writ of mandamus, separation of powers challenge to the composition of the Court of Military Commission Review while proceedings before military commission were ongoing and noting that petitioner's arguments could be raised and fully aired on appeal from final judgment); In re Khadr, 823 F.3d 92 (D.C.Cir. 2016) (same).

─────────

NOTE ON BOUMEDIENE AND THE TERRITORIAL REACH OF HABEAS CORPUS

Page 1259. Add a new footnote * at the end of the penultimate paragraph of Paragraph (1):

*   For an argument that Anglo-American habeas jurisprudence includes important statutory foundations separate and apart from common law developments, see Tyler, p. 110, *supra* (detailing the significance of the English Habeas Corpus Act of 1679).

Page 1259. Add a new footnote ** at the end of Paragraph (1):

**   Tyler, p. 109, *supra*, posits that "Hamdi and Boumediene should be understood as posing distinct questions". In her view, Hamdi was incorrectly decided insofar as it stands at odds with the animating purpose behind the Suspension Clause—namely, to preclude the government from detaining someone deemed to owe allegiance outside the criminal process in the absence of a valid suspension. In Boumediene, by contrast, no Justice questioned the government's authority to detain enemy combatants outside the criminal process as part of the war on terrorism. Boumediene, accordingly, solely implicated the question "what procedural rights attach in habeas proceedings." Tyler then questions "whether there is room for both cases under the umbrella of Suspension Clause jurisprudence" while also asking whether "the Suspension Clause and due process elements of the war on terrorism decisions should be rendered conceptually distinct." *Cf.* Tyler, p. 110, *supra* (underscoring the importance of geography as well as the bond of allegiance with respect to the reach and application of the English Habeas Corpus Act during the American Revolutionary War).

Page 1259. Add at the end of Paragraph (1):

In Department of Homeland Security v. Thuraissigiam, 140 S.Ct. 1959 (2020), the Court held that the Suspension Clause did not apply to a petitioner seeking asylum in this country who was captured 25 yards inside the border and then ordered removed via expedited administrative proceedings. Writing for the Court, Justice Alito framed the Court's analysis as asking whether petitioner's claims would have come within the reach of the Suspension Clause as it was understood in 1789. (The Court framed its inquiry this way after quoting the petitioner's brief to say that " 'there is no reason' to consider whether the Clause extends any further" (p. ___ (quoting Brief for Respondent 26, n. 12)).) Finding no support for the proposition that "the writ of habeas corpus was understood at the time of the adoption of the Constitution to permit a petitioner to claim the right to enter or remain in a country or to obtain administrative review potentially leading to that result", the Court held that the Suspension Clause did not apply (p. ___ (observing that at the Founding, "[t]he writ simply provided a means of contesting the lawfulness of restraint and securing release")). For the Thuraissigiam majority, that was the end of the matter.*** Compare the Court's approach in Boumediene, which moved beyond a historical record that it viewed as providing no clear analogy to explore functional considerations in determining the application of the Suspension Clause in the case.

   *** It was irrelevant, moreover, that during the Founding period and for decades thereafter, federal policy provided an " 'open door to the immigrant' " (citation omitted), rendering it such that a challenge to a limitation on review of immigration determinations would never have arisen during that period. Concurring in the judgment in Thuraissigiam but reserving judgment on future cases that might present different considerations, Justices Breyer and Ginsburg relied upon Boumediene for the proposition that habeas corpus "is an 'adaptable remedy,' and the 'precise application and scope' of the review it guarantees may change 'depending upon the circumstances' " (p. ___ (quoting Boumediene v. Bush, 553 U. S. 723, 779 (2008)).

Page 1260. Add a new footnote 1a at the end of Paragraph (2)(b):

   [1a] See also Kent, *Piracy and Due Process*, 39 Mich.J.Int'l L. 385 (2018) (exploring the political and legal treatment of piracy in the period leading up to and immediately following ratification and concluding that the history cuts against any historically inflected arguments supporting the concept of global due process).

Page 1261. Add to the end of Paragraph (2)(c):

The Supreme Court's most recent intervention in this debate came in Agency for International Development v. Alliance for Open Society International, Inc., 140 S.Ct. 2082 (2020), in which it rejected the proposition that foreign affiliates of American organizations could bring a First Amendment challenge to conditions that Congress attached to funding grants to combat HIV/AIDS abroad. Writing for the Court, Justice Kavanaugh (joined by Chief Justice Roberts and Justices Thomas, Alito, and Gorsuch), posited that "it is long settled as a matter of American constitutional law that foreign citizens outside U. S. territory do not possess rights under the U. S. Constitution" (citations omitted).[1b] He distinguished the situation of foreign citizens inside the United States, who "may enjoy certain constitutional rights", such as "the right to due process in a criminal trial." Finally, Justice Kavanaugh set apart those cases in which "under some circumstances, foreign citizens in the U. S. Territories—or in 'a territory' under the 'indefinite' and 'complete and total control' and 'within the constant jurisdiction' of the United States—may possess certain constitutional rights" (pp. ___–___ (quoting Boumediene, 553 U. S. at 755–71)). In dissent, Justice Breyer, joined by Justices Ginsburg and Sotomayor, opined that the plaintiffs should not be understood as foreign organizations but as instead affiliates of their American counterparts. Regardless, however, he rejected the Court's assessment of prior caselaw on matters of extraterritoriality, writing that it "does not reflect the current state of the law." "At most, one might say that [foreign citizens abroad] are unlikely to enjoy very often extraterritorial protection under the Constitution. Or one might say that the matter is undecided. But this Court has studiously avoided establishing an absolute rule that forecloses that protection in all circumstances" (p. ___). The dissent further cited Boumediene's rejection of a "formalistic" approach and its holding that " 'questions of extraterritoriality turn on objective factors and practical concerns' present in a given case" (p. ___). Arguing that questions of territoriality were not presented or briefed in the case, the dissent would have left open such questions in light of the many complications that they may raise (p. ___ (listing examples of potential future cases presenting different circumstances)).

¹ᵇ In reaching this conclusion, the majority emphasized that "[i]f the rule were otherwise, actions by American military, intelligence, and law enforcement personnel against foreign organizations or foreign citizens in foreign countries would be constrained by the foreign citizens' purported rights under the U. S. Constitution. That has never been the law" (p. ___ (citing Verdugo-Urquidez, 494 U. S. at 273–74; Eisentrager, 339 U. S. at 784)).

Page 1261. Add a new Paragraph (2)(f):

(f)   In applying the Suspension Clause, how should a court determine whether a petitioner in inside the United States? In Department of Homeland Security v. Thuraissigiam, 140 S.Ct. 1959 (2020), the Court concluded that an alien seeking asylum in the United States should be treated differently than one who is "already in the country [and] held in custody pending deportation." Unlike the alien in the latter scenario, one seeking entry stands on a different footing for purposes of the application of both the Suspension Clause and due process principles. This conclusion followed from Congress's "plenary authority to decide which aliens to admit" (citation omitted).[3] It was therefore of no relevance to the inquiry that petitioner had actually crossed the border and been apprehended some 25 yards inside the United States. The decision reveals that the border remains an important factor in constitutional analysis and that the Court defers extensively to Congress in the immigration context. As several Justices observed in Thuraissigiam, the decision could have important ramifications for those who enter the United States without legal authorization who are apprehended years later and put into removal proceedings. See id. (Breyer, J., concurring in the judgment); id. (Sotomayor, J., dissenting). For additional discussion of Thuraissigiam, see pp. 54–55, 112, 113–114, *supra*.

[3]   The Thuraissigiam Court distinguished Boumediene as involving individuals who "had been 'apprehended on the battlefield in Afghanistan' and elsewhere, not while crossing the border" (p. ___ (quoting Boumediene, 553 U. S., at 734)), and observing that "[t]hey sought only to be released from Guantanamo, not to enter this country."

----

3. COLLATERAL ATTACK ON CRIMINAL CONVICTIONS

A. COLLATERAL ATTACK ON STATE CONVICTIONS

INTRODUCTORY NOTE ON THE OPERATION OF FEDERAL HABEAS CORPUS JURISDICTION FOR STATE PRISONERS

Page 1268. Add at the end of footnote 13:

Updated 2018 figures from the Administrative Office of the U.S. Courts reveal similar numbers. Specifically, in the one-year period ending September 30, 2018, of 12,724 petitions on which courts took action, courts terminated 12,653 "before pretrial", 64 "during or after pretrial", and only 7 "during or after trial." Administrative Office of the U.S. Courts, 2018 Judicial Business, Table C-4.

Page 1271. Add at the end of footnote 23:

Between 2017–2018, the district courts took action on 160 capital habeas petitions, disposing of all but one before trial. Administrative Office of the U.S. Courts, 2018 Judicial Business, Table C-4.

INTRODUCTORY NOTE ON THE HISTORICAL DEVELOPMENT OF FEDERAL RELITIGATION IN CRIMINAL CASES

Page 1274. Add at the end of Paragraph (4):

Professor Vázquez notes that during the nineteenth century, those convicted in state courts enjoyed direct appeal as of right to the Supreme Court of any federal question decided against them. Surveying the cases between the 1916 introduction of discretionary review of state court criminal cases by the Supreme Court and the Brown decision in 1953 that follows on Seventh Edition p. 1275, Vázquez concludes that during this period the Justices debated whether review of such questions remained the exclusive province of the Supreme Court on direct appeal or whether lower federal courts could examine them in habeas proceedings. Thus, Vázquez argues, disagreement centered not on whether a federal court would review such questions generally, but instead over which federal forum should do so. See Vázquez, *Habeas as Forum Allocation: A New Synthesis*, 71 U. Miami L.Rev. 645 (2017).[8a]

[8a] Vázquez's conclusion therefore contrasts with that reached by Professor Bator in his survey of the same period. See Bator, Seventh Edition p. 1283.

NOTE ON THE RULE OF BROWN V. ALLEN AND ON HABEAS CORPUS POLICY

Page 1284. Add a new footnote 7a at the end of Section C, Paragraph (1)(b):

[7a] Two recent contributions to this debates include Huq, *Habeas and the Roberts Court*, 81 U.Chi.L.Rev. 519 (2014) (criticizing King and Hoffman's broader proposals to scale back collateral federal habeas corpus review and questioning the plausibility of the fiscal tradeoffs they propose); and Wiseman, *What is Federal Habeas Worth?*, 67 Fla.L.Rev. 1157 (2015) (estimating expenditures associated with non-capital habeas review in the federal courts to constitute "a tiny fraction" of criminal justice spending).

NOTE ON RETROACTIVITY AND NEW LAW IN HABEAS CORPUS

Page 1298. Add to the end of Paragraph (4)(b):

The Court will revisit this matter in Edwards v. Vannoy, cert. granted, ___ S.Ct. ___ (2020) (No. 19–5807), which presents the question whether Teague's second exception encompasses a claim brought by a habeas petitioner seeking to benefit from the Court's recent holding that the Sixth Amendment's requirement of a unanimous jury applies to the states under the Fourteenth Amendment. See Ramos v. Louisiana, 140 S.Ct. 1390 (2020) (overruling Apodaca v. Oregon, 406 U.S. 404 (1972)).[6a]

[6a] Notwithstanding the Supreme Court's failure to date to recognize any watershed procedural rules within the meaning of Teague's second exception since Teague, a number of state court decisions have done so. See Fox & Stein, *Constitutional Retroactivity in Criminal Procedure*, 91 Wash.L.Rev. 463 (2016).

Page 1299. Substitute the following for the last sentence of Paragraph (4)(c):

The Court extended this reasoning in Montgomery v. Louisiana, 136 S.Ct. 718 (2016), holding that its decision in Miller v. Alabama, 567 U.S. 460 (2012), was substantive for Teague purposes. Miller had held that a juvenile convicted of a homicide offense could not be sentenced to life in prison without parole absent consideration of whether the defendant's crimes reflect " 'irreparable corruption' " (p. 2469) (quoting Roper v. Simmons, 543 U.S. 551, 573 (2005)). The same Term, the Court extended its decision in Bousley v. United States, 523 U.S. 614 (1998), holding retroactive its decision in Johnson v. United States, 135 S.Ct. 2551 (2015), which struck down as unconstitutionally vague a provision calling for enhanced sentences in cases involving possession of a firearm by a felon. See Welch v. United States, 136 S.Ct. 1257 (2016).[6b] Given these extensions of Teague's first exception, and so long as Teague's second exception remains a null set, it would be accurate to restate Teague and its exceptions this way: new substantive rules apply retroactively; new procedural rules do not.

[6b] For additional discussion of Montgomery, see pp. 120–134, *infra*. For additional discussion of Welch, see pp. 141–143, *infra*.

Page 1300. Add a new Paragraph (5) to Section C:

(5) Teague's Foundations. What is the basis for Teague's mandate? The Constitution or the federal habeas statute? The Court explored this important question in Danforth v. Minnesota, 552 U.S. 264 (2008), and Montgomery v. Louisiana, 136 S.Ct. 718 (2016), included below as a principal case. See also pp. 61–62 and 78–79, *supra*; pp. 120–134, *infra*.

Page 1301. Add at the end of Section D:

The Court revisited the questions raised in Danforth v. Minnesota, 552 U.S. 264 (2008), in Montgomery v. Louisiana, 136 S.Ct. 718 (2016). In Montgomery, the Court held that Teague's first exception establishes a constitutional rule that state courts must apply in collateral proceedings. Writing for the Court, Justice Kennedy concluded that "[i]f a State may not constitutionally insist that a prisoner remain in jail on federal habeas review, it may not constitutionally insist on the same result in its own postconviction proceedings." For further discussion, see pp. 61–62, and 78–79, *supra*; pp. 120–134, *infra*.

In applying Griffith and Teague, the threshold question of whether a state court proceeding is direct or collateral is significant. In McKinney v. Arizona, 140 S.Ct. 702 (2020), a closely divided Court concluded that where a federal habeas court orders a state court to reweigh aggravating and mitigating factors in determining the appropriateness of a death sentence, the subsequent proceeding should be treated as collateral for Teague purposes. Accordingly, Griffith did not apply, and the state court was not required to apply intervening Supreme Court decisions that postdated the conclusion of the petitioner's original direct appeal. Citing the state supreme court's labeling of the reweighing proceeding as occurring on "collateral review," the Court found "no good reason" to second guess that classification. Dissenting for four Justices, Justice Ginsburg read the majority opinion "not

[to] hold that the classification a state supreme court assigns to a proceeding is inevitably dispositive of a retroactivity question." Instead, she understood the test to "look[ ] first to the State's classification of a proceeding, and then ask[ ] whether the character of the proceeding warrants the classification." Applying that test, Justice Ginsburg viewed the reweighing proceeding as a reinstatement of petitioner's direct appeal: the state supreme court conducted a *de novo* review of McKinney's sentence, used the docket number from his original direct appeal, and labeled McKinney's original appeal as " 'reinstated.' " In her view, McKinney was therefore entitled to the benefit of all relevant Supreme Court decisions that predated the reweighing proceeding (Ginsburg, J., dissenting) ("Whether the Constitution requires the application of law now in force is a question of federal constitutional law, not an issue subject to state governance."). McKinney raises several questions. First, will any new proceedings ordered by a federal habeas court short of a full retrial alter the date of finality for Teague purposes? Second, is there a convincing distinction to be drawn between McKinney's circumstances and those presented in Magwood v. Patterson, 561 U.S. 320 (2010)? In Magwood, the Court held that where a federal habeas court orders a state court to resentence the petitioner, the ensuing proceeding results in a "new" judgment for purposes of AEDPA and a subsequent federal habeas petition is therefore not "second or successive" to any prior petition; instead, the petition should be treated as "challeng[ing] a new judgment for the first time." For additional discussion of Magwood, see p. 139, *infra*.

NOTE ON TERRY WILLIAMS V. TAYLOR AND 28 U.S.C. § 2254(d)(1)

Page 1314. Add a new footnote * at the end of the first paragraph of Paragraph (2):

* Two Terms ago, a divided Court remanded for reconsideration a capital case on appeal from state post-conviction proceedings after having previously reversed the federal court of appeals' grant of relief to the same petitioner for similar claims. See Madison v. Alabama, 139 S.Ct. 718 (2019); Dunn v. Madison, 138 S.Ct. 9 (2018) (per curiam). Explaining the difference in outcomes with respect to the claims, which turned on the application of Ford v. Wainwright, 477 U.S. 399 (1986), and Panetti v. Quarterman, 551 U.S. 930 (2007), to a capital defendant suffering from dementia, the Court majority emphasized that "[b]ecause the case now comes to us on direct review of the state court's decision (rather than in a habeas proceeding), AEDPA's deferential standard no longer governs." Madison, 139 S.Ct. at 726; id. at 725 (contrasting the Court's earlier decision as "premised on AEDPA's 'demanding' and 'deferential standard' ") (quoting Madison, 138 S.Ct. at 11).

In a recent article, Professor Vázquez contends that the Court's approach in these cases is the product of its erroneous interpretation in *Terry Williams v. Taylor* of the standard set forth in § 2254(d)(1). In support of Justice Stevens' minority position, Vázquez contends that the *Williams* Court "could just as plausibly have read 'unreasonable' to mean 'contrary to' " when parsing AEDPA's text. He further argues that the weight of the legislative history and President Clinton's signing statement both strongly support the conclusion that AEDPA was not intended to alter the prior *de novo* review standard applied by federal courts to questions of federal law in collateral habeas corpus cases. Vázquez, *AEDPA as Forum Allocation: The Textual and Structural Case for Overruling* Williams v. Taylor, 56 Am.Crim.L.Rev. 1 (2019).

Page 1314. Add a new footnote ** at the end of the fifth sentence of the second paragraph of Paragraph (2):

** The Court found § 2254(d)(1) satisfied in McWilliams v. Dunn, 137 S.Ct. 1790 (2017). Reversing the Court of Appeals, the Court held, 5–4, that Alabama's provision of mental health assistance to a capital defendant "fell so dramatically short" of the requirements set forth in Ake v. Oklahoma, 470 U.S. 68 (1985) (holding that where certain threshold criteria are met, states must provide indigent defendants with access to a mental health expert to "assist in evaluation, preparation, and presentation of the defense"), that petitioner had made the requisite showing under § 2254(d)(1).

Page 1314. Add a new footnote *** at the end of the second paragraph of Paragraph (2):

*** The Court's decisions from the 2014 and 2015 Terms continued the trend. During this period, the Court decided eight cases implicating 28 U.S.C. § 2254(d). In all but one, the Court reversed lower court decisions granting relief. Four of those cases came out of the Ninth Circuit, and three came out of the Sixth Circuit. See Kernan v. Hinojosa, 136 S.Ct. 1603 (2016) (per curiam); Woods v. Etherton, 136 S.Ct. 1149 (2016) (per curiam); White v. Wheeler, 136 S.Ct. 456 (2015) (per curiam); Davis v. Ayala, 576 U.S. 257 (2015); Woods v. Donald, 575 U.S. 312 (2015) (per curiam); Glebe v. Frost, 574 U.S. 21 (2014) (per curiam); Lopez v. Smith, 574 U.S. 1 (2014) (per curiam). In one, the Court concluded by "again advis[ing] the Court of Appeals that the provisions of AEDPA apply with full force even when reviewing a conviction and sentence imposing the death penalty." Wheeler, *supra*, at 462. More recent Terms have witnessed additional reversals of lower court decisions granting habeas relief as insufficiently deferential under § 2254(d). See Shoop v. Hill, 139 S.Ct. 504 (2019) (per curiam) (vacating award of relief under § 2254(d) where court of appeals relied in part on a Supreme Court decision rendered after the date on which defendant-petitioner's conviction became final); Dunn v. Madison, 138 S.Ct. 9 (2018) (per curiam) (reversing the lower court's granting of habeas relief in a death penalty case for failing to give sufficient deference to state court judgment under § 2254(d)); Sexton v. Beaudreaux, 138 S.Ct. 2555 (2018) (per curiam) (reversing lower court for failing to accord sufficient deference under § 2254(d) to state court's resolution of Strickland claim). Further, several of the Court's recent opinions highlight that state court decisions involving underlying claims that are generally reviewed deferentially are entitled to "double" deference under AEDPA. See, *e.g.,* Etherton, *supra* (applying deference under § 2254(d)(1) in addition to the "strong" presumption of Strickland v. Washington, 466 U.S. 668 (1984), that counsel provided adequate representation); Wheeler, *supra* (applying "doubly deferential" review under AEDPA to claim challenging trial judge's decision to excuse a juror for cause).

Page 1316. Add at the end of Paragraph (4):

In Wilson v. Sellers, 138 S.Ct. 1188 (2018), the Court revisited the question of how federal habeas courts applying § 2254(d) should interpret summary dispositions by state courts. After a Georgia trial court rejected Wilson's post-conviction challenge to the effectiveness of his counsel during the sentencing phase of his capital trial, the Georgia Supreme Court summarily denied his application for a certificate of probable cause to appeal. Writing for the Court, Justice Breyer concluded that in applying § 2254(d), which requires deferring to state court decisions "on the merits," a federal habeas court should " 'look through' the unexplained decision to the last related state-court decision that does provide a relevant rationale," and "presume that the unexplained decision adopted the same reasoning." The Court also held, however, that this default proposition may be overcome where a party can demonstrate that the summary affirmance "relied or most likely did rely on different grounds than the lower state court's decision, such as alternative grounds for affirmance that were briefed or argued to the state supreme court or obvious in the record it reviewed." This "look through" presumption, the Court posited, is most consistent with earlier habeas jurisprudence as articulated in Ylst v. Nunnemaker, 501 U.S. 797 (1991), Seventh Edition p. 507, which held that a federal habeas court should presume that where the last reasoned state court decision in a case determined that a federal claim had been procedurally defaulted, that reasoning similarly informed any summary affirmances by higher state courts.

Dissenting for three Justices, Justice Gorsuch argued that the presumption adopted by the majority was at odds with the presumption applied in summary dispositions of federal court decisions, which posits that summary affirmances may be construed solely as approving of a lower court's judgment and not its reasoning. See Comptroller v. Wynne, 575 U.S. 542 (2015). The dissent also contended that the majority's presumption "requires [federal habeas courts] to treat the work of state court colleagues with disrespect we would not tolerate for our own." Nonetheless, Justice Gorsuch concluded that regardless of which default rule controls, the majority's invitation to federal habeas courts in appropriate cases to review materials beyond the last reasoned state court decision renders the debate over the proper presumption not especially significant. Is Justice Gorsuch right, or is the majority's default presumption likely to govern in most cases given the amount of labor and potential speculation that could be involved where a federal habeas court looks beyond the last reasoned opinion in reviewing state court judgments? And, *contra* Justice Gorsuch's suggestion, can it be said that the majority's presumption, which enables state courts to clarify where their decisions do not conform with the last reasoned opinion, respects the state courts? *Cf.* Michigan v. Long, Seventh Edition p. 494.

Page 1316. Add a new sentence at the beginning of Paragraph (5):

In Shoop v. Hill, 139 S.Ct. 504 (2019) (per curiam), the Court unanimously held that "clearly established law" for purposes of § 2254(d) does not encompass Supreme Court decisions rendered after the date on which defendant-petitioner's conviction became final. In doing so, the Court vacated a court of appeals decision granting habeas relief that "lean[ed] heavily" on such a decision.

Page 1319. After Paragraph (9), add the following principal case and accompanying Notes:

————

INTRODUCTORY NOTE: RETROACTIVITY AND THE OBLIGATIONS OF STATE AND FEDERAL COURTS IN COLLATERAL REVIEW PROCEEDINGS

In Montgomery v. Louisiana, below, the Court explored the question of the retroactive application of new constitutional holdings in state court postconviction proceedings. As indicated in the Note following the case, the decision is likely to bear significantly on federal habeas corpus proceedings and the questions raised in Tyler v. Cain, Seventh Edition p. 1318, particularly Justice O'Connor's concurring opinion.

————

Montgomery v. Louisiana

577 U.S. ___, 136 S.Ct. 718, 193 L.Ed.2d 599 (2016).
Certiorari to the Supreme Court of Louisiana.

■ JUSTICE KENNEDY delivered the opinion of the Court.

This is another case in a series of decisions involving the sentencing of offenders who were juveniles when their crimes were committed. * * *

I

Petitioner is Henry Montgomery. In 1963, Montgomery killed Charles Hurt, a deputy sheriff in East Baton Rouge, Louisiana. Montgomery was 17 years old at the time of the crime. [After his first conviction and death sentence was reversed on appeal, Montgomery was retried and a jury found him "guilty without capital punishment." Under Louisiana law, Montgomery automatically received a life sentence without possibility of parole. At the time, therefore,] Montgomery had no opportunity to present mitigation evidence to justify a less severe sentence. That evidence might have included Montgomery's young age at the time of the crime; expert testimony regarding his limited capacity for foresight, self-discipline, and judgment; and his potential for rehabilitation. Montgomery, now 69 years old, has spent almost his entire life in prison.

Almost 50 years after Montgomery was first taken into custody, this Court decided Miller v. Alabama, 576 U.S. 460 (2012). Miller held that mandatory life without parole for juvenile homicide offenders violates the Eighth Amendment's prohibition on " 'cruel and unusual punishments.' " Miller required that sentencing courts consider a child's "diminished culpability and heightened capacity for change" before condemning him or her to die in prison. Although Miller did not foreclose a sentencer's ability to impose life without parole on a juvenile, the Court explained that a lifetime in prison is a disproportionate sentence for all but the rarest of children, those whose crimes reflect " 'irreparable corruption.' " (quoting Roper v. Simmons, 543 U.S. 551, 573 (2005)).

After this Court issued its decision in Miller, Montgomery sought collateral review of his mandatory life-without parole sentence. [One form of collateral review available under Louisiana law "allows a prisoner to bring a collateral attack on his or her sentence by filing a motion to correct an illegal sentence." The relevant state statute provides that "[a]n illegal sentence may be corrected at any time by the court that imposed the sentence."]

Louisiana's collateral review courts will * * * consider a motion to correct an illegal sentence based on a decision of this Court holding that the Eighth Amendment to the Federal Constitution prohibits a punishment for a type of crime or a class of offenders. [Here, however, the trial court denied Montgomery's motion for collateral relief on the ground that Miller was not retroactive on collateral review, and the

Louisiana Supreme Court then denied his application for a supervisory writ.]

II

[The Court first addressed the question whether it had jurisdiction to decide the case.]

[The argument against jurisdiction proceeds as follows:] [A] State is under no obligation to give a new rule of constitutional law retroactive effect in its own collateral review proceedings. As those proceedings are created by state law and under the State's plenary control * * * , it is for state courts to define applicable principles of retroactivity. * * *

If, however, the Constitution establishes a rule and requires that the rule have retroactive application, then a state court's refusal to give the rule retroactive effect is reviewable by this Court. *Cf.* Griffith v. Kentucky, 479 U.S. 314, 328 (1987) (holding that on direct review, a new constitutional rule must be applied retroactively "to all cases, state or federal"). States may not disregard a controlling, constitutional command in their own courts. See Martin v. Hunter's Lessee, 1 Wheat. 304, 340–341, 344 (1816). * * *

Justice O'Connor's plurality opinion in Teague v. Lane, 489 U.S. 288 (1989), set forth a framework for retroactivity in cases on federal collateral review. [The argument against jurisdiction rests on the proposition that] Teague was an interpretation of the federal habeas statute, not a constitutional command; and so, the argument proceeds, Teague's retroactivity holding simply has no application in a State's own collateral review proceedings. [But] Teague originated in a federal, not state, habeas proceeding; so it had no particular reason to discuss whether any part of its holding was required by the Constitution in addition to the federal habeas statute. * * *

The Court now holds that when a new substantive rule of constitutional law controls the outcome of a case, the Constitution requires state collateral review courts to give retroactive effect to that rule. Teague's conclusion establishing the retroactivity of new substantive rules is best understood as resting upon constitutional premises. That constitutional command is, like all federal law, binding on state courts. This holding is limited to Teague's first exception for substantive rules; the constitutional status of Teague's exception for watershed rules of procedure need not be addressed here.

* * * Justice Harlan defined substantive constitutional rules as "those that place, as a matter of constitutional interpretation, certain kinds of primary, private individual conduct beyond the power of the criminal law-making authority to proscribe." Mackey v. United States, 401 U.S. 667, 692 (1971) (opinion concurring in judgments in part and dissenting in part). In Penry v. Lynaugh, decided four months after Teague, the Court recognized that "the first exception set forth in Teague should be understood to cover not only rules forbidding criminal

punishment of certain primary conduct but also rules prohibiting a certain category of punishment for a class of defendants because of their status or offense." 492 U.S. 302, 330 (1989). Penry explained that Justice Harlan's first exception spoke "in terms of substantive categorical guarantees accorded by the Constitution, regardless of the procedures followed." *Id.*, at 329. Whether a new rule bars States from proscribing certain conduct or from inflicting a certain punishment, "[i]n both cases, the Constitution itself deprives the State of the power to impose a certain penalty." *Id.*, at 330.

Substantive rules, then, set forth categorical constitutional guarantees that place certain criminal laws and punishments altogether beyond the State's power to impose. It follows that when a State enforces a proscription or penalty barred by the Constitution, the resulting conviction or sentence is, by definition, unlawful. [Here, the Court contrasted procedural rules and observed that "a trial conducted under a procedure found to be unconstitutional in a later case does not, as a general matter, have the automatic consequence of invalidating a defendant's conviction or sentence."]

By holding that new substantive rules are, indeed, retroactive, Teague continued a long tradition of giving retroactive effect to constitutional rights that go beyond procedural guarantees. See Mackey, *supra*, at 692–693 (opinion of Harlan, J.) ("[T]he writ has historically been available for attacking convictions on [substantive] grounds"). Before Brown v. Allen, 344 U.S. 443 (1953), "federal courts would never consider the merits of a constitutional claim if the habeas petitioner had a fair opportunity to raise his arguments in the original proceeding." Desist v. United States, 394 U.S. 244, 261 (1969) (Harlan, J., dissenting). Even in the pre-1953 era of restricted federal habeas, however, an exception was made "when the habeas petitioner attacked the constitutionality of the state statute under which he had been convicted. Since, in this situation, the State had no power to proscribe the conduct for which the petitioner was imprisoned, it could not constitutionally insist that he remain in jail." *Id.*, at 261, n. 2 (Harlan, J., dissenting). * * * It follows, as a general principle, that a court has no authority to leave in place a conviction or sentence that violates a substantive rule, regardless of whether the conviction or sentence became final before the rule was announced.

[The Court next conceded that the precedents "do not directly control the question the Court now answers for the first time," although noting that they nonetheless "have important bearing on the analysis necessary in this case."]

There is no grandfather clause that permits States to enforce punishments the Constitution forbids. To conclude otherwise would undercut the Constitution's substantive guarantees. * * * If a State may not constitutionally insist that a prisoner remain in jail on federal habeas review, it may not constitutionally insist on the same result in its own postconviction proceedings. Under the Supremacy Clause of the Constitution, state collateral review courts have no greater power than federal habeas courts to mandate that a prisoner continue to suffer punishment barred by the Constitution. If a state collateral proceeding is open to a claim controlled by federal law, the state court "has a duty to grant the relief that federal law requires." Yates v. Aiken, 484 U.S. 211, 218 (1988). * * *

As a final point, it must be noted that the retroactive application of substantive rules does not implicate a State's weighty interests in ensuring the finality of convictions and sentences. Teague warned against the intrusiveness of "*continually* forc[ing] the States to marshal resources in order to keep in prison defendants whose trials and appeals conformed to then-existing constitutional standards." 489 U.S., at 310. This concern has no application in the realm of substantive rules, for no resources marshaled by a State could preserve a conviction or sentence that the Constitution deprives the State of power to impose. See Mackey, 401 U.S., at 693 (opinion of Harlan, J.) ("There is little societal interest in permitting the criminal process to rest at a point where it ought properly never to repose"). * * *

III

* * * Miller announced a substantive rule that is retroactive in cases on collateral review.

The "foundation stone" for Miller's analysis was this Court's line of precedent holding certain punishments disproportionate when applied to juveniles. 567 U.S., at 470, n. 4. Those cases include Graham v. Florida, *supra*, which held that the Eighth Amendment bars life without parole for juvenile nonhomicide offenders, and Roper v. Simmons, 543 U.S. 551, which held that the Eighth Amendment prohibits capital punishment for those under the age of 18 at the time of their crimes. [The Court discussed the holdings in Miller, Roper, and Graham, observing that Miller "took as its starting premise the principle established in Roper and Graham that 'children are constitutionally different from adults for purposes of sentencing.'" The Court continued by noting that Miller "made clear that 'appropriate occasions for sentencing juveniles to this harshest possible penalty will be uncommon.'"]

Miller, then, did more than require a sentencer to consider a juvenile offender's youth before imposing life without parole; it established that the penological justifications for life without parole collapse in light of "the distinctive attributes of youth." *Id.*, at 2465. Even if a court considers a child's age before sentencing him or her to a lifetime in prison, that sentence still violates the Eighth Amendment for a child whose crime reflects "'unfortunate yet transient immaturity.'" *Id.*, at 2469 (quoting Roper, 543 U.S., at 573). * * * [Miller therefore] rendered life without parole an unconstitutional penalty for "a class of defendants because of their status"—that is, juvenile offenders whose crimes reflect the transient immaturity of youth. Penry, 492 U.S., at 330. As a result, Miller announced a substantive rule of constitutional law. Like other substantive rules, Miller is retroactive because it " 'necessarily carr[ies] a significant risk that a defendant' "—here, the vast majority of juvenile offenders—" 'faces a punishment that the law cannot impose upon him.' " Schriro v. Summerlin, 542 U.S. 348, 352 (2004) (quoting Bousley v. United States, 523 U.S. 614, 620 (1998)).

Louisiana nonetheless argues that Miller is procedural because it did not place any punishment beyond the State's power to impose; it instead required sentencing courts to take children's age into account before condemning them to die in prison. * * * Miller, it is true, did not bar a punishment for all juvenile offenders, as the Court did in Roper or Graham. Miller did bar life without parole, however, for all but the rarest of juvenile offenders, those whose crimes reflect permanent incorrigibility. For that reason, Miller is no less substantive than are Roper and Graham. * * *

To be sure, Miller's holding has a procedural component. * * * There are instances in which a substantive change in the law must be attended by a procedure that enables a prisoner to show that he falls within the category of persons whom the law may no longer punish. * * * The procedure Miller prescribes is no different. * * *

[The Court next defended Miller's decision not to require trial courts to make findings of fact regarding a child's incorrigibility: "When a new substantive rule of constitutional law is established, this Court is careful to limit the scope of any attendant procedural requirement to avoid intruding more than necessary upon the States' sovereign administration of their criminal justice systems."]

* * * Giving Miller retroactive effect, moreover, does not require States to relitigate sentences, let alone convictions, in every case where a juvenile offender received mandatory life without parole. A State may remedy a Miller violation by permitting juvenile homicide offenders to be considered for parole, rather than by resentencing them. See, *e.g.*, Wyo. Stat. Ann. § 6–10–301(c) (2013) (juvenile homicide offenders eligible for parole after 25 years).

Extending parole eligibility to juvenile offenders does not impose an onerous burden on the States, nor does it disturb the finality of state convictions. Those prisoners who have shown an inability to reform will continue to serve life sentences. * * *

* * * In light of what this Court has said in Roper, Graham, and Miller about how children are constitutionally different from adults in their level of culpability, however, prisoners like Montgomery must be given the opportunity to show their crime did not reflect irreparable corruption; and, if it did not, their hope for some years of life outside prison walls must be restored.

■ JUSTICE SCALIA, with whom JUSTICE THOMAS and JUSTICE ALITO join, dissenting.

The Court has no jurisdiction to decide this case, and the decision it arrives at is wrong. I respectfully dissent.

I.   Jurisdiction

* * * [A] majority of this Court, eager to reach the merits of this case, resolves the question of our jurisdiction by deciding that the Constitution *requires* state postconviction courts to adopt Teague's exception for so-called "substantive" new rules and to provide state-law remedies for the violations of those rules to prisoners whose sentences long ago became final. This conscription into federal service of state postconviction courts is nothing short of astonishing.

A

Neither Teague nor its exceptions are constitutionally compelled. Unlike today's majority, the Teague-era Court understood that cases on collateral review are fundamentally different from those pending on direct review because of "considerations of finality in the judicial process." Shea v. Louisiana, 470 U.S. 51, 59–60 (1985). That line of finality demarcating the constitutionally required rule in Griffith from the habeas rule in Teague supplies the answer to the not-so-difficult question whether a state postconviction court must remedy the violation of a new substantive rule: No. A state court need only apply the law as it existed at the time a defendant's conviction and sentence became final. See Griffith, *supra*, at 322. And once final, "a new rule cannot reopen a door already closed." James B. Beam Distilling Co. v. Georgia, 501 U.S. 529, 541 (1991) (opinion of Souter, J.). Any relief a prisoner might receive in a state court after finality is a matter of grace, not constitutional prescription.

B

The majority can marshal no case support for its contrary position. * * *

[T]he Supremacy Clause cannot possibly answer the question before us here. It only elicits another question: What federal law is supreme? Old or new? The majority's champion, Justice Harlan, said the old rules apply for federal habeas review of a state-court conviction: "[T]he habeas court need only apply the constitutional standards that prevailed at the time the original proceedings took place," Desist, 394 U.S., at 263 (dissenting opinion), for a state court cannot "toe the constitutional mark" that does not yet exist, Mackey, 401 U.S., at 687 (opinion of Harlan, J.). Following his analysis, we have clarified time and again—recently in Greene v. Fisher, 565 U.S. 34, 38–40 (2011)—that *federal* habeas courts are to review state-court decisions against the law and factual record that existed at the time the decisions were made. "Section 2254(d)(1) [of the federal habeas statute] refers, in the past tense * * *. This backward-looking language requires an examination of the state-court decision at the time it was made." Cullen v. Pinholster, 563 U.S. 170, 181–182 (2011).

Until today, no federal court was *constitutionally obliged* to grant relief for the past violation of a newly announced substantive rule. Until today, it was Congress's prerogative to do away with Teague's exceptions altogether. Indeed, we had left unresolved the question whether Congress had already done that when it amended a section of the habeas corpus statute to add backward-looking language governing the review of state-court decisions. See Antiterrorism and Effective Death Penalty Act of 1996, § 104, 110 Stat. 1219, codified at 28 U.S.C. § 2254(d)(1); Greene, 565 U.S. at 39, n. A maxim shown to be more relevant to this case, by the analysis that the majority omitted, is this: The Supremacy Clause does not impose upon state courts a constitutional obligation it fails to impose upon federal courts.

C

All that remains to support the majority's conclusion is that all-purpose Latin canon: *ipse dixit*. The majority opines that because a substantive rule eliminates a State's power to proscribe certain conduct or impose a certain punishment, it has "the automatic consequence of invalidating a defendant's conviction or sentence." What provision of the Constitution could conceivably produce such a result? The Due Process Clause? It surely cannot be a denial of due process for a court to pronounce a final judgment which, though fully in accord with federal constitutional law at the time, fails to anticipate a change to be made by this Court half a century into the future. The Equal Protection Clause? Both statutory and (increasingly) constitutional laws change. If it were a denial of equal protection to hold an earlier defendant to a law more stringent than what exists today, it would also be a denial of equal protection to hold a later defendant to a law more stringent than what existed 50 years ago. No principle of equal protection requires the criminal law of all ages to be the same.

The majority grandly asserts that "[t]here is no grandfather clause that permits States to *enforce punishments the Constitution forbids*." (emphasis added). Of course the italicized phrase begs the question. There most certainly is a grandfather clause—one we have called *finality*—which says that the Constitution does not require States to revise punishments that were lawful when they were imposed. Once a conviction has become final, whether new rules or old ones will be applied to revisit the conviction is a matter entirely within the State's control; the Constitution has nothing to say about that choice. * * *

The majority's imposition of Teague's first exception upon the States is all the worse because it does not adhere to that exception as initially conceived by Justice Harlan—an exception for rules that "place, as a matter of constitutional interpretation, certain kinds of primary, private individual *conduct* beyond the power of the criminal lawmaking authority to proscribe." Mackey, 401 U.S., at 692 (emphasis added).

Rather, it endorses the exception as expanded by Penry. * * * [But t]he "evolving standards" test concedes that in 1969 the State had the power to punish Henry Montgomery as it did. Indeed, Montgomery could at that time have been sentenced to death by our yet unevolved society. * * *

II.   The Retroactivity of Miller

* * * Having distorted Teague, the majority simply proceeds to rewrite Miller.

* * * Miller stated, quite clearly * * *: "Our decision does not categorically bar a penalty for a class of offenders or type of crime—as, for example, we did in Roper or Graham. Instead, it mandates only that a sentencer *follow a certain process*—considering an offender's youth and attendant characteristics—before imposing a particular penalty." 567 U.S., at 483 (emphasis added).

* * * Under Miller, bear in mind, the inquiry is whether the inmate was seen to be incorrigible when he was sentenced—not whether he has proven corrigible and so can safely be paroled today. What silliness. (And how impossible in practice, see Brief for National District Attorneys Assn. et al. as Amici Curiae 9–17.) * * *

But have no fear. The majority does not seriously expect state and federal collateral-review tribunals to engage in this silliness, probing the evidence of "incorrigibility" that existed decades ago when defendants were sentenced. What the majority expects (and intends) to happen is set forth in the following not-so-subtle invitation: "A State may remedy a Miller violation by permitting juvenile homicide offenders to be considered for parole, rather than by resentencing them." Of course. This whole exercise, this whole distortion of Miller, is just a devious way of eliminating life without parole for juvenile offenders. The Court might have done that expressly (as we know, the Court can decree *anything*), but that would have been something of an embarrassment. After all, one of the justifications the Court gave for decreeing an end to the death penalty for murders (no matter how many) committed by a juvenile was that life without parole was a severe enough punishment. See Roper, 543 U.S., at 572. How could the majority—in an opinion written by the very author of Roper—now say *that* punishment is *also* unconstitutional? The Court expressly refused to say so in Miller, 567 U.S., at 479. So the Court refuses again today, but merely makes imposition of that severe sanction a practical impossibility. And then, in Godfather fashion, the majority makes state legislatures an offer they can't refuse: Avoid all the utterly impossible nonsense we have prescribed by simply "permitting juvenile homicide offenders to be considered for parole." Mission accomplished.

■ JUSTICE THOMAS, dissenting.

* * * We have jurisdiction under 28 U.S.C. § 1257 only if the Louisiana Supreme Court's decision implicates a federal right. * * *

I

A

No provision of the Constitution supports the Court's holding. The Court invokes only the Supremacy Clause, asserting that the Clause deprives state and federal postconviction courts alike of power to leave an unconstitutional sentence in place. But that leaves the question of what provision of the Constitution supplies that underlying prohibition.

The Supremacy Clause does not do so. That Clause merely supplies a rule of decision: *If* a federal constitutional right exists, that right supersedes any contrary provisions of state law. Accordingly, as we reaffirmed just last Term, the Supremacy Clause is no independent font of substantive rights. Armstrong v. Exceptional Child Center, Inc., 575 U.S. 320, 324–25 (2015).

[Justice Thomas then discussed other possible bases for the Court's decision. Article III, he wrote, "defines the scope of *federal* judicial power. It cannot compel *state* postconviction courts to apply new substantive rules retroactively." Turning to due process, Justice Thomas noted that "[q]uite possibly, ' "[d]ue process of law" was originally used as a shorthand expression for governmental proceedings according to the "law of the land" *as it existed at the time of those proceedings*' " (quoting In re Winship, 397 U.S. 358, 378 (Black, J., dissenting) (emphasis added)).]

[The Equal Protection Clause] prohibits a State from "deny[ing] to any person within its jurisdiction the equal protection of the laws." Amdt. XIV, § 1. But under our precedents "a classification neither involving fundamental rights nor proceeding along suspect lines . . . cannot run afoul of the Equal Protection Clause if there is a rational relationship between the disparity of treatment and some legitimate governmental purpose."

The disparity the Court eliminates today—between prisoners whose cases were on direct review when this Court announced a new substantive constitutional rule, and those whose convictions had already become final—is one we have long considered rational. * * *

B

The Court's new constitutional right also finds no basis in the history of state and federal postconviction proceedings. Throughout our history, postconviction relief for alleged constitutional defects in a conviction or sentence was available as a matter of legislative grace, not constitutional command.

The Constitution mentions habeas relief only in the Suspension Clause, which specifies that "[t]he Privilege of the Writ of *Habeas Corpus* shall not be suspended, unless when in Cases of Rebellion or Invasion the public Safety may require it." Art. I, § 9, cl. 2. But that Clause does not specify the scope of the writ. And the First Congress, in prescribing federal habeas jurisdiction in the 1789 Judiciary Act, understood its

scope to reflect "the black-letter principle of the common law that the writ was simply not available at all to one convicted of crime by a court of competent jurisdiction." Bator, *Finality in Criminal Law and Federal Habeas Corpus for State Prisoners*, 76 Harv.L.Rev. 441, 466 (1963). Early cases echoed that understanding. *E.g.*, Ex parte Watkins, 3 Pet. 193, 202 (1830) ("An imprisonment under a judgment cannot be unlawful, unless that judgment be an absolute nullity; and it is not a nullity if the court has general jurisdiction of the subject, although it should be erroneous").
* * *

II

A

Not only does the Court's novel constitutional right lack any constitutional foundation; the reasoning the Court uses to construct this right lacks any logical stopping point. If, as the Court supposes, the Constitution bars courts from insisting that prisoners remain in prison when their convictions or sentences are later deemed unconstitutional, why can courts let stand a judgment that wrongly decided any constitutional question? * * *

B

There is one silver lining to today's ruling: States still have a way to mitigate its impact on their court systems. * * *

Only when state courts have chosen to entertain a federal claim can the Supremacy Clause conceivably command a state court to apply federal law. As we explained last Term, private parties have no "constitutional . . . right to enforce federal laws against the States." Armstrong, 575 U.S., at 325. Instead, the Constitution leaves the initial choice to entertain federal claims up to state courts, which are "tribunals over which the government of the Union has no adequate control, and which may be closed to any claim asserted under a law of the United States." Osborn v. Bank of United States, 9 Wheat. 738, 821 (1824).

States therefore have a modest path to lessen the burdens that today's decision will inflict on their courts. States can stop entertaining claims alleging that this Court's Eighth Amendment decisions invalidated a sentence, and leave federal habeas courts to shoulder the burden of adjudicating such claims in the first instance. Whatever the desirability of that choice, it is one the Constitution allows States to make. * * *

NOTE ON MONTGOMERY V. LOUISIANA AND RETROACTIVITY IN STATE POSTCONVICTION AND FEDERAL COLLATERAL REVIEW

(1) The Montgomery Case and the Constitution. The Montgomery decision raises a number of complicated questions about the intersection of new law, retroactivity, and collateral review of "final" criminal convictions in both the state and federal courts. What is the basis for Montgomery's holding that "Teague's conclusion establishing the retroactivity of new substantive rules is best understood as resting upon constitutional premises" and, accordingly, that Miller must be applied retroactively to cases that would otherwise be considered final?[1] The Supremacy Clause? Due Process? Equal Protection? The Suspension Clause? Might the Eighth Amendment have some bearing on the retroactivity question? How convincing are the arguments of Justices Scalia and Thomas that the Constitution contains no mandate to reopen final convictions? *Cf.* Harper v. Virginia Dept. of Taxation, 509 U.S. 86 (1993), and Reynoldsville Casket Co. v. Hyde, 514 U.S. 749 (1995), discussed at Seventh Edition pp. 758–59. How do (a) the Court's discussion of the role of the Supremacy Clause in Testa v. Katt, 330 U.S. 386 (1947), see Seventh Edition p. 437, and (b) Justice Thomas's dissent in Haywood v. Drown, 556 U.S. 729 (2009), see Seventh Edition p. 444, factor into the equation?

In Griffith v. Kentucky, 479 U.S. 314 (1987), see Seventh Edition pp. 55, 1294, the Court relied on Justice Harlan's view of retroactivity for two propositions: (1) to " 'disregard current law in adjudicating cases' " still on direct review would be " 'quite simply an assertion that our constitutional function is not one of adjudication but in effect of legislation' " (quoting Mackey v. United States, 401 U.S. 667, 679 (1971) (Harlan, J., concurring in part and dissenting in part), see Seventh Edition p. 1294); and (2) "selective application of new rules violates the principle of treating similarly situated defendants the same" (citing Desist v. United States, 394 U.S. 244, 258–59 (1969) (Harlan, J., dissenting in part), see Seventh Edition p. 1294). Does this reasoning apply equally to cases like Montgomery that are no longer pending on direct review? For further consideration of these aspects of Montgomery v. Louisiana, see pp. 61–62 and 78–79, *supra.*[2]

(2) Substance v. Procedure. Despite having announced in Miller that the decision "does not categorically bar a penalty for a class of offenders or type of crime" but "mandates only that a sentencer follow a certain process", the Montgomery Court classified Miller's holding as substantive for Teague

---

[1] In Danforth v. Minnesota, 552 U.S. 264 (2008), the Court posited that the Teague doctrine was properly understood as "an exercise of th[e] Court's power to interpret the federal habeas statute" (p. 278).

[2] In the wake of Montgomery, the Supreme Court held that its decision in Johnson v. United States, 135 S.Ct. 2551 (2015), is a substantive decision that applies retroactively to federal prisoner cases on collateral review. See Welch v. United States, 136 S.Ct. 1257 (2016). Johnson held that the residual clause of the Armed Career Criminal Act, 18 U.S.C. § 924(e)(2)(B)(ii) (ACCA), which served as a basis for sentencing enhancement in cases involving possession of a firearm by a felon, was unconstitutionally vague. In Welch, with Justice Kennedy once again writing for the majority, the Court held that Johnson had announced a new rule that "changed the substantive reach of the ACCA, altering 'the range of conduct or the class of persons that the [Act] punishes' " (quoting Schriro v. Summerlin, 542 U.S. 348, 353 (2004)). Because "[t]he residual clause is invalid under Johnson," the Court held, "it can no longer mandate or authorize any sentence." The Court continued that "whether a new rule is substantive or procedural" requires a consideration of "the function of the rule," and it rejected the argument that the inquiry depends on whether "the underlying constitutional guarantee [being asserted by the petitioner] is characterized as procedural or substantive." As in Montgomery, Justice Thomas dissented, arguing that the first Teague exception had become unmoored from its origins in the jurisprudence of Justice Harlan. For further discussion of Welch, see pp. 141–143, *infra.*

purposes. Is there a valid distinction to be drawn, as Justice Scalia suggests, between cases involving constitutionally protected conduct and cases involving sentences later deemed to be in violation of the Constitution? Relying on Teague's extension to cases like Penry v. Lynaugh, 492 U.S. 302 (1989), Seventh Edition p. 1298, the Montgomery Court reasoned that such a distinction was unfounded. More generally, does Montgomery reveal the elusiveness of the distinction between substantive and procedural rules?

(3) Justice Thomas's Dissent and Its Implications. Before Montgomery could pursue federal habeas relief, he had to exhaust all available state remedies. Justice Thomas argues that states can simply eliminate postconviction proceedings to avoid implementing the Court's decision in Miller.[3] Can his position be reconciled with the majority's apparent holding that the Constitution forbids a state from continuing to insist that a prisoner whose claim falls under Teague's first exception remain in jail? *Cf.* Case v. Nebraska, 381 U.S. 336 (1965), Seventh Edition p. 1290 n. 15; Martinez v. Ryan, 566 U.S. 1 (2012), Seventh Edition p. 1339; Haywood v. Drown, 556 U.S. 729 (2009), Seventh Edition p. 444. If Justice Thomas is right, is Congress under an *obligation* to provide for collateral habeas review of Miller claims in federal court?

Professors Vázquez and Vladeck argue that post-Montgomery, state courts must provide postconviction relief for petitioners seeking the benefit of new rules of substantive constitutional law where all avenues of direct review are foreclosed. See Vázquez & Vladeck, *The Constitutional Right to Collateral Post-Conviction Review*, 103 Va.L.Rev. 905 (2017). The authors argue that imposing such an obligation upon federal habeas courts would upend longstanding assumptions underlying Article III, including the Madisonian Compromise and the widely held view that "federal habeas corpus [is] constitutionally gratuitous as a means of postconviction review." Fallon & Meltzer, Seventh Edition p. 1293 n. 2, at 1813. Nor do Vázquez and Vladeck read the Court's line of cases following from Testa v. Katt, 330 U.S. 386 (1947), see Seventh Edition p. 437, as foreclosing the conclusion that state courts must be open in such cases. In their view, any limitation on state court jurisdiction to provide collateral relief to prisoners claiming the benefit of a new rule of substantive federal law "would be based, at bottom, on disagreement with the policies underlying the Constitution, as interpreted in Montgomery," and therefore would not constitute a "valid excuse" under Testa as applied in Haywood v. Drown, 556 U.S. 729 (2009), see Seventh Edition p. 444. This conclusion also follows, in the authors' view, under the Court's decision in General Oil Co. v. Crain, 209 U.S. 211 (1908), see Seventh Edition p. 759, which held that a state court's determination regarding its jurisdiction to award a potentially constitutionally-required remedy is not an adequate and independent state ground precluding Supreme Court review of the decision. In support of their conclusion, the authors read Haywood to limit the range of "neutral" rules or "valid excuses" that will justify closing

---

[3] In a different case the same Term, Justice Alito posited that "[s]tates are under no obligation to permit collateral attacks on convictions that have become final, and if they allow such attacks, they are free to limit the circumstances in which claims may be relitigated." Foster v. Chatman, 136 S.Ct. 1737, 1759 (2016) (Alito, J., concurring in the judgment).

state courts to federal claims. They also reject the proposition that closing state courts entirely to a particular class of claims based on state law necessarily will justify the same jurisdictional limitation with respect to analogous federal claims.[4]

What is left of the "valid excuse" doctrine under the authors' interpretation of Testa and Haywood, given that they reject the proposition that state legislatures could eliminate entirely state postconviction review?

(4) The Intersection of Montgomery, Teague, and AEDPA. Looking ahead, federal courts will have to determine the application of Montgomery and Miller to habeas proceedings in federal court. Consider two habeas petitioners: (a) one who, because of a failure to meet state procedural requirements, has lost the ability to raise, on direct review in state court, the Eighth Amendment claim later embraced in Miller, and (b) one who raised and thereby preserved the claim throughout direct proceedings before Miller. Would the two petitioners fare differently in federal habeas? Should they? With respect to the latter petitioner whose claim was presumably rejected on the merits by the state courts, does § 2254(d)(1) permit a federal habeas court to grant relief from a mandatory life sentence? Post-Montgomery, courts will have to wrestle with how Teague and Montgomery intersect with both habeas procedural default jurisprudence and § 2254(d)(1)'s "backward-looking language". Cullen v. Pinholster, 563 U.S. 170, 182 (2011). See also Paragraph (6), Seventh Edition p. 1317. Consider also the litigant who has already pursued federal habeas relief on a prior occasion and must overcome the limits on successive petitions set forth in § 2244(b)(2). See Note on Successive and Abusive Habeas Petitions, Seventh Edition pp. 1346–49. For the petitioner who has not previously presented the claim in federal habeas, does Montgomery, when combined with Miller, establish "a new rule of constitutional law, made retroactive to cases on collateral review by the Supreme Court that was previously unavailable" under § 2244(b)(2)(a)? For discussion of these and other questions raised by the intersection of Montgomery with AEDPA and the procedural default doctrine, along with an argument that some court must be available to award relief where a petitioner seeks the benefit of a new rule of substantive constitutional law, see Vázquez & Vladeck, p. 132, *supra.*

(5) Jurisdictional Infirmities and Montgomery. How, if at all, does the rationale of Montgomery v. Louisiana apply when the original court in which the state successfully prosecuted a criminal defendant lacked jurisdiction? In McGirt v. Oklahoma, 140 S.Ct. 2452 (2020), the Supreme Court held that because a large swathe of Oklahoma constitutes land within the boundaries of Indian reservations, or "Indian country," as a matter of federal law, state courts lack jurisdiction to try crimes committed by Native Americans within that territory. Instead, only federal or tribal courts possess jurisdiction over

---

[4]   For elaboration on the ramifications of Montgomery for debates over the role of state courts as enforcers of federal rights, see Vladeck, p. 110, *supra* (positing that "Montgomery may represent the beginning of the Supreme Court's habeas jurisprudence coming full circle—and the vindication of Professor Hart's famous conclusion about the centrality of state, rather than federal, courts to the protection of federal constitutional rights").

such matters. Will petitions for habeas relief predicated upon McGirt fall within the first Teague exception?

(6) The Role, if Any, of 28 U.S.C. § 2241. In Felker v. Turpin, 518 U.S. 651 (1996), the Court noted that a potential bypass of AEDPA's limitations on successive petitions may be found in the Court's original writ. Several courts of appeals, moreover, have suggested that § 2241, the modern descendant of the original provision for habeas jurisdiction, § 14 of the 1789 Judiciary Act, may serve as a proper vehicle for relief in certain federal cases where AEDPA otherwise appears to preclude relief. See Seventh Edition pp. 1362–63. Against this backdrop, if AEDPA is read to preclude relief for a petitioner seeking the retroactive benefit of Miller or another substantive decision falling under Teague's first exception, there is an argument to be made that § 2241's broad language would give a court a proper basis for awarding relief notwithstanding AEDPA's limitations. See 28 U.S.C. § 2241 (providing that a writ of habeas corpus "may be granted" where a petitioner "is in custody in violation of the Constitution or laws or treaties of the United States").

(7) Reopening Judgments Under Federal Rule of Civil Procedure 60(b). Federal Rule of Civil Procedure 60(b) permits a district court to reopen "a final judgment, order, or proceeding" for various reasons, including the discovery of new evidence that was previously unavailable and "any other reason that justifies relief." The Supreme Court has interpreted the rule to permit reopening a judgment on the basis of "extraordinary circumstances," although noting that "[s]uch circumstances will rarely occur in the habeas context." Gonzalez v. Crosby, 545 U.S. 524 (2005). In Buck v. Davis, 137 S.Ct. 759 (2017), with Chief Justice Roberts writing for the majority, the Court held 6–2 that extraordinary circumstances justified reopening a 2006 judgment denying relief to a state prisoner in what was then his first federal habeas petition. In moving to reopen the judgment, petitioner sought the benefit of the Court's decisions in Martinez v. Ryan, 566 U.S. 1 (2012), see Seventh Edition p. 1339, and Trevino v. Thaler, 569 U.S. 413 (2013), see Seventh Edition p. 1341, to excuse his failure to raise in state postconviction proceedings a claim of ineffective assistance of counsel in his capital sentencing proceedings. The underlying claim related to the decision of petitioner's own counsel to introduce an expert report and related testimony that characterized petitioner's race as a factor increasing his likelihood of future violence. After criticizing the court of appeals for misunderstanding the standard for granting a certificate of appealability,[5] the Court concluded that counsel's performance at his sentencing "fell outside the bounds of competent representation" and thereby prejudiced the petitioner. Turning to the Rule 60(b) inquiry, the Court posited that "extraordinary circumstances" may justify reopening a judgment where there is a " 'risk of injustice to the parties' " or a " 'risk of undermining the public's confidence in the judicial

---

[5]　Specifically, the Court criticized the court of appeals for conflating the merits of petitioner's arguments with the decision whether to grant a certificate of appealability, an inquiry that asks " 'only if the District Court's decision was debatable' " (quoting Miller-El v. Cockrell, 537 U.S. 322, 327 (2003)). See Seventh Edition p. 1269. The Court left open the question whether an appeal of the denial of a motion under Rule 60(b) requires a certificate of appealability.

process' " in leaving a judgment intact (quoting Liljeberg v. Health Services Acquisition Corp., 486 U.S. 847, 863–64 (1988)). Finding these factors present in the case, the Court held that the district court had abused its discretion in denying the Rule 60(b) motion. This conclusion followed, in the Court's view, from the fact that the State had confessed error in other cases in which it had relied upon the same expert and the fact that "Buck may have been sentenced to death in part because of his race." Finally, the Court held that the State had waived any Teague arguments relating to petitioner's reliance on Martinez and Trevino for relief. In so doing, the Court declined to speak to the retroactive application of the decisions.

Buck v. Davis potentially opens a new avenue of relief for habeas petitioners seeking to rely on new law after the conclusion of federal habeas proceedings. Note, however, that Buck involved (1) the introduction of deeply objectionable and highly prejudicial expert testimony; (2) a confession of error by the State in related cases; and (3) waiver by the State of any Teague arguments relating to the new law on which petitioner sought to rely. The Supreme Court again took up a prisoner's attempt to reopen his federal habeas proceedings under Rule 60(b) in Tharpe v. Sellers, 138 S.Ct. 545 (2018) (per curiam). After a district court denied a Rule 60(b) motion and the court of appeals denied a COA, the Supreme Court reversed. The case involved evidence suggesting that race may have played a role in a juror's vote to convict and sentence the petitioner to death. As in Buck, the Court stressed "the unusual facts" of the case. Ultimately, however, the Court remanded, acknowledging that the petitioner still "faces a high bar in showing that jurists of reason could disagree" with the district court's conclusion that under § 2254(e)(1) it should defer to the state court's rejection of the import of the relevant evidence. Similarly, the Court observed that "[i]t may be that, at the end of the day [petitioner] should not receive a COA." Deeming the Court's treatment of the case nothing more than "ceremonial handwringing," a dissent for three Justices written by Justice Thomas would have affirmed the district court's denial of relief. Although Tharpe supports the conclusion that the Court's approval of using Rule 60(b) to reopen habeas proceedings potentially opens a significant new avenue for challenging convictions in successive proceedings, Tharpe's disposition suggests that such an avenue will only be available in extraordinary circumstances.

NOTE ON RELITIGATING THE FACTS IN HABEAS CORPUS PROCEEDINGS

Page 1320. Add a new footnote 1a after Paragraph (2)(a):

[1a] In Brumfield v. Cain, 576 U.S. 305 (2015), the Court rejected a state court's factual findings under 28 U.S.C. § 2254(d)(2) as unreasonable. In the wake of Atkins v. Virginia, 536 U.S. 304 (2002), which held that application of the death penalty to persons with intellectual disabilities violates the Eighth Amendment, Brumfield sought a hearing in state court to prove his intellectual disability. Surveying the evidence presented during Brumfield's capital sentencing procedure, the state court denied his request. Although recognizing that AEDPA requires that state court findings be given "substantial deference", a five-Justice majority concluded that the state court's denial of a hearing was unreasonable when held up against the evidence in the record. The majority emphasized that under the state's implementing standard

for Atkins, Brumfield need only raise a reasonable doubt as to whether he had an intellectual disability in order to secure a full hearing on the question. In dissent, Justice Thomas argued first that the majority had recharacterized a question involving "the application of law to fact" as a "determination of the facts themselves" in contradiction of the Court's § 2254(d)(1) jurisprudence, and second that even if § 2254(d)(2) proved the correct standard of review, Brumfield had failed to satisfy it.

Page 1322. Substitute the following for the last sentence of the first paragraph in Paragraph (4):

In affirming, the Ninth Circuit en banc ruled that a habeas court could consider evidence adduced in a federal evidentiary hearing permitted by § 2254(e)(2) when determining, under § 2254(d)(1), whether the state court's rejection of a constitutional claim was contrary to, or an unreasonable application of, clearly established federal law.

Page 1322. Substitute the following paragraph for the third paragraph in Paragraph (4):

Justice Sotomayor's dissent on the relationship between § 2254(d)(1) and § 2254(d)(2) stressed that evidentiary hearings are held in only 4 of every 1,000 non-capital cases and 9.5 of every 100 capital cases and that hearings are permitted by § 2254(e)(2) only when the prisoner was diligent or when very restrictive requirements are satisfied. In these limited circumstances, she argued, consideration of new evidence does not upset the balance established by AEDPA. She further contested the majority's linguistic argument by noting that § 2254(d)(2) expressly requires district courts to base their review on the state court record. See 28 U.S.C. § 2254(d)(2) (precluding relief unless the state court adjudication "resulted in a decision that was based on an unreasonable determination of the facts in light of the evidence presented in the State court proceeding"). This direction, she argued, would be unnecessary if the use of the past tense in § 2254(d)(1), which makes no reference to the state court record, required the same result. When § 2254(e)(2) permits a hearing, some courts of appeals had held (incorrectly, she declared) that § 2254(d)(1) simply does not apply; others had followed the approach of the Ninth Circuit, which permits consideration of new evidence adduced in a federal court hearing when assessing the reasonableness of the state court decision. No court of appeals, however, had followed the majority's approach, which, she said, has the potential to prevent diligent petitioners from introducing evidence in federal habeas proceedings where the state courts are closed to that petitioner.

Page 1323. Add a new footnote 5 at the end of Paragraph (4):

[5] With AEDPA dramatically limiting the opportunities for relief available to habeas petitioners, some scholars have called upon the Supreme Court to take more criminal appeals on direct review. See, e.g., Vázquez, p. 118, *supra*. Some jurists, meanwhile, have lamented that the standards governing most habeas cases are statutory, as opposed to judge-made, with the former far more difficult to adjust as circumstances warrant. See, e.g., Fletcher, *Symposium Introduction*, 107 Calif.L.Rev. 999 (2019). In the absence of expanded direct review by the Court of state criminal convictions, AEDPA's inflexible deferential standards of review give state courts the last word on most questions of federal constitutional law that arise in state criminal cases.

INTRODUCTORY NOTE ON FEDERAL HABEAS CORPUS AND STATE PROCEDURAL DEFAULT

Page 1326. Add a new footnote 1 at the end of Paragraph (3):

¹ For additional background on Fay v. Noia and the companion cases that made Noia's claims especially sympathetic, see Yackle, *The Story of Fay v. Noia: Another Case About Another Federalism*, in Federal Courts Stories (Jackson & Resnik eds. 2010), at 191.

NOTE ON FEDERAL HABEAS CORPUS AND STATE COURT PROCEDURAL DEFAULT

Page 1338. Add at the end of footnote 8:

The Court revisited the question of attorney abandonment in Christeson v. Roper, 574 U.S. 373 (2015) (per curiam), a capital case in which counsel appointed by the district court to represent a habeas petitioner failed to meet with his client and file a petition on his behalf within the one-year AEDPA filing deadline. Reversing the district court's refusal to grant petitioner's motion to substitute new counsel, the Court concluded that substitution served the "interests of justice." Petitioner's only chance to secure habeas review of his underlying claims was to prevail on an argument that appointed counsel's missteps warranted equitable tolling of the one-year filing deadline—an argument that the same appointed counsel unsurprisingly did not make. As Justice Alito noted in his dissent, however, even with new counsel, petitioner still had to satisfy the standard for equitable tolling, no easy task. See Holland v. Florida, 560 U.S. 631, 653 (2010) (holding that equitable tolling of AEDPA's one-year limitations period may be had only upon a showing of diligence and "extraordinary circumstances").

Page 1341. Substitute the following for the final three sentences of Paragraph (5):

In Martinez, the Court stressed that the right is a "bedrock principle" of the criminal justice system. But what about the right to effective assistance of counsel in a criminal defendant's first appeal as of right? The Supreme Court took up this question in Davila v. Davis, 137 S.Ct. 2058 (2017), and sided with the majority of circuits in holding that Martinez and Trevino should be limited to their particular circumstances.[12a]

Writing for a five-Justice majority, Justice Thomas stressed that "Martinez did not purport to displace Coleman as the general rule governing procedural default. Rather, it 'qualifie[d] Coleman by recognizing a narrow exception'" applying only to ineffective assistance of trial counsel claims and only where those claims "'must be raised in an initial-review collateral proceeding.'" Because Martinez and Trevino were focused on trial errors and because "[c]laims of ineffective assistance of appellate counsel" fail to "pose the same risk that a trial error—of any kind—will escape review altogether," the Court concluded that the default of claims by allegedly ineffective appellate counsel should not be excused. In support of its refusal to extend Martinez and Trevino, the Court posited that "[i]f an unpreserved trial error was so obvious that appellate counsel was constitutionally required to raise it on appeal, then trial counsel likely provided ineffective assistance by failing to object to it in the first instance." In such circumstances, the Court noted, Martinez and Trevino would authorize excusing any default of claims relating to the trial counsels' ineffectiveness. As further support for declining to extend the Martinez line, Justice Thomas cited the likelihood that "[a]dopting petitioner's argument could flood the federal courts with defaulted claims of appellate ineffectiveness" and that such claims in turn "could serve as the gateway to federal review of a host of trial errors."

Writing for four Justices in dissent, Justice Breyer emphasized that prisoners have a constitutional right to effective assistance of counsel "at both trial and during an initial appeal" and that the Court's decisions have labeled the effective assistance of appellate counsel—just like effective assistance of trial counsel—as "critically important." Turning to the majority's claims, Justice Breyer cited several scenarios in which the ineffectiveness of appellate counsel could result in underlying claims never being reviewed by any court. (Among other things, Justice Breyer noted that this would be true under the majority's reasoning with respect to Brady claims that only became apparent after trial.) He also challenged the majority's assertion that a different holding would open up the floodgates with respect to the filing of new habeas petitions.

Given that the Court has labeled both the effective assistance of trial and appellate counsel as critically important to a fair trial, is there a principled distinction underlying the differing results in Martinez and Davila? In any event, does Davila close off avenues of relief for defaulted claims that were not available to a prisoner at the time of trial?[12b]

[12a] See, *e.g.*, Dansby v. Hobbs, 766 F. 3d 809 (8th Cir.2014) (positing that the "right to appeal is " 'of relatively recent origin' " and "so a claim for equitable relief in that context is less compelling") (citations omitted); but see Ha Van Nguyen v. Curry, 736 F.3d 1287 (9th Cir.2013) ("There is nothing in our jurisprudence to suggest that the Sixth Amendment right to effective counsel is weaker or less important for appellate counsel than for trial counsel.").

[12b] To date, those circuits that have reached the question have declined to extend the reasoning of Martinez and Trevino to Brady claims discovered after trial. See, *e.g.*, Hunton v. Sinclair, 732 F.3d 1124 (9th Cir.2013).

Page 1344. Add at the end of footnote 17:

A divided Court extended the reasoning of Flores-Ortega in Garza v. Idaho, 139 S.Ct. 738 (2019), to hold that where an attorney fails to notice an appeal, despite express instructions from a defendant to do so, prejudice to the defendant under the Strickland standard is presumed " 'with no further showing from the defendant of the merits of his underlying claims,' " even where the defendant has signed an appeal waiver as part of a plea agreement (quoting Flores-Ortega, 528 U.S., at 484).

Page 1346. Add a new footnote 19a at the end of Paragraph (2):

[19a] In Johnson v. Lee, 136 S.Ct. 1802 (2016) (per curiam), the Supreme Court reiterated that a state's " 'procedural bar may count as an adequate and independent ground for denying a federal habeas petition even if the state court had discretion to reach the merits despite the default' " (quoting Walker v. Martin 562 U.S. 307, 311 (2011)). See also Beard v. Kindler, 558 U.S. 53 (2009), discussed at Seventh Edition pp. 541–42. For further discussion, see p. 65, *supra*.

NOTE ON SUCCESSIVE AND ABUSIVE HABEAS PETITIONS

Page 1349. Add a new Paragraph 4a:

(4a) Reopening Judgments Under Federal Rules of Civil Procedure 59(e) and 60(b). Federal Rule of Civil Procedure 59(e) permits a litigant to file a "motion to alter or amend a judgment * * * no later than 28 days after the entry of the judgment." In Banister v. Davis, 140 S.Ct. 1698 (2020), the Supreme Court held that a Rule 59(e) motion does not qualify as a second or successive petition for purposes of 28 U.S.C. § 2244(b). Justice Kagan stressed the limited nature of Rule 59(e) motions in writing for a seven-Justice majority. First, such motions must be filed within 28 days of entry of judgment, without possibility of extension, Fed. Rule Civ. Proc. 6(b)(2) (prohibiting extensions to Rule 59(e)'s deadline). Second, the Court has recognized that the Rule allows a district court " 'to rectify its own mistakes in the period immediately following' " its decision and that federal courts generally have invoked the rule "only" to "reconsider[ ] matters properly encompassed in a decision on the merits" (quoting White v. New Hampshire Dept. of Employment Security, 455 U. S. 445 (1982)). Thus, in reviewing Rule 59(e) motions, courts do not address new arguments or evidence that the moving party could have raised before the decision issued (citing 11 Wright, Miller & Kane, Federal Practice and Procedure § 2810.1, at 163–64 (3d ed. 2012)). Finally, the timely filing of a Rule 59(e) motion " 'suspends the finality of the original judgment' for purposes of an appeal" (quoting FCC v. League of Women Voters of Cal., 468 U. S. 364, 373, n. 10 (1984)). Putting these factors together, the Court held that Rule 59(e) motions pertain to the same, original underlying judgment with respect to the habeas petitioner's first federal petition.

The Court also relied in part upon "historical habeas doctrine and practice" and AEDPA's purposes, which aim to limit " 'piecemeal litigation' " (quoting Panetti v. Quarterman, 551 U. S. 930 (2007)). Justice Kagan distinguished Gonzalez v. Crosby, 545 U. S. 524 (2005), in which the Court held that a motion filed under Federal Rules of Civil Procedure 60(b)[4a] seeking "relie[f] from a final judgment" that denied habeas relief counts as a second or successive habeas application for purposes of AEDPA in certain contexts. Specifically, Gonzalez held that where a Rule 60(b) motion " 'attacks the federal court's previous resolution of a claim on the merits,' " it shall be deemed second or successive. Holding that Rules 59(e) and 60(b) differ "in just about every way that matters to the inquiry" relating to successive petitions, the Banister Court distinguished Rule 60(b) motions as not governed by any strict time limits with respect to when they may be filed[4b]; for giving rise to a separate appeal than an appeal from the original judgment; and for "attack[ing] an already completed judgment."[4c]

The Court's decision in Gonzalez did not encompass Rule 60(b) motions that attack "some defect in the integrity of the federal habeas proceedings," such as a court's incorrect application of a statute of limitations. Although

---

[4a] Rule 60(b) provides that a court may grant relief from a final judgment if a party can show (1) mistake, inadvertence, surprise, or excusable neglect; (2) newly discovered evidence that, with reasonable diligence, could not have been discovered in time to move for a new trial under Rule 59(b); (3) fraud * * * misrepresentation, or misconduct by an opposing party; (4) the judgment is void; (5) the judgment has been satisfied, released, or discharged [or] reversed or vacated * * *; or (6) "any other reason that justifies relief."

[4b] Federal Rules of Civil Procedure 60(c)(1) provides that Rule 60(b) motions may be filed within a "reasonable time."

[4c] Banister is consistent with the Court's earlier decision in Magwood v. Patterson, 561 U.S. 320 (2010). There, the Court held that if a prisoner secures relief resulting in a material change to the original judgment, such as an order requiring resentencing, the ensuing judgment is deemed "new" and any federal habeas petition that follows is not treated as second or successive.

Gonzalez posited that motions of this kind should only be permitted in "extraordinary circumstances" that "will rarely occur in the habeas context," the Court held, 6–2, in Buck v. Davis, 137 S.Ct. 759 (2017), that such circumstances existed. In Buck, the petitioner sought to reopen the judgment in his first federal habeas petition eight years after the fact based on the intervening Supreme Court decisions in in Martinez v. Ryan, 566 U.S. 1 (2012), see Seventh Edition p. 1339, and Trevino v. Thaler, 569 U.S. 413 (2013), see Seventh Edition p. 1341. Writing for the majority, Chief Justice Roberts emphasized the extraordinary circumstances of petitioner's claims, which suggested that "Buck may have been sentenced to death in part because of his race."[4d] In so doing, the Court suggested that it is appropriate to reopen a judgment under Rule 60(b) where there is a " 'risk of injustice to the parties' " or a " 'risk of undermining the public's confidence in the judicial process' " in leaving a judgment intact (quoting Liljeberg v. Health Services Acquisition Corp., 486 U.S. 847, 863–64 (1988)). In reaching its holding, the Buck Court did not discuss whether petitioner's Rule 60(b) motion was successive and emphasized that the State had waived any Teague arguments in the case. See also Tharpe v. Sellers, 138 S.Ct. 545 (2018) (per curiam) (reversing and remanding the denial of a Rule 60(b) motion in another habeas case).[4e]

[4d]   For additional discussion of Buck, see pp. 134–135, *supra*.

[4e]   For additional discussion of Tharpe, see p. 135, *supra*.

NOTE ON PROBLEMS OF CUSTODY AND REMEDY

Page 1355. Add at the end of footnote 7:

In Ziglar v. Abbasi, 137 S.Ct. 1843 (2017), the Supreme Court lent support to the proposition that at least some form of injunctive relief should be available to prisoners challenging conditions of confinement. The case involved a Bivens lawsuit for damages brought against federal officials by individuals detained as part of the investigations into the attacks of September 11, 2001. Writing for a 4–2 majority, Justice Kennedy held that the prisoners could not proceed with their Bivens claims alleging abusive detention conditions in part because other avenues of relief were available to them. "To address" decisions related to the prisoners' conditions of confinement, Justice Kennedy posited, "detainees may seek injunctive relief." The Court left open whether such relief should be specifically available in habeas proceedings, noting that it has never resolved the question. It nonetheless held out "the habeas remedy" as "a faster and more direct route to relief than a suit for money damages" in such cases. In dissent, Justice Breyer contended that "[n]either a prospective injunction nor a writ of habeas corpus . . . will normally provide plaintiffs with redress for harms they have already suffered," and more generally questioned the ability of prisoners denied, as the respondents alleged they were, "access to most forms of communication with the outside world" to pursue habeas proceedings during their detentions. Given the custody requirement for habeas jurisdiction to lie, how effective would a habeas remedy be under the circumstances presented in cases like Abbasi? For additional discussion of Ziglar, see pp. 79–81 and 95–96, *supra*.

B. COLLATERAL ATTACK ON FEDERAL CONVICTIONS

NOTE ON 28 U.S.C. § 2255 AND ITS RELATIONSHIP TO FEDERAL HABEAS CORPUS

Page 1359. Add to the end of Paragraph (5)(a):

In Welch v. United States, 136 S.Ct. 1257 (2016), the Court relied on Bousley v. United States, Seventh Edition pp. 1358–59, to hold retroactive the rule of Johnson v. United States, 135 S.Ct. 2551 (2015). Johnson had held that the residual clause of the Armed Career Criminal Act, 18 U.S.C. § 924(e)(2)(B)(ii) (ACCA), which provides for enhanced sentences in cases of possession of a firearm by a felon, was unconstitutionally vague in violation of due process.[4a] After pleading guilty to one count of being a felon in possession of a firearm, Welch received an enhanced sentence under the Act based on three prior violent felony convictions. Throughout the proceedings that followed, Welch contended that one of his prior convictions fell outside the reach of the ACCA, rendering him ineligible for a sentence enhancement. After losing the argument before the district court in a motion under 28 U.S.C. § 2255, Welch applied to the Court of Appeals for a certificate of appealability, which it denied. Shortly thereafter, the Supreme Court decided Johnson. Welch then sought certiorari review before the Court of the merits of his claim as well as the question whether Johnson announced a substantive rule that should be given retroactive effect to cases on collateral review.

Reaching only the second question raised by Welch's petition, Justice Kennedy concluded that Johnson had announced a new rule for purposes of Teague. He then turned to the question whether Johnson's rule "falls within one of the two categories that have retroactive effect under Teague." Relying on Schriro v. Summerlin, 542 U.S. 348, 353 (2004), and Montgomery v. Louisiana, 136 S.Ct. 718 (2016), pp. 121–130, *supra*, he concluded that it did. The Court had long indicated that a substantive rule under Teague " 'includes decisions that narrow the scope of a criminal statute by interpreting its terms' " (quoting Schriro, 542 U.S. at 353). Because of Johnson, the ACCA's residual clause "can no longer mandate or authorize any sentence" for those who might otherwise fall under that provision. It followed, in the Court's view, that the decision in Johnson was substantive in nature.

The Court explained that its Teague jurisprudence determines "whether a new rule is substantive or procedural by considering the function of the

---

[4a] The ACCA imposes a sentence enhancement of five years or more where a felon is found to possess a firearm and after three or more convictions for a "serious drug offense" or a "violent felony," the latter of which is defined in two ways. First, the "elements clause" defines a violent felony as involving any crime that "has as an element the use, attempted, use, or threatened use of a physical force against the person of another". Second, the "residual clause" provides that the crimes of burglary, arson, and extortion, and crimes involving the "use of explosives" qualify as violent felony, as well as crimes involving "conduct that presents a serious potential risk of physical injury to another." 18 U.S.C. § 924(e)(2)(B). Johnson held that the "serious potential risk" residual language gave insufficient guidance as to the scope of its application. For further discussion of Johnson, see pp. 24–25, *supra*.

rule." The Teague analysis, Justice Kennedy wrote, does not depend on whether "the underlying constitutional guarantee [being asserted by the petitioner] is characterized as procedural or substantive." Finally, citing Bousley, Justice Kennedy deemed it irrelevant to the Teague analysis that Congress retained power "to enact a new version of the residual clause that imposes the same punishment on the same persons for the same conduct, provided the new statute is precise enough to satisfy due process."

Justice Thomas dissented on two grounds. First, he argued that the lower courts never had before them the question whether Johnson (which had not yet been decided) applied retroactively, a fact that precluded the Court's review of the claim. On this view, the Court of Appeals correctly denied a certificate of appealability.[4b] Second, Justice Thomas complained that the majority had "erode[d] any meaningful limits on what a 'substantive' rule is" under Teague. Because "the Government remains as free to enhance sentences for federal crimes based on the commission of previous violent felonies after Johnson as it was before", Justice Thomas argued, Johnson's rule should not be deemed substantive under the Court's precedents. Bousley "applied only to new rules reinterpreting the text of federal criminal statutes in a way that narrows their reach." Johnson, by contrast, "announced only that there is no way in which to narrow the reach of the residual clause without running afoul of the Due Process Clause." Reading Johnson as substantive, on this view, will mean that "if any decision has the effect of invalidating substantive provisions of a criminal statute," it will be treated as substantive, "no matter what the reason for the statute's invalidation."

In closing, Justice Thomas argued that the Court's Teague jurisprudence, while "profess[ing] to venerate Justice Harlan's theory of retroactivity", has moved well beyond the limited category of substantive claims Justice Harlan viewed as entitled to retroactive application. In support, Justice Thomas pointed to the Court's extension of Teague's first exception to rules prohibiting certain punishments in cases like Penry v. Lynaugh, 492 U.S. 302 (1989), Seventh Edition p. 1298; to federal prisoners challenging the reach of federal criminal statutes, as in Bousley; and to state postconviction proceedings, as the Court did over his dissent in Montgomery v. Louisiana, 136 S.Ct. 718 (2016), pp. 121–130, *supra*. "With the Court's unprincipled expansion of Teague," Justice Thomas complained, "every end is instead a new beginning."

Does Justice Thomas successfully distinguish Bousley? Regardless, is he correct that the Court has moved far beyond Justice Harlan's definition of substantive rules warranting retroactive application? See Mackey v. United States, 401 U.S. 667, 692 (1971) (Harlan, J., concurring in part and dissenting in part) (referring to rules that render "certain kinds of primary, private individual conduct beyond the power of the criminal law-making authority to proscribe"); see also Seventh Edition p. 1294 (Paragraph (3)). For discussion of some of the complications likely to arise as prisoners seek the benefit of Johnson and Welch, see Paragraph (8), at Seventh Edition pp. 1362–63.

[4b] The majority reversed the Court of Appeals' denial of a certificate of appealability on the basis that "reasonable jurists at least could debate whether Welch is entitled to relief" under Johnson. Justice Thomas's dissent labeled the Court's conclusion "preposterous" given that

Welch had sought the benefit of Johnson for the first time in an untimely motion for reconsideration of the Court of Appeals' prior denial of his application for a certificate. In Justice Thomas' view, the Court of Appeals could not be criticized for "denying Welch the opportunity to 'appeal' a claim that he failed to raise," which was based on "a decision that did not yet exist." Justice Thomas argued that the majority's standard means that a lower court can avoid being reversed in such circumstances only with "judicial clairvoyance" and "by inventing arguments on the movant's behalf."

Page 1361. Substitute the following for footnote 9:

[9]   Section 2255(h) requires that in order to proceed, any "second or successive motion must be certified as provided in section 2244 by a panel of the appropriate court of appeals" to be predicated upon "newly discovered evidence that, if proven and viewed in the light of the evidence as a whole, would be sufficient to establish by clear and convincing evidence that no reasonable factfinder would have found the movant guilty of the offense" or "a new rule of constitutional law, made retroactive to cases on collateral review by the Supreme Court, that was previously unavailable." Thus, by its terms, § 2255 permits a successive petition based on newly discovered evidence of innocence without § 2244(b)(2)(B)(i)'s further requirement that "the factual predicate for the claim could not have been discovered previously through the exercise of due diligence."

With respect to second or successive motions that involve claims previously presented, courts have interpreted § 2255 to incorporate the restrictions on successive petitions found in 2244(b)(1) & (2), despite the fact that those provisions are expressly limited to claims "presented in a second or successive habeas corpus application under section 2254." See, *e.g.*, In re Baptiste, 828 F.3d 1337 (11th Cir.2016) (per curiam) (holding that § 2255 incorporates § 2241(b)(1)'s requirement that claims presented in a prior motion be dismissed); White v. United States, 371 F.3d 900 (7th Cir.2004) (same). Along similar lines, many circuits have concluded that denials of certification under § 2255(h) to proceed with a second or successive petition may not be appealed, incorporating the standard of § 2244(b)(3)(E), which is not expressly limited to petitions filed under § 2254. See, *e.g.*, In re Graham, 714 F.3d 1181 (10th Cir.2013) (per curiam); Lykus v. Corsini, 565 F.3d 1 (1st Cir.2009) (en banc) (per curiam).

Page 1363. Add to the end of Paragraph (8):

Some circuits have extended this reasoning to encompass petitions brought pursuant to § 2241 for relief based on new decisions that would have rendered the petitioner ineligible for sentencing enhancements that were imposed at sentencing. See, *e.g.*, United States v. Wheeler, 886 F.3d 415 (4th Cir.2018); Hill v. Masters, 836 F.3d 591 (6th Cir.2016). But see McCarthan v. Director of Goodwill Industries-Suncoast, Inc., 851 F.3d 1076 (11th Cir.2017) (en banc) (holding that "a change in caselaw does not make a motion to vacate a prisoner's sentence 'inadequate or ineffective to test the legality of his detention' " under § 2255(e)).

CHAPTER XII

ADVANCED PROBLEMS IN JUDICIAL FEDERALISM

---

1. PROBLEMS OF RES JUDICATA

INTRODUCTORY NOTE

Pages 1365–66. Replace the text of Paragraph (1) with the following:

(1) Claim Preclusion. Under the doctrine of claim preclusion, once a court has entered a valid final judgment, a subsequent action on the same claim by any party to that judgment, or by one in "privity" with a party, is normally precluded. The underlying intuition rests at least in part on waiver: the precluded party could and should have raised the matter in the earlier litigation and has now waived the opportunity to do so. Today, most courts embrace the Restatement 2d view that a claim should be defined in terms of the transaction or transactions that were the subject of the dispute, not in terms of the particular theory of recovery that was advanced. The applicability of claim preclusion does not ordinarily depend on whether the claim in question was actually litigated in a prior proceeding. Rather, the question is whether it could and should have been litigated.

A range of exceptions to the rule of claim preclusion covers such matters as the existence of "consent" to the splitting of a claim and instances in which the prior judgment rested on such preliminary grounds as lack of jurisdiction or improper venue. The exceptions for lack of jurisdiction or venue help to illustrate that the theory of claim preclusion is based on waiver. But if the claim could not have been heard in the prior proceeding—because the court there lacked jurisdiction or venue, or, to take another example, because the claim had not yet accrued—then claim preclusion does not apply, as the litigant can hardly be taxed for having failed to raise a claim that could not have been resolved in that proceeding.

Page 1367. Add a new Paragraph (7):

(7) Preclusion of Defenses. It is unclear whether claim preclusion bars a defendant from raising a defense that might have been, but was not, raised in prior litigation. The Supreme Court touched on this issue in Lucky Brand Dungarees, Inc. v. Marcel Fashions Group, Inc., 140 S.Ct. 1589 (2020). It explained that "defense preclusion" is not "a standalone category of res judicata, unmoored from the two guideposts of issue preclusion and claim preclusion." Rather, any preclusion of a defense "must, at a minimum, satisfy the strictures of issue preclusion or claim preclusion." That principle was enough for the unanimous Court to reject the plaintiff's argument that the defendant was precluded from asserting a defense to an alleged trademark violation it did not raise in prior litigation between the parties, since the two lawsuits "were grounded on different conduct, involving different marks, occurring at different times", and thus "did not share a 'common nucleus of operative facts'" (citing Restatement 2d § 24 cmt. b, at 199).

In a footnote, the Court raised the possibility that claim preclusion may never apply to defenses, since "'[v]arious considerations, other than actual merits, may govern' whether to bring a defense, 'such as the smallness of the amount or the value of the property in controversy, the difficulty of obtaining the necessary evidence, the expense of the litigation, and [a party's] own situation'" (alterations in original) (quoting Cromwell v. County of Sac, 94 U.S. 351, 356 (1877)). It declined to reach the issue, however, since the plaintiff had not satisfied the "identity of claims" requirement.

Should defense preclusion ever be available? On the one hand, it appears to promote efficiency and finality by forcing parties to litigate defenses as early as possible. On the other hand, as the Court suggested, parties often have good reasons for not raising all conceivable defenses, and forcing them to do so on pain of preclusion might unnecessarily expand the earlier lawsuit and raise overall litigation costs. How should the Court sort out these competing policy arguments? What sources of law should it look to?

———

A.   LITIGATION WITH THE FEDERAL GOVERNMENT

NOTE ON RES JUDICATA IN FEDERAL GOVERNMENT LITIGATION AND ON THE PROBLEM OF ACQUIESCENCE

Page 1374. Add at the end of Paragraph (1):

Another question is whether the growing spate of federal district court injunctions that bar the federal government from enforcing federal statutes or regulations against nonparties in other districts and circuits is consistent with Mendoza. In recent years courts have been particularly aggressive in enjoining the government "nationwide" from enforcing immigration laws in contexts ranging from the Trump administration's sanctuary city policy, *see, e.g.,* City of Chicago v. Barr, 961 F.3d 882 (7th Cir.2020), and executive order limiting entry into the United States, see Hawaii v. Trump, 878 F.3d 662 (9th Cir.2017) (third executive order), reversed, Trump v. Hawaii, 138 S.Ct. 2392 (2018), to the Obama administration's program to establish lawful presence for aliens for various federal-law purposes, see Texas v. United States, 86 F.Supp. 3d 591 (S.D.Tex.), aff'd, 809 F.3d 134 (5th Cir.2015), aff'd by an equally divided Court, 136 S.Ct. 2271 (2016) (mem.). But the nationwide injunction trend is not limited to immigration. See Bray, *Multiple Chancellors: Reforming the National Injunction,* 131 Harv.L.Rev. 417, 428–45, 457–61 (2017) (documenting rise and prevalent use of nationwide injunctions in numerous contexts).

By preventing the government from litigating the enjoined issue in other courts against other parties, a nationwide injunction operates like nonmutual offensive collateral estoppel against the government. It flips Mendoza's policy priorities by elevating efficiency concerns and by frustrating the percolation of legal issues before different courts and in different factual contexts that Mendoza found vital to optimal Supreme Court decision-making and the proper development of federal law. It also has an adverse asymmetrical impact on the government, which is frequently involved in lawsuits against different parties involving the same issues, and which has powerful incentives to appeal every adverse nationwide injunction or risk foreclosing further review of the issue everywhere. In an opinion concurring in the Supreme Court's grant of a stay of a nationwide injunction, Justice Gorsuch, joined by Justice Thomas, mentioned most of these factors as reasons to oppose nationwide injunctions, but he did not invoke Mendoza. See Dep't of Homeland Security v. New York, 140 S.Ct. 599 (2020).

Does it follow from these considerations that Mendoza rules out nationwide injunctions? The proper policy balance in the context of developing a federal common law of preclusion against the government is an analytically separate issue from the proper balance of the equities for purposes of assessing the scope of injunctive relief against the government in a particular context. Which set of concerns should have priority, and how should the concerns be integrated? For arguments that Mendoza is an impediment to nationwide injunctions, see Morley, *Disaggregating Nationwide Injunctions*, 71 Ala.L.Rev. 1, 31 (2019) (stressing that "[n]ationwide defendant-oriented injunctions are flatly inconsistent with Mendoza"); Bray, *supra*, at 469–81 (invoking Mendoza's policy rationale among other considerations to argue that injunctions should protect the plaintiff but not non-parties); Berger, *Nationwide Injunctions Against the Federal Government: A Structural Approach*, 92 N.Y.U.L.Rev. 1068, 1090 (2017) (invoking Mendoza's policy rationale among other considerations to argue that injunctions against the federal government should be geographically limited by circuit); *cf.* Trammell, *Demystifying Nationwide Injunctions*, 98 Tex.L.Rev. 67, 97–101 (2019) (arguing that Mendoza's policy considerations should guide judges in crafting nationwide injunctions). For arguments that downplay Mendoza's relevance, see Sohoni, *The Lost History of the "Universal" Injunction*, 133 Harv.L.Rev. 920, 994–95 n.487 (2020) (suggesting that Mendoza is relevant but not dispositive); Clopton, *National Injunctions and Preclusion*, 118 Mich.L.Rev. 1, 20–44 (2019) (maintaining that Mendoza is not a strong argument against nationwide injunctions, but proposing that it be overruled in any event); Frost, *In Defense of Nationwide Injunctions*, 93 N.Y.U.L.Rev. 1065, 1112–13 (2018) (arguing that Mendoza can be squared with nationwide injunctions).

CHAPTER XIII

THE DIVERSITY JURISDICTION OF THE FEDERAL DISTRICT COURTS

_____

1. INTRODUCTION

NOTE ON THE HISTORICAL BACKGROUND AND CONTEMPORARY UTILITY OF THE DIVERSITY JURISDICTION

Page 1416. Add at the end of footnote 1:

For an argument that emphasizes the Framers' experience judging prize case appeals during the Revolutionary War, see Mask & MacMahon, *The Revolutionary War Prize Cases and the Origins of Diversity Jurisdiction*, 63 Buff.L.Rev. 477 (2015).

Page 1419. Add at the end of footnote 9:

See also Dodson, *Beyond Bias in Diversity Jurisdiction*, 69 Duke L.J. 267 (2019) (arguing that bias against out-of-state litigants no longer justifies diversity jurisdiction but "[p]romoting aggregation [of litigation] across state lines" may do so).

_____

2. ELEMENTS OF DIVERSITY JURISDICTION

NOTE ON COMPLETE VERSUS MINIMAL DIVERSITY AND ON ALIGNMENT OF PARTIES

Page 1428. Replace footnote 8 with the following:

⁸ The Supreme Court clarified the scope of Section 1453(b) in Home Depot U.S.A., Inc. v. Jackson, 139 S.Ct. 1743 (2019). The issue in Home Depot was whether a third-party counterclaim defendant—that is, a new party brought into the suit by the original defendant's counterclaim against the original plaintiff—can remove a suit that otherwise qualifies for original federal jurisdiction. In an opinion by Justice Thomas, the Court ruled that a third-party counterclaim defendant cannot remove because it is not a "defendant" under the relevant removal statutes. The Court first addressed removal under 28 U.S.C. § 1441(a), which permits a "defendant" to remove a "civil action * * * of which the district courts" have "original jurisdiction". It reasoned that since the original complaint alone determines whether a federal court has original jurisdiction over a civil action, the defendant who can remove is the one named in the original complaint, not a party named in a counterclaim. The Court then turned to Section 1453(b), which presented "a closer question" primarily because its broader language permits removal by "any defendant" to a "class action". It concluded that removal was not available under this Section either. The Court explained that the clauses in Section 1453(b) that use the term "any defendant" concern CAFA's relaxed removal requirements—namely, its elimination of both the requirement that all defendants in a diversity case must consent to removal, see 28 U.S.C. § 1446(b)(2)(A), and the bar on removal if any defendant is a citizen of the state where the action is brought, see 28 U.S.C. § 1441(b)(2). But nothing in Section 1453(b) alters Section 1441(a)'s limitation on what type of party can remove. Section 1453(b) thus does not expand who is a "defendant" under the removal statutes, but rather clarifies what restrictions apply to

eligible parties seeking removal for certain class actions. The Court noted that this conclusion was reinforced by the fact that Sections 1453(b) and 1441(a) both rely on the procedures for removal in 28 U.S.C. § 1446, which employs the term "defendant" and thus suggests that that term should have the same meaning in both Sections. In dissent, Justice Alito disagreed sharply with the Court's statutory analysis of both removal provisions, and argued that the Court created an unjustified "loophole" in Section 1453(b) to Congress's clear aim of making class action removal easier. For a useful discussion of the issues in Home Depot, see Tidmarsh, *Finding Room For State Class Actions in a Post-CAFA World: The Case of the Counterclaim Class Action*, 35 W.St.U.L.Rev. 193 (2007).

Page 1429. Add at the end of the first paragraph of footnote 10:

Wolff, *Choice of Law and Jurisdictional Policy in the Federal Courts*, 165 U.Pa.L.Rev. 1847 (2017) (arguing that Klaxon is no barrier to federal courts developing federal choice-of-law rules in CAFA cases to resolve state-law conflicts).

NOTE ON THE TREATMENT OF CORPORATIONS, UNINCORPORATED ENTITIES, AND LITIGATION CLASSES IN THE DETERMINATION OF DIVERSITY

Page 1435. Eliminate the last sentence of Paragraph (1) and replace Paragraph (2) with the following:

(2) Partnerships, Business Trusts, and Other Unincorporated Entities. In Americold Realty Trust v. ConAgra Foods, Inc., 136 S.Ct. 1012 (2016), the Court reaffirmed Bouligny and ruled broadly that "[w]hile humans and corporations can assert their own citizenship, other entities take the citizenship of their members." The question in Americold was whether the citizenship for diversity purposes of a Maryland "real estate investment trust" should be determined by the citizenship of the trust or of its members. The Court described Letson's identification of corporate citizenship with the state of incorporation as a "limited exception", ratified by Congress in 28 U.S.C. § 1332(c), to Deveaux's general rule that "only a human could be a citizen for jurisdictional purposes." The Court thus affirmed that the citizenship of all "artificial entities other than corporations, such as joint-stock companies or limited partnerships", is determined by the citizenship of all of its members. The Court further explained that the appropriate "membership" of unincorporated entities is determined by state law, and that under the law of Maryland, which created the investment trust, the relevant members were its shareholders. The Court distinguished Navarro Sav. Ass'n v. Lee, 446 U.S. 458 (1980), which some lower courts had interpreted to hold that a trust possesses the citizenship of its trustees alone rather than the shareholder beneficiaries. It clarified that Navarro held only that when trustees file suit in their name (as opposed to the trust's name), their jurisdictional citizenship is the state to which they belong. But when the trust itself is a litigant, its citizenship is determined by its members in accordance with state law.